1982

Judea,
Samaria, and Gaza

Judea, Samaria, and Gaza: Views on the Present and Future

Edited by Daniel J. Elazar

American Enterprise Institute for Public Policy Research
Washington and London

Daniel J. Elazar is president of the Jerusalem Institute for Federal
Studies.

Library of Congress Cataloging in Publication Data

Main entry under title:

Judea, Samaria, and Gaza.
    (AEI studies ; 334)

    1. Israel-Arab War, 1967—Occupied territories—
Addresses, essays, lectures. I. Elazar, Daniel Judah.
II. Series.
DS127.6.03J83   956'.046   81-10929
ISBN 0-8447-3458-6   AACR2
ISBN 0-8447-3459-4 (pbk.)

AEI Studies 334

Printed in the United States of America

102,820

Acknowledgments

This book was developed and written in the Jerusalem Institute for Federal Studies as part of its continuing exploration of possible solutions for the administered territories: Judea, Samaria, and the Gaza Strip. Its chapters were prepared by the fellows, associates, and staff of the JIFS or by colleagues otherwise involved in the larger project. Special thanks are due JIFS Associate Shmuel Sandler for his assistance in working with the authors in the preparation of their manuscripts. Judy Cohen, the institute coordinator, Hannah Kliger, and Holly Dorman of the institute's staff in the United States handled the technical aspects of preparing the papers with their usual high competence. Sarah Lederhendler, the JIFS translator, dealt with the technical materials in the excellent manner we have come to expect.

Needless to say, the views in the chapters are those of the authors alone and not necessarily those of their respective institutions or the JIFS.

DANIEL J. ELAZAR

Contributors

Moshe Drori served as a legal adviser to the Judea and Samaria Regional Command (military government) from 1970 to 1974. Since then he has been engaged in legal research at the Hebrew University of Jerusalem, publishing many articles as well as a comprehensive book on law in the administered territories. His *Local Government, Democracy, and Elections in Judea and Samaria: Legal Aspects* was published in 1980 by the Jerusalem Institute for Federal Studies, of which he is an associate.

Elisha Efrat has served as geographer and planner with the Israel Ministry of the Interior since 1960 and has taught geography at Tel Aviv University since 1967. Professor Efrat's books include *The Israel Physical Master Plan, Israel toward the Year 2000*, and the forthcoming *Settlement Geography of Israel*, among others.

Daniel J. Elazar is president of the Jerusalem Institute for Federal Studies, Senator N. M. Paterson Professor of Intergovernmental Relations at Bar-Ilan University, Ramat Gan, and senior fellow of the Center for the Study of Federalism at Temple University, Philadelphia. Among his recent books are *Federalism and Political Integration* and *Self-rule/Shared Rule: Federal Solutions to the Middle East Conflict*.

Hillel Frisch holds a master's degree in international affairs from Columbia University and is a research associate of the Jerusalem Institute for Federal Studies. His publications include "Bolstering the Regime from Within: Egyptian Intellectuals behind the Sadat Initiative," and he is coauthor of "Project Renewal: An Introduction to the Issues and Actors."

Avraham (Anthony) Lavine holds a master's degree in Middle East area studies. He was a contributor to the *Encyclopedia Judaica* and since 1970 has directed the Department of International Relations of the Israel Ministry of Labor and Social Affairs. His work includes liaison with representatives of international voluntary agencies active in the administered territories.

SASSON LEVI recently retired from active service in the Israel Defense Forces with the rank of colonel. A native of Egypt, Colonel Levi specialized in Arab affairs and served in a key capacity in the military government of Judea and Samaria. He has a B.A. in political science from Bar-Ilan University.

MORDECHAI NISAN completed his Ph.D. in international relations at McGill University and presently teaches political science in the School for Overseas Students of the Hebrew University of Jerusalem. His writings include *Israel and the Territories: A Study in Control 1967–1977* and many articles on Middle East politics.

SHMUEL SANDLER, who earned his Ph.D. at Johns Hopkins University, teaches international relations at Bar-Ilan University and is an associate of the Jerusalem Institute for Federal Studies. He has published articles on American foreign policy and on Israeli politics. Currently his Ford Foundation–supported research focuses on alternative federal solutions to the Arab-Israeli conflict.

JEHOSHUA SCHWARZ is a water resources engineer with TAHAL Consulting Engineers Ltd., Israel Water Planners, and has published several articles under their auspices.

REPHAEL VARDI served as coordinator of operations in the administered territories for the Ministry of Defense from 1974 to 1976. Holder of an M.A. in jurisprudence, General Vardi has served as comptroller of the Defense Establishment (Israel) since 1980.

Contents

Introduction

Daniel J. Elazar

Eretz Israel/Palestine is a unique land in many ways, not least in its geography. On the one hand, it is well known as the crossroads of the old world, where Eurasia and Africa come together culturally and physically. The continental divide between the Atlantic basin and the Indian Ocean–Pacific basins crosses the full length of the land from north to south. Yet the Jordan River basin, which is the heart of the land and contains most of the territory historically considered to be part of it, actually drains into neither of the world's two great ocean systems but is hydrologically self-contained. It drains into the Dead Sea and never leaves the land except to evaporate heavenward.

This physical fact testifies to the land's unity from the Mediterranean to the eastern desert and may even be seen as testifying to its separate character. It also points toward the source of its tragic history as a center of both local and international conflict.

Today that conflict occurs on multiple levels. Most immediate is the struggle between the Jews of Israel and the Palestinian Arabs for a homeland that they, perforce, share. This struggle is part of a larger one between the Jewish people and the Arab world over the right of the Jews—the oldest of peoples—not only to their ancient homeland but also to their very status as a people. Beyond those local and regional dimensions, the conflict has been absorbed into the struggles between the free world and the Communist world and between the third world and the West.

The unity of the land was recognized in international law as recently as 1921 when the League of Nations defined the British mandate over Palestine to include both banks of the Jordan River. The character of the local conflict was imprinted on the map with almost equal rapidity when the new mandatory power in 1922 separated Transjordan from western Palestine for administrative purposes. According to Winston Churchill, who was responsible for that act, its purpose was to give the two peoples their own areas within the land for national development.

As a result of the 1947 partition and 1948 war, the Arab segment of the land was enlarged to include the greater part of what historically had been the heartland of Eretz Israel on both sides of the Jordan, all under Jordanian rule, while the Jews were left principally with the original Palestine (that is, the land of the Philistines) along the Mediterranean coast. As in 1922, the armistice lines demarcating the border were to be temporary, pending a final settlement. Only the perimeters surrounding both states—the old League of Nations boundaries—had any status in international law.

In 1967 the Israeli victory in a war forced upon it, changed the country's political map again, bringing the cease-fire lines back to the 1922 arrangement. In western Eretz Israel/Palestine, some 3 million Jews and 1.5 million Arabs found themselves in a new situation: the two great concentrations of Arab population brought under Israeli control in the Judean and Samarian hills, the Jordan Valley, and the Gaza Strip became the focal point of a mélange of ambivalent relationships involving both cooperation and confrontation. While the Palestinian Arabs continue to oppose Israeli rule on the political level, they have in day-to-day matters worked together with Israelis to achieve a higher level of freedom, safety, and prosperity than they have ever known before. Similarly, while the Israelis have been very active in the administered territories in matters of security and settlement, they have been more than content to leave day-to-day governance in local hands under a policy of minimum coercion/maximum consent. As a result, life in the territories continues on two seemingly contradictory levels. If a final settlement still seems distant in light of an irrepressible and unresolvable conflict, the two peoples are living together and out of necessity trying to make the best of it.

In the meantime, the map of the territories occupied by Israel as a result of the 1967 war has been changed. From 1967 to 1977, under the Labor government, a band of Jewish settlements was established in the Jordan Valley to serve as a security belt for an Israel more vulnerable than ever before because of the introduction of new levels of weaponry into the conflict. The cluster of pre-1948 Jewish settlements in the Etzion Hills, south of Jerusalem, was reestablished, Jews returned to the Hebron area for the first time since the late 1930s and built neighboring Kiryat Arba, and a ring of Jewish neighborhoods was built in territories surrounding the Arab sections of Jerusalem.

With the Likud victory in May 1977, a new phase of Jewish

settlement began, with clusters and bands of settlements founded in the mountains of Samaria and Judea and in the Gaza Strip. These new settlements, which became front-page news overnight, were set down according to plan in an effort to create "facts" that would eliminate once and for all the possibility of repartitioning the land west of the Jordan River. For better or worse, four years of that effort have changed the map of the country. A new reality has been created, which will affect any future settlement. This volume offers a set of Israeli perspectives on this new reality.

The chapters in this volume describe this life on two levels as it has persisted for well over a decade. The authors focus on developments that hold promise for a future settlement of the conflict or that must be taken into account if any such settlement is to be achieved. Part 1 looks at the land itself: who lives on it, who owns it, and how is it watered. In part 2 the authors consider governance, economy, and social services, each of which has been reshaped since 1967. Part 3 focuses on planning for the future, examining Israel's security needs, the Jordanian connection, and, finally, the elements that have shifted the thrust of the search for peace in Eretz Israel/Palestine from partition to sharing.

The first consideration in this inquiry must be the pattern of settlement on the land itself, the subject of part 1. In chapter 1, Elisha Efrat, one of Israel's leading geographers, examines spatial patterns in the interrelationship between Jews and Arabs in Judea and Samaria. Professor Efrat carefully maps out both the Arab and the Jewish settlement patterns in the territories and the changes that took place in the periods 1947–1967 and since 1967. He pays particular attention to Jerusalem and environs. In his conclusion Professor Efrat presents six different scenarios for the future as they would be reflected in changes in the spatial patterns and their likely consequences.

Despite the seeming certainty that characterizes so many pronouncements about "the West Bank," the legal status of the territories is by no means clear, having been left in limbo in 1948. In chapter 2, Moshe Drori, former chief legal officer of the military government in Judea and Samaria, examines legal aspects of the Israeli settlements in Judea and Samaria. Beginning with an exploration of the legal status of Judea and Samaria, he focuses in turn on the land issue, the legal status of the Israeli settlements, their municipal organization and powers, and the personal status of the Israeli settlers. The chapter also examines the history of Israeli taxation of Jews and Arabs in Judea and Samaria. In conclusion, he recommends the development of a legal extraterritorial status for the Israeli settlers that will be consistent with any future autonomy arrangements.

The interrelationship between land and water hardly needs to be stressed in the discussions of human settlement and rule over particular pieces of territory. The issue is even more acute in the territories under discussion because of the dominance of the Jordan River basin and the sharing of a common hydrological system even beyond that drainage basin. In chapter 3, J. Schwarz, one of Israel's leading water experts, describes the hydrological situation in the territories, documenting in a detailed way how the land is a single land when it comes to water. This analysis also suggests how close to the limits of use the population has come as its prosperity is fed by finite water resources. Whatever the future may bring in the way of a political settlement, both Jews and Arabs will have to cooperate in water matters or pay a heavy price.

Part 2 begins with chapter 4, in which Sasson Levi, a reserve colonel in the Israeli Army and for many years a leading figure in the military government in Judea and Samaria, examines local government in the administered territories. As part of the policy of minimum coercion/maximum consent, the Israeli authorities encouraged self-government on the municipal level and indeed expanded the powers of local government in the territories relative to what they were under Jordanian and Egyptian rule. Both the latter were highly centralized states by nature even apart from the suspicions or hostilities they harbored toward what were for them peripheral territories with dangerous populations. While the Israelis could have taken the same approach, for better or worse, they instead opened the door to greater democratization and participation in local government affairs, including a considerably widened franchise for local elections and greater independence for municipal authorities to act, as Levi documents. While this policy did have the effect of reducing to a minimum the necessity for day-to-day intervention in matters of governance in the territories, it also brought forth in the end a new generation of leadership who rejected the older generation of conservative notables and identified with the Palestine Liberation Organization, thereby increasing tensions and even violence in recent years.

Chapter 5 begins with an examination of the political economy of the administered territories by Shmuel Sandler, with Hillel Frisch, both of the Jerusalem Institute for Federal Studies. The authors have been actively studying means to develop shared-rule solutions to the problem of the territories. Chapter 5 depicts economic developments in the territories since 1948, and especially since 1967, as well as the differing assessments of those developments by the various parties involved. The results of the authors' inquiry show that, while under Jordanian rule the economy of the West Bank declined as a result of deliberate government policies to concentrate growth east of the Jordan, the Israeli occupation brought a boom between 1967 and 1973 and then stagnation, more or less, after 1973 because of similar conditions in the Israeli economy to which the territories were, perforce, linked. Perhaps the most important conclusion to be drawn from their work is that whatever the political solution attained, the economy of the territories will necessarily be integrated with one or the other of its neighbors and will be profoundly affected by that relationship. Thus, there must be some interest among the residents of the territories in at least having a role in determining overall economic policy with the partner or partners they are fated to have. On the other hand, it would be unrealistic for them to expect to be able to forge an independent economic future even if they were to achieve political independence.

If the operative principle in matters of local government was to leave things as much as possible in the hands of the existing municipalities and their indigenous leaders, as far as social services are concerned, Israel has made a serious effort to raise standards and benefits. Here, too, administration has been left largely to the residents of the territories, with Arab social service professionals working closely with their Israeli counterparts in order to improve service to their own people. In chapter 6, Avraham Lavine, of Israel's Ministry of Labor and Social Affairs, reports on the system of social services that has been developed in Judea, Samaria, and Gaza since 1967, indicating the changes that have taken place and something of their measurable impact. Lavine details the social changes that have occurred under Israeli rule and contributed to the changes in the way social services had to be delivered, how the latter changes were introduced, and their results. A major feature of his examination is the combination of cooperative and complementary activity on the part of Israeli, international, and local social service agencies.

Uppermost in the minds of Israelis when considering the future of the administered territories (see part 3) is their security. This is true for those who are committed to the maintenance of the full historical Jewish connection with the territories as much as for those for whom security is the paramount goal. Because of the immediacy and the sensitivity of the security issue, it cannot help but be a major sticking point in any change in the status of the territories. In chapter 7, on the administered territories and the internal security of Israel, Major General (Reserves) Rephael Vardi, for twelve years the head of the military government in the territories, presents what is in all likelihood the dominant Israeli view on the subject. His analysis reveals the problem in all its starkness. The solutions he suggests can be taken to be close to those of whatever Israeli government is likely to be in power, although his own statement is personal and unofficial.

Beyond immediate security considerations there is the whole question of the Jordanian connection, often treated—quite erroneously—as if it were a matter of bringing in a third party. There is a tendency outside the region to fail to recognize the strong links between the population of the territories and those to the east of the Jordan. As the land is one country, so, too, is the Arab population one population—with the notable exception of the Hashemite royal family. In chapter 8, Mordechai Nisan discusses "the Jordanian connection." Dr. Nisan, a recognized expert on the subject and the author of *Israel and the Territories: A Study in Control*, makes a strong case for considering the population of both banks as one when it comes to determining the future peace settlement. His argument is that, demographically speaking, there already is a Palestinian state, although the Palestinians do have reason to resent the fact that Jordan's government is not their government, despite their heavy representation in the Jordanian polity and society.

In the last analysis, the political prerequisite for peace seems to be that Jews and Arabs each have an independent state in historical Eretz Israel/Palestine and share the disputed territory in the middle. I not only advocate such a position in chapter 9 but also do so by reviewing the permanent and transient elements to be taken into consideration in the search for a Mideast peace, the shift in direction from partition to sharing, and finally the basis for a shared-rule solution. Whether such a solution is attainable is another question. What remains clear in the rather disappointing aftermath of the Israeli-Egyptian Peace Treaty is that no other solution comes as close to dealing with the essential issues.

In case after case, these chapters point to the necessity of sharing, at least in light of the changes since 1967. Had the Six Day War not occurred—had King Hussein not chosen to go to war—the situation would no doubt have been different. But there is no going back on history. On the other hand, necessity can be the mother of invention. Unfortunately, in human affairs this is not always the case. Invention is what is sorely needed in this land, and all too often it has been sorely lacking. Politicians may be optimistic or pessimistic as the need arises. An academic assessment such as this one attempts to be realistic and to allow readers to draw their own conclusions.

PART ONE

The Land and Its Resources

1

Spatial Patterns of Jewish and Arab Settlements in Judea and Samaria

Elisha Efrat

Since the Six Day War, the demographic, settlement, and economic structure of Judea and Samaria has been considerably altered. Settlements were established in the Jordan Valley and in the mountains of Judea and Samaria, the Etzion Block of settlements was enlarged, many new roads were built, and Jerusalem's municipal boundaries were extended to permit the construction of new residential quarters. Many of these development activities were carried out by different planning and administrative bodies without much coordination among them. This chapter analyzes the changes that have taken place and proposes a series of future spatial patterns for the various sections of Judea and Samaria, all suitable for a state of peace while reflecting the different priorities of Jews and Arabs.

The chapter begins with a description of the settlement changes in Judea and Samaria between 1947 and 1967 and then analyzes the settlement changes brought about by the Israeli military administration after 1967. Finally, it describes, with maps, possible spatial patterns for the implementation of autonomy, including a scale of priorities.[1]

Changes in Settlement Patterns, 1947–1967

Between Israel's War of Independence of 1948 and the Six Day War of 1967, the region of Judea and Samaria—an integral part of Eretz Israel/Palestine—was bounded by the armistice lines between

[1] I have prepared a more comprehensive study of this subject in the framework of the Tel-Aviv University Research Project on Peace.

9

Israel and Jordan, but no physical or economic links connected it with the State of Israel. After 1948 the region no longer had access to the Mediterranean Sea or to the coastal plain and the Gaza Strip; its only link was with the Kingdom of Jordan to the east. This delineation caused changes in the pattern of towns and villages that were reflected in their number, population, interrelationship, and eastward orientation. Geographical changes in the settlement pattern were the result of the unnatural political conditions, which affected the physical, economic, and social factors of this area.

The Geographical Dispersion of the Villages. In the Hebron Mountains the dispersion of the villages is linear and concentrated, owing to the geographical features of the area. To the east the influence of the desert is very noticeable; the annual precipitation is between 100 and 300 mm (4–12 inches), the vegetation is sparse, there are few springs and little soil. All these factors severely limit the extension of human settlement beyond a line about 5 km (3 miles) east of the mountain crest. To the south, the influence of the Negev Desert penetrates some distance into the Hebron Mountains, and as a result the number of villages falls off as one nears the border of the desert.

The villages in the Hebron Mountains are dispersed along a line parallel to the watershed, but at some distance from it, near deposits of good soft building stone. The villagers also refrained from settling on fertile land on the plateau. To the west, a number of villages are located along a tectonic axis parallel to the general orientation of the mountain. Their position on the edge of the mountainous backbone ensures geographical advantages and adequate supplies of spring water.[2] The larger villages, of 3,000–5,000 inhabitants, are found mainly in the southwest, while in the central part of the region the average village has only 500–1,000 inhabitants. The larger population of the border villages may be explained by the need for protecting the settled farmers against the predations of desert nomads and by the gradual intermingling, over the years, of farmers and nomads in settlements that enjoy favorable soil and water conditions.[3] We can therefore visualize the settlement pattern in the Hebron Mountains as having crystallized along well-defined axes, as a result of the geographical character of the hill country and its agricultural possibilities (see figure 1).

[2] On the dispersion of villages, see E. Efrat, "Dispersion of Settlements in Judea and Samaria," *Hamizrah Hehadash* (Hebrew), vol. 20 (1979), pp. 257-65.

[3] For a detailed and up-to-date account of the settlement process of desert nomads, see A. Shmueli, *The Settlement of the Judean Desert Bedouin* (Tel Aviv: Gomé, 1971; in Hebrew).

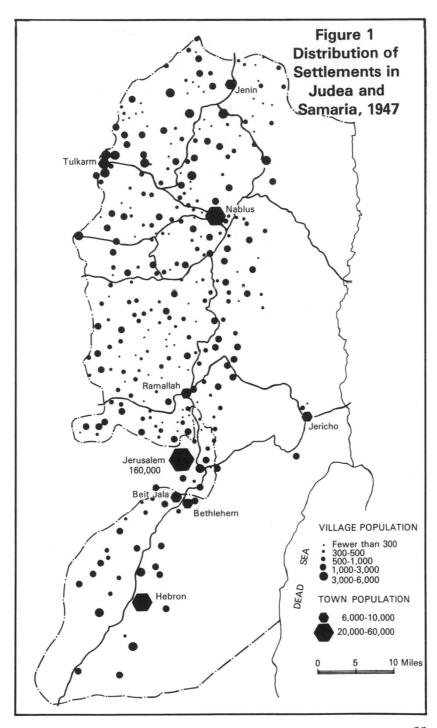

**Figure 1
Distribution of
Settlements in
Judea and
Samaria, 1947**

Jenin

Tulkarm

Nablus

Ramallah

Jericho

Jerusalem
160,000

Beit Jala

Bethlehem

DEAD SEA

VILLAGE POPULATION

· Fewer than 300
· 300-500
● 500-1,000
● 1,000-3,000
● 3,000-6,000

TOWN POPULATION

⬢ 6,000-10,000

⬢ 20,000-60,000

Hebron

0   5   10 Miles

11

The pattern of settlement in Samaria is more scattered and covers almost the entire area. The broken mountainous topography has resulted in a network of villages located on hilltops and mountain spurs, where they dominate the surrounding country. The valleys are as a rule not settled, since they contain fertile sedimentary soil suitable for intensive cultivation.[4] The wide dispersion of villages in the Samaria hills is made possible by the presence of a large number of springs, a result of the many fault lines that are characteristic of these mountains. The villages are generally small (500–1,000 inhabitants); only a few fall into the 3,000–5,000 category.

The Number and Location of Villages. Against the background of the physical conditions of the region, it is interesting to compare the number of villages in Judea and Samaria at the end of the British Mandate (1947) and at the end of the Jordanian rule (1967). See figure 2 and table 1.

It follows that the total increase was 132 villages (50 percent), but the increase for Samaria was only 25 percent, while the corresponding figure for Judea reached 144 percent. Though most of the new villages in Judea were small, they are nevertheless a striking feature in the spatial distribution of villages in this region.[5] Table 2 shows the distribution of the villages by subdistricts in 1947 and 1967. It can be seen that there was a great increase in the number of villages in the Hebron and Jerusalem subdistricts, while in Samaria only the Jenin subdistrict showed a striking increase.

The distribution in table 2 shows that during this twenty-year period, there was a tendency to further settlement in Judea, special stress being laid on settling the frontier with Israel in the south and southwest. An effort was also made to strengthen border settlement at the edge of the desert, east of the Hebron and the Jerusalem mountains.

The distribution of villages in Samaria was more balanced, but here, too, the north and west were favored as compared with the east. As to the settlements near the armistice line, they underwent considerable demographic and physical changes. The armistice line cut them off from their lands in the coastal plain, and the villagers began therefore to cultivate patches of land in the hills. The lack

---

[4] An analysis of the soil characteristics of this region can be found in Y. Dan, *Soils of the Judean Mountains and the Samaria Mountains* (Rehovoth: Volcani Institute for Agricultural Research, 1968; in Hebrew).

[5] Based on "List of Villages of the Region with Their Land Areas" (Jerusalem: Israel Lands Administration, List of Settlements in the West Bank, August 1967; in Hebrew).

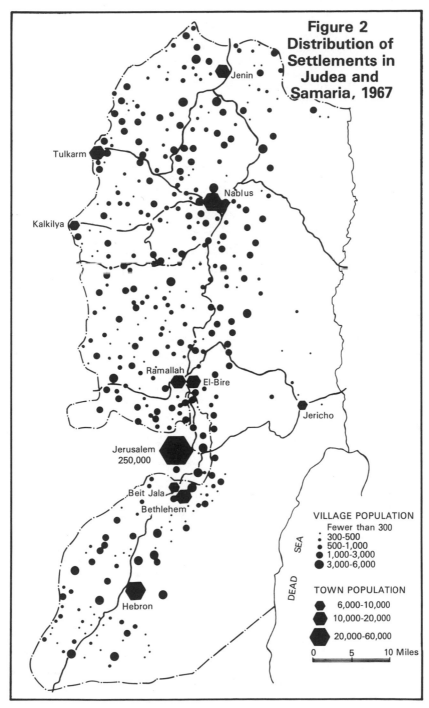

**Figure 2
Distribution of
Settlements in
Judea and
Samaria, 1967**

Jenin

Tulkarm

Nablus

Kalkilya

Ramallah
El-Bire

Jericho

Jerusalem
250,000

Beit Jala
Bethlehem

DEAD SEA

VILLAGE POPULATION
Fewer than 300
300-500
500-1,000
1,000-3,000
3,000-6,000

TOWN POPULATION
6,000-10,000
10,000-20,000
20,000-60,000

Hebron

0   5   10 Miles

13

TABLE 1
NUMBER OF VILLAGES IN JUDEA AND SAMARIA, 1947 AND 1967

Area	1947	1967	Increase	Percent Increase
Judea	54	132	78	144
Samaria	210	264	54	25
Total	264	396	132	50

SOURCES: 1947 data from the Mandatory "Village Statistics" of 1945; 1967 data from the 1967 population census of Judea and Samaria carried out by the Israel Defense Forces.

TABLE 2
NUMBER OF VILLAGES IN JUDEA AND SAMARIA SUBDISTRICTS, 1947 AND 1967

Subdistrict	1947	1967	Increase	Percent Increase
Nablus	91	97	6	6.5
Jenin	29	55	26	89
Tulkarm	34	42	8	23
Ramallah	56	70	14	25
Jerusalem	34	66	32	94
Hebron	20	66	46	230
Total	264	396	132	50

of markets in the west and the absence of roads to the east brought about a decline in agriculture and the lowering of living standards. Some villages turned eastward toward the interior of the region. The emigration of young villagers to the Persian Gulf countries raised the living standards of the inhabitants, leading to greater prosperity and to the construction of new buildings, so that the same border villages which in the late 1940s had suffered from isolation recovered later and increased their built area.[6] The construction of new security roads and the widening of existing roads also contributed to the prosperity of the border villages.

[6] M. Brawer, *Changes in Location and Pattern of Border Villages*, Proceedings of the Symposium in Rural Geography, University of Baroda, 1968.

TABLE 3
POPULATION OF JUDEA AND SAMARIA BY SUBDISTRICTS, 1947 AND 1967

Subdistrict	1947	1967	Percent Increase
Nablus	62,500	152,400	144
Jenin	49,000	78,300	60
Tulkarm	35,000	72,300	106
Ramallah	50,700	88,800	75
Jerusalem	39,400	88,400	124
Hebron	47,000	118,300	151
Total	283,600	598,500	111
Judea	86,400	206,700	139
Samaria	197,200	391,800	99

SOURCES: 1947 estimate based on the Mandatory "Village Statistics" of 1945; 1967 data from the 1967 population census carried out by the Israel Defense Forces.

In spite of these artificial settlement activities, there was, interestingly enough, little change in the geographical distribution of the villages. Only few new settlements succeeded in gaining a foothold on the threshold of the desert or on the shore of the Dead Sea. Neither were many new settlements established in the Jordan Valley, owing to unfavorable soil conditions and lack of water resources.[7]

Population of the Villages. A comparison of the village population between the two years 1947 and 1967 (table 3) reveals some striking features.

In 1947 the rural population numbered 283,600, and in 1967, after an increase of 111 percent in twenty years, it had risen to 598,500. There is a striking difference between the rate of increase in Judea (139 percent) and in Samaria (99 percent), which is probably due to the internal migration of refugees and to the settlement of nomads. While in 1947 the population was more or less uniformly distributed among the several subdistricts, the figures for 1967 show a marked change in the Nablus and Hebron subdistricts. The population of the Hebron subdistrict rose by 151 percent and that of Nablus by

[7] For a more detailed exposition of the planning considerations governing the establishment of settlements in this region, see E. Efrat, *Judea and Samaria, Guidelines for Regional and Physical Planning* (Jerusalem: Ministry of the Interior, Planning Department, 1970), pp. 67-86.

15

144 percent—that is, the highest population growth took place in the two principal centers of the region, one in the south and the other in the north, and especially along the armistice line. It should also be noted that during the Mandate there was a normal distribution of the population among the villages, only few of which numbered less than 500 or more than 3,000 inhabitants, the majority lying in the 500–1,000 range. Today this distribution has been to some extent distorted by the marked increase of small villages of 100–300 inhabitants.

The Geographical Pattern of the Towns. In Judea the geographical dispersion of the towns coincides generally with the watershed and follows the line Hebron, Bethlehem, Beit Jala, Jerusalem, Ramallah, and El-Bire. These towns are the administrative, commercial, marketing, and service centers for the surrounding villages. Jerusalem has the additional function of being the capital of both Judea and Samaria, while Hebron is the main center for the southern hills. Bethlehem and Beit Jala to the south and Ramallah and El-Bire to the north serve as secondary centers, which depend on the capital, particularly as regards their economy. The town distribution pattern in Judea is linear and is characterized by the division of functions between the various towns.

In Samaria, on the other hand, the towns developed either on the hills facing the Valley of Esdraelon and the Sharon Plain, or at focal points and crossroads of intra- and interregional traffic arteries. The dispersion pattern of the towns emphasizes the central position of Nablus, the capital of Samaria, with Jenin to the north, Tulkarm to the west, and Kalkilya to the southwest. The towns of Samaria are not particularly large, and they are not a very important factor in the population of the region. Table 4 shows the comparison between the population of the towns in 1947 and 1967.

The urban population increased at a rate of only 45 percent, as compared with a rise of 111 percent in the rural population (table 3). Thus, the urbanization index is still very low (in Israel, 87 percent), and the rural population increase is still predominant. All the towns were small in the past and have remained so today, and even the main centers, such as Hebron and Nablus, do not exceed 40,000 inhabitants. During this period, two villages, Kalkilya and El-Bire, were raised to the status of towns, but their populations did not reach the 10,000 mark. The rate of growth of towns was lower in Judea than in Samaria, while in the villages the position was reversed. The reason may have been that the towns in Judea had less commercial and social connection with Transjordan than did their counterparts in Samaria. The greater part of the urban population

16

TABLE 4
Population of Towns in Judea and Samaria, 1947 and 1967

Town	1947	1967	Percent Increase
Jenin	4,000	8,346	109
Nablus	23,250	41,537	78
Tulkarm	8,000	10,157	27
Kalkilya	(5,850)[a]	8,922	52
Ramallah	5,000	12,030	141
El-Bire	(2,920)[a]	9,568	228
East Jerusalem	65,000[b]	69,857	—
Bethlehem	9,000	14,439	60
Beit Jala	3,700	6,041	63
Hebron	24,600	38,091	55
Jericho	3,000	5,200	73
Total	154,320	224,188	45

[a] A village in 1947.

[b] The estimate includes those parts of the 1947 city that were reunited with the western part in 1967.

SOURCES: 1947 estimate based on the Mandatory "Village Statistics" of 1945; 1967 data from the 1967 population census carried out by the Israel Defense Forces.

increase was accounted for by the migration of refugees or by the movement from village to town, and to a smaller degree by the internal growth in the town itself. East Jerusalem did not grow, and there was a continuous trickle of population to the neighboring towns and villages, such as Ramallah and El-Bire. Jericho was an exception, owing to its location on the main route between Transjordan and Jerusalem and to its being a winter resort.

The Jordanian government during the nineteen years of its rule did little to develop the resources and the economy of Judea and Samaria or to encourage physical planning, as it saw this region merely as a forward area on the frontier with Israel. As a result, the development of the settlements was limited and determined mainly by the geography of the region. The lack of new water supplies and the absence of the exploitation of mineral resources or of industrial development left the region to contend with the influence of the desert in the east, with a mountainous terrain and with an artificial boundary to the west, north, and south. New neighborhoods were constructed in the main centers of attraction, East Jerusalem and Amman, and building construction was intensified as a result of the economic prosperity of persons who were forced to migrate owing to the lack of suitable economic opportunities in the region itself. All this led, as mentioned above, to a new pattern of settlement, influenced on one side by the armistice line and on the other side by the lack of governmental economic encouragement.

Approaches to Israel Settlement Policy. After the Six Day War in 1967, Jewish settlements were gradually established in Judea and Samaria. These were initially defense strongholds and military agricultural settlements. Later, they achieved the status of permanent settlements. A glance at the map shows that the main concentrations of settlements were and are in the Jordan Valley, the Dead Sea shore, and the eastern slope of the Samaria Mountains. Lately there has been some settlement in western Samaria.

The settlements planted in Judea and Samaria are political in nature, their main object being to obtain a hold on areas which may some time in the future face being cut off from the State of Israel. Most of the settlements are located in the eastern part of the region and at selected points in the west and in the hill country, where land is available and where there are few inhabitants, so the existing population is minimally affected.

There are various approaches to the question of settlement in Judea and Samaria, some traditional and obsolete, others more modern and ambitious. I shall examine four of these approaches, note their advantages and shortcomings, and explain the general process of settlement in the whole region against the background of its geography and the existing Arab agricultural settlement.

The Traditional Arab Settlement. The Arab agricultural settlement in Judea and Samaria is a primary geographical phenomenon resulting from the physical nature of the region and its technological underdevelopment. However, the location of these settlements, their dispersion pattern, and the manner in which the physical conditions have been exploited to enable the inhabitants to support themselves and to keep to their way of life may be used as a starting point for all new settlers in this region, even if they come equipped with the most modern know-how and technology.

The dispersion of the villages in the Hebron Mountains is not free or ramified, like that in the plains or in the valleys, but is linear, clustered, and concentrated, owing to the limitations imposed by nature and to the mountainous topography. These limit the eastward expansion of settlement beyond a line passing through Bani

Na'im, Beit Fajjar, and Beit Sahur. In the south, the desert influence of the Negev is very noticeable. It penetrates between the Dahiriyeh and Tel Kerayot ridges and makes itself felt by the decrease in rainfall and population density as one approaches the threshold of the desert. Towards the west, the concentration of settlements is limited by morphological and geographical factors. A number of villages are strung out along the Hebron Mountain backbone in a northeast-southwest direction, parallel to the crest of the mountain. These are: Idna, Tarquimiye, Beit Ayla, Kharas, Surif, Nahalin, Husan, and Battir.

The villages on the mountain crest take advantage of the local topography, avoid the main highway as much as possible and do not encroach on agricultural land. As conditions on the plateau are relatively favorable for agriculture, the villages were located at the edge of the plateau, at a convenient distance from the fields, and preferably in such areas, between the mountain crest and the slopes, where soft building stone is available and cultivation terraces can easily be built. Thus, Shuyukh, Beit Fajjar, Si'ir, Beit Kahil, Beit Ummar, Khadr, and others are all built near the mountain crest. In the north, the village network is bounded by the descent of the Hebron Mountains towards the Jerusalem hills. The village pattern of the Hebron Mountains can be seen as tending to crystallize and cluster along well-defined axes, owing to the character of the mountain and the location of areas suitable for cultivation.

The dispersion of settlements in Samaria is different from that in Judea or the other mountainous parts of Eretz Israel. While Judea is sparsely populated, with most of the villages located on two or three longitudinal axes, in Samaria the settlements are more widely dispersed. Here, too, the settlement pattern is influenced by climate, topography, soil, water, and roads. There is a sharp division between the rainy Mediterranean climate in the west and the semiarid desert climate in the east. The dividing line coincides more or less with the 300 mm isohyet (a line drawn on a map connecting points receiving equal rainfall), and there are almost no settlements east of the line that passes through the villages Mughaiyir, Majdal Bani Fadil, Beit Dajan, Tammun, and Tayasir. Owing to the structure of the Samaria Mountains, which are open to the west, the Mediterranean climate and consequently the boundaries of the agricultural area penetrate farther east than is the case in Judea. There are no settlements in the semiarid Jordan Valley except Jericho in the south, which was in the past based on an oasis.

The nature of the terrain in Samaria determines the location of the settlements, which are situated mainly on the hilltops, on the spurs or on the anticlines, which afford them relative security. There are also some villages in valleys or on their fringes. Villages in the hilly terrain are found mainly in the western part of the Samaria Mountains, following the mountain spurs which descend in the direction of the coastal plain, and also in the eastern part, near the threshold of the desert. In central Samaria, on the other hand, near the longitudinal valleys, the villages are located in the middle or at the foot of the slope. The same holds good for the area south of Nablus and the whole region between Nablus and Jenin, where better security and greater ease of cultivation enabled the villagers to choose a lower location. The lower the topography, the more scattered the villages. The dispersion is fairly even between Ramallah and Nablus, and less so between Nablus and Jenin.

In contrast to the Hebron and the Jerusalem mountains, only one-third of the villages in Samaria are located on hilltops, while over 20 percent are at the foot of a slope or on the edge of a valley. The soil found in the valleys is an important factor for the villages in the Samaria Mountains. The valleys themselves are not settled, since they contain fertile sedimentary soil suitable for intensive cultivation. In the Mikhmetat, Dotan, and Sanur valleys, the villages lie on the fringes of the valley, close to the mountain slope, making use of every inch of available soil for cultivation. The wide dispersion of villages in the Samaria Mountains is also made possible by the abundance of springs, which are the result of the many fault lines characteristic of this region.

The traditional Arab settlement in the Judean and Samarian hills demonstrates that the climatic frontier of the desert constitutes a barrier to the extension of the settlements and causes the concentration and sedentariness of the population at the edge of the desert, which is evidenced by both the size of the villages and the extent of their landholdings. The dispersal of the settlements, particularly in Judea, is governed almost entirely by geographical factors, and no evidence can be found of artificial or planned Arab development activity, such as that in the new Jewish settlement areas. A striking case is that of the Jordan Valley, where irrigation and soil improvement are preconditions for any settlement. Here, where human endeavor is more important than natural conditions, there has been no development at all. The villages in this area and their interrelationship show no signs of any special coordination, but rather of isolation and dependence on the immediate local resources of soil, water, and means of communication.

As for urban settlement in this region, there have not been any notable signs of urbanization. Neither the nature of the terrain nor the

agricultural economic background was conducive to urban development. The towns are relatively small and are located along the
main traffic artery of the mountain. The towns in Judea and Samaria
form a kind of mirror image north and south of Jerusalem, with
Bethlehem and Beit Jala opposite Ramallah and El-Bire, while Hebron,
the Hebron Mountain capital, is the counterpart of Nablus, the
northern capital. The remaining towns are located as bridge points
pointing toward the neighboring regions: Jericho toward Transjordan,
Jenin toward the Valley of Esdraelon, and Tulkarm toward the Sharon
Plain.

Regional Settlement. The Israeli solution for the settlement of an
entire region is to build a regionwide network of settlements, even if
it runs contrary to the natural balance of population over a wider
area or if it involves establishing new settlements in previously
uninhabited areas that may be less suitable for development than
other places now settled by Arabs. The only condition necessary
for such settlement is a large investment of capital resources in order
to bring about such changes in the natural environment as are needed
to adapt it for settlement. This approach was first applied to a
section of the Jordan Valley, from a point south of Bet Shean Valley
to the northern end of the Dead Sea.

The Jordan Valley was one of the areas in Judea and Samaria
which had remained sparsely populated, though it was potentially
suitable for settlement. After the Six Day War, the Israeli settlement
authorities immediately started to draw up plans with a view to
settling Jews in this area. These plans were based on the establishment of a number of agricultural village settlements which would be
based on the climatic advantages of the Jordan Valley—a mild winter
and the possibility of growing tropical vegetables and fruit.[8]

Thus an exceptional opportunity presented itself to develop an
area by means of a comprehensive regional approach and to establish a
group of settlements based on the physical characteristics of the
valley. It was also necessary to plan the infrastructure required for
a continuous chain of settlements extending over the whole length
of the valley that would constitute a defense barrier parallel to the
Jordan River and facing Jordanian territory.

The Jordan Valley is estimated to contain 16,500 acres of cultivable land, unevenly distributed along the length of the valley.

[8] This description of the Jordan Valley development is by N. Markovsky, "Jewish
Settlement in the Jordan Valley: Its Character and Development," in *Judea and
Samaria*, ed. A. Shmueli, D. Grossman, and R. Ze'evi (Jerusalem: Cana'an, 1977;
in Hebrew), pp. 630-39.

The northern part is more suitable for intensive cultivation than the southern part, near the Dead Sea shore, and therefore more settlements were established in the north than in the south. The settlement pattern was also influenced by the longitudinal structure of the valley. Settlements could be located either in the main valley itself or in the lateral valleys which descend from the Judean Mountains and also contain soil suitable for cultivation.

The availability of local water resources was less decisive than that of land, since it was possible to supply water by artificial means. Of the total of 42 million cubic meters, which is the annual water potential of the Jordan Valley, the major portion is to be found in the north, while in the south there are only smaller quantities of water of inferior quality.

The amount of land and water available determined the number of agricultural units and settlements that could be planned for the valley. On the basis of 7.5 acres of land and 30,000 cubic meters per annum of water for each unit, we arrive at a potential of 2,000 units; if we assume 80 units per settlement, the number of agricultural settlements would approach eighteen to twenty-five.

The settlements were necessarily located next to the cultivable areas. Most of them were initially *Nahal* ("Fighting Pioneer Youth") outposts, some of which have already become permanent settlements. The type of settlement was determined in each case by local conditions, such as soil and water, and by the type of pioneering organization providing the settlers. Owing to the comprehensive approach to the planning of the whole region, it was possible to bring to it settlers from all sectors of the population, with varied backgrounds of agricultural knowledge and experience. The group of fourteen settlements in the north and center of the valley is called in Hebrew *Hevel Adam* (the "Adam district"), while the region north of the Dead Sea will contain three agricultural settlements and two tourist centers on the Dead Sea shore, one at Kaliya and the other at the mouth of Nahal Deragot.

Agriculture, in its various branches, provides most of the employment in the region. Industries and crafts were established in cooperative settlements in order to supplement income and to provide alternative employment during slack seasons. Owing to the paucity of agricultural resources in the southern part of the valley, the settlements there will be based mainly on tourism. The settlement pattern in the Jordan Valley is more or less similar to that found in other parts of the country—namely, a combination of farming and industry wherever this has been found to be necessary.

The regional settlement of the Jordan Valley is, as already noted, based on the political concept of a continuous chain of settlements parallel to the Jordan River, constituting a defense boundary in accordance with the Allon Plan, and on avoiding Jewish settlement in those parts of Judea and Samaria which have a dense Arab population. According to this concept, economic benefits could be derived from those geographic factors which had previously prevented settlement in the Jordan Valley. The idea was that with the aid of large-scale capital investment in the development of water resources and the use of agrotechnical know-how that had not been available to Arab farmers, it would be possible to raise large crops of winter vegetables and fruit which could be sold at high prices in the European market. This has indeed proved to be the case.

The settlement plan also ensures the geographical continuity of the settlements, which greatly facilitates the supply of services, as does the fact that all the settlements are close, to either the Jordan Valley or the East Samaria highway. One notable omission has been the lack of a large urban center, and there is concern that the building of such a center now, at Ma'aleh Efrayim, has come too late, as the settlers have in the meantime established links with other, more distant, centers. This, by the way, is a classic instance in Israel of the belated appearance of urban centers in regional settlement schemes.

"Spot" Settlement. Agricultural settlement in Judea and Samaria after the Six Day War has not been confined to the Jordan Valley. New settlements were recently established at several points in western Samaria, such as Rehan, Bet Homot, Shimron, Kedumim, Sal'it, Elqana, Karnei Shomron, Tappuah, Ari'el, and Neve Tzuf, and in the northwest of the Jerusalem Corridor, such as Kefar Mattityahu, Shilat, and Mevo Horon. New settlements in the Etzion Block are El'azar, Rosh Tzurim, Migdal 'Oz, and Allon Shevut, as well as Kefar Etzion itself, which was resettled (see figure 3).

These settlements were of necessity established on unoccupied state land, and since the greater part of the suitable land is already being cultivated in one way or another, the new settlements were in most cases set up in places with unfavorable agricultural conditions and often distant from existing roads. This raises difficult problems, especially as regards education and health services, electricity supply, and the like, which are not only a heavy burden on the national budget, but also deter potential investors, not to speak of the difficulty in maintaining a satisfactory social life in a community that does not exceed a few dozen souls.

Israel's extensive settlement experience proves the advantages

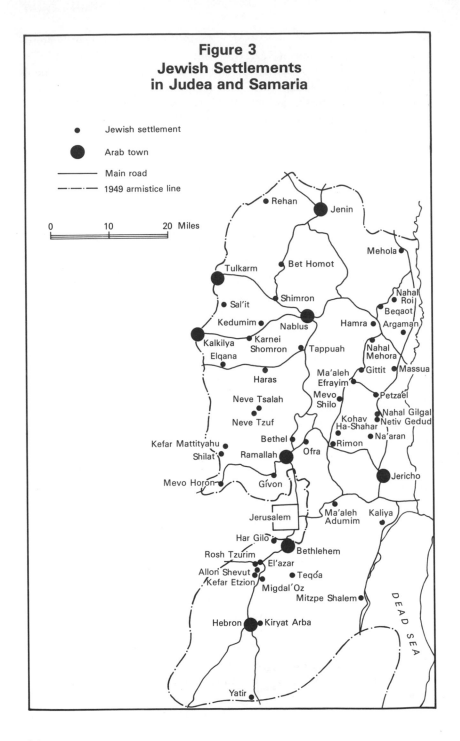

Figure 3
Jewish Settlements
in Judea and Samaria

- Jewish settlement
- Arab town
- Main road
- 1949 armistice line

0   10   20 Miles

Rehan
Jenin
Mehola
Tulkarm
Bet Homot
Shimron
Sal'it
Nahal Roi
Beqaot
Kedumim
Nablus
Hamra
Argaman
Kalkilya
Karnei Shomron
Tappuah
Nahal Mehora
Elqana
Gittit
Massua
Haras
Ma'aleh Efrayim
Neve Tsalah
Mevo Shilo
Petza'el
Neve Tzuf
Kohav Ha-Shahar
Nahal Gilgal
Netiv Gedud
Kefar Mattityahu
Bethel
Rimon
Na'aran
Shilat
Ofra
Ramallah
Mevo Horon
Givon
Jericho
Jerusalem
Ma'aleh Adumim
Kaliya
Har Gilo
Rosh Tzurim
Bethlehem
El'azar
Allon Shevut
Teqóa
Kefar Etzion
Migdal'Oz
Mitzpe Shalem
Hebron
Kiryat Arba
DEAD SEA
Yatir

24

of the cooperative system not only in agriculture but also in industry under certain circumstances. The cooperative system also is instrumental in integrating the settlers as a community. It is very difficult to maintain the cohesion of a small community far removed from the center of the country, and in such circumstances settlement becomes something in the nature of a permanent demonstration. This is particularly difficult if the individual settler does not succeed in putting down economic roots. Moreover, the single settlement can never repay the public funds invested in it. Most serious of all is the question of lack of sufficient land. Even nonagricultural settlements cannot absorb hundreds of additional settlers unless their area is enlarged by many hundreds of acres. In most cases it will not be possible to acquire this land, mainly because there has been no planning for orderly and unpublicized land purchases. As a result it will be necessary to expropriate private property or to take possession of public land, which involves the risk of litigation by neighboring farmers claiming right of possession of the land as its cultivators.

As yet, no clear pattern of this type of settlement activity has emerged, and it does not form part of any regional plan, with the exception of the group of settlements in the Etzion Block, which are intended to form one cohesive unit. The settlements are established without a predetermined plan as to timing and location, the main object being political, namely to occupy lands which otherwise might some day be in danger of being cut off from the State of Israel.

The future of this type of settlement activity is difficult to foretell. Will it grow or decline, and will it stand the test of changing political circumstances? Just as in the past, agricultural settlements within Israel had geographical significance when it came to determining the borders between Israel and its neighbors, it can be assumed that in the future as well, the settlements beyond the 1949 armistice line will influence political territorial decisions.

Urban Settlement. Proposals have been aired lately for the establishment of urban settlements around Jerusalem, as well as urban and semiurban settlements in different parts of the region. From a social and economic point of view, urban development has the advantage over all other kinds of development in being able to absorb many people in a relatively small area. Beginnings in urban settlement were made in East Jerusalem as early as 1967, but it is only lately that the scale of these developments has increased.

After the reunification of Jerusalem it became urgently necessary to make decisions regarding the planning of the city and its environs, but for the first few months after the Six Day War there was no clear-cut policy in this respect. No time was lost in pulling down the barriers between both parts of the city, and the city fathers saw to the immediate physical joining of East and West Jerusalem and to the management of the whole city on the basis of the existing infrastructure. First priority in building and reconstruction was given to those parts of the city where adverse strategic conditions, existing since the War of Independence, needed correction. Thus, the Sanhedria quarter in the eastern part of the city was enlarged, and the Ramot Eshqol, Giv'at Hamivtar, Ma'alot Dafna, and Giv'at Shapira quarters were developed, so as to create a continuous built-up area between the city and Mount Scopus. The decision was then also made to rebuild the Jewish quarter of the Old City, independently of any considerations regarding other parts of East Jerusalem.

Shortly afterward it was decided to build four residential neighborhoods within the new municipal boundaries, two in the north (Neve Ya'aqov and Ramot), one in the south (Giloh), and one in the east (East Talpiyot). These quarters were built on high ground enclosing the city from these directions. The Jerusalem municipality also planned the industrial zone of 'Anatot and began to develop another industrial zone in 'Atarot, near the airport. These steps were contrary to established planning policy of consolidating the city itself and preventing its spreading over a wide area, but political and historical reasons dictated the steps taken at that time.

After these quarters had been built, Israeli policy makers turned their attention to ensuring a Jewish majority in Jerusalem. According to the National Plan for the Dispersion of the Population, the population of the Jerusalem district in the mid-1990s should be 12 percent of the total population of Israel, while today it accounts for only 9.5 percent. The government decided to work toward increasing the population of the city in order to preserve the present numerical balance between Jews and non-Jews, which means increasing the annual growth rate by 3.7 percent.

The present policy may be termed the "thickening of Jerusalem." Government and other public bodies have initiated plans to widen the Jerusalem Corridor northward, beyond the Ma'aleh Bet Horon road, and southward beyond the 'Adullam–Etzion Block road. This will provide room around the city and allow future metropolitan development, including new suburbs, rural settlements, and even new towns, in the area extending from the Etzion Block in the south to Ma'aleh Adumim in the east, Har Ba'al Hatzor in the north, and Lower Bet Horon in the west.[9]

[9] For further detail, see *Jerusalem Surroundings: Their Impact on Urbanization* (Jerusalem: Municipal Planning Policy Department, 1977; in Hebrew).

The guiding principle in the development of the Jerusalem surroundings is the control of the heights, such as Giloh and Ramot, and of traffic crossroads on the mountain backbone, such as the Etzion Block or Giv'on. Of particular importance in the view of the planners is control of the main northwest and southwest traffic axes which connect Jerusalem with the lowland and the coastal plain. This can be achieved by clusters of settlements rather than by settlements forming a continuous linear pattern. It is thought that in order to ensure control of the area, there must be a correlation between the number of settlers and the number of settlements.

In the Jerusalem area there are two segments which have significant Jewish populations—namely, the city itself and the Jerusalem Corridor. All other segments are sparsely populated by Jews. Within the area there are several boundaries, each with a different significance: There is West Jerusalem, where there has been intensive Jewish development; there is the municipal area of Jerusalem, where Israeli law applies and whose boundary has political significance. The surroundings of Jerusalem have more of a functional importance; administratively, they are part of Judea and Samaria. They are a suitable subject for regional planning and for determining the zone of influence near the city. In the expanded corridor to the west of Jerusalem there is room for the development of agricultural settlement.

The above outline indicates the common denominator of the various settlement bodies with regard to the Jerusalem area. Development will be based on the existing road network, in particular the Bet Horon–Ma'aleh Adumim and 'Emeq Ha'elah–Etzion Block axes. The circle of new quarters within the municipal area of Jerusalem will be completed. Villages will be built on the heights overlooking the city, such as Nabi Samuel and Beit Jala, and in places which dominate the main traffic arteries connecting the mountains with the lowland and the coastal plain. The development of settlements in this area will be along an axis northward from Ma'aleh Hahamisha, and from Ramallah to Jericho, with Giv'on and Ma'aleh Adumim at the center of the area. The Etzion Block settlements will be strengthened, and the settlement of Teqo'a will be built as an outpost in the southwestern part of the Hebron Mountains.

Conclusions. The main difficulty encountered when planning the settlement of Judea and Samaria is that it is not empty but inhabited by about 600,000 Arabs who are not prepared to leave any place of their own free will. In contrast to past experience when Jews settled in other parts of Eretz Israel, the Arabs of Judea and Samaria are not at the mercy of absentee "effendi" landowners who are willing to sell their land. New approaches had therefore to be found to make possible settlement in this region, and the planners had to contend with innumerable restraints.

Traditional Arab settlement in the region is the most widespread and deep-rooted, and it occupies most of the cultivable land. It cannot, however, serve as a model for modern Jewish settlement. The system of regional settlement has a history of success within the pre-1967 lines, is an accepted technique in other countries, and has given rise to well-defined settlement models. It is efficient and very promising, but cannot serve as a model for all of Judea and Samaria, only for the Jordan Valley. This is its main weakness from a political point of view. The system of "spot" settlement has a wider application, and is perhaps more significant politically, but its economic and social weaknesses are so considerable as to raise doubts regarding its viability and its ability to achieve a spatial hold on the region, in the wider sense of the term. Of all types of settlement, urban settlement is the most compact in terms of population, the most economical with regard to land utilization, and generally also the one having the most promising economic future. Its main weakness is its high cost; enormous sums have to be invested in preparing an urban infrastructure. To this must be added the doubt as to whether there exists a potential for the tens of thousands of people required for the urban settlement of the area.

It is interesting to note that the four approaches that we have described reflect the application, in the short period of thirteen years, of a cross section of settlement processes utilized in Eretz Israel over the past century. When Zionist settlement first started, at the end of the nineteenth century, the traditional Arab approach was predominant, and this constituted a challenge to the early Jewish settlers. The "spot" approach reminds us of the "stockade and tower" pioneer settlements of the 1930s, both on the frontier and in the midst of the Arab population. The regional approach brings to mind the settlement undertakings in the Valley of Esdraelon and the Bet Shean Valley, and, later, in the Lakhish region and the northwestern Negev. The urban approach, which was first applied to the building of the development towns, is being repeated now in Judea and Samaria.

Spatial Patterns of Jewish-Arab Interrelationships

The existence of dominant geographic features in Judea and Samaria, which could be the basis for Jewish-Arab interrelationships, can also be used as a foundation for the development of various autonomy arrangements. These features are:

- the concentration of Arab settlement in the mountainous parts of Judea and Samaria
- the absence of Arab settlement in the Jordan Valley and the Judean Desert
- the concentration of Jewish settlement in the Jordan Valley
- the haphazard distribution of Israeli settlement in the hill country
- the existence of the Etzion Block between Jerusalem and Hebron
- the network of medium-sized Arab towns spread all over the region
- the prominence of Arab urban settlement on the backbone of the Judea and Samaria mountains
- the state of "rivalry" between the traditional Arab and the new Jewish patterns of settlement
- the continuous and fairly intensive growth of building activity in most Arab towns
- the rapid development and construction of Jewish semiurban centers, and the means taken to encourage people to settle in them
- the creation of an improved road network and the improved interrelationship between the various parts of the region

With these features as a background, it is possible to develop spatial patterns for a number of interrelationship or autonomy arrangements, with each pattern representing a combination of dominant elements, Israeli or Arab, both physical and demographic, while stressing their interrelationship. Such patterns can be presented on a rising scale, from a spatial minimum to a spatial maximum, or vice versa.

The various plausible spatial situations are presented below as six patterns of autonomy, with particulars of the geographic and demographic elements of each pattern. The six proposed patterns are:

1. Return to the pre-1967 spatial pattern
2. Return to the pre-1967 spatial pattern, excluding East Jerusalem
3. Return to the pre-1967 spatial pattern, excluding East Jerusalem, with minimal border revisions
4. Return to the pre-1967 spatial pattern, excluding East Jerusalem and the Jordan Valley, with minimal border revisions

5. Division of the region between Jews and Arabs, excluding East Jerusalem and the Jordan Valley, with minimal border revisions
6. Enforcement of Israeli sovereignty over the entire region of Judea and Samaria

These are basic patterns whose political implications have to be considered carefully. There are of course also other possible variants, which incorporate elements from one or another of the above patterns.

Pattern 1: Return to the Pre-1967 Spatial Pattern. In view of the many physical changes that have taken place in Judea and Samaria since the Six Day War, a return to the 1949 armistice line boundary would bring about a situation in which many existing elements would be cut off from their ties with Israel and from their continuity with the state. (See figure 4.)

• The new Jewish quarters surrounding Jerusalem, such as Giloh, Ramot, Shapiro Quarter, Neve Ya'aqov, East Talpiyot, and Greater Sanhedria, would be left outside the municipal boundaries of Jerusalem. These quarters house today about 15,000 inhabitants, and this number will eventually rise to 35,000. The large public building complex recently built on Mount Scopus (which was an Israeli enclave between 1948 and 1967) will also be cut off from the Israeli part of the city.
• Kiryat Arba will be cut off from its surroundings and will remain as an isolated quarter next to Arab Hebron. Its distance from Jerusalem, 35 km (22 miles), will, in the absence of a continuous connection, lead to a falling off in population and development.
• The semiurban settlements, some of which are already being built, while others are yet in the planning stage, will remain without a functional center in their vicinity. The severance of their link with Jerusalem and the State of Israel will render their existence pointless. There are at present eight such settlements, among them Ma'aleh Adumim, Giv'on, Ari'el, and Elqana. Others, such as Efrat, are in an advanced planning stage.
• The Jerusalem–Tel Aviv freeway may again be cut between Sha'ar Ha-Gai and Latrun. Jerusalem will cease to be linked by road to Nablus, the Jordan Valley, the Dead Sea, and Beersheba by way of Hebron. The connection between Gaza and Hebron through Beersheba will probably also be affected.
• The 'Atarot airfield, with its improved landing strip, will no longer be able to serve Israeli aviation, which will not be able to

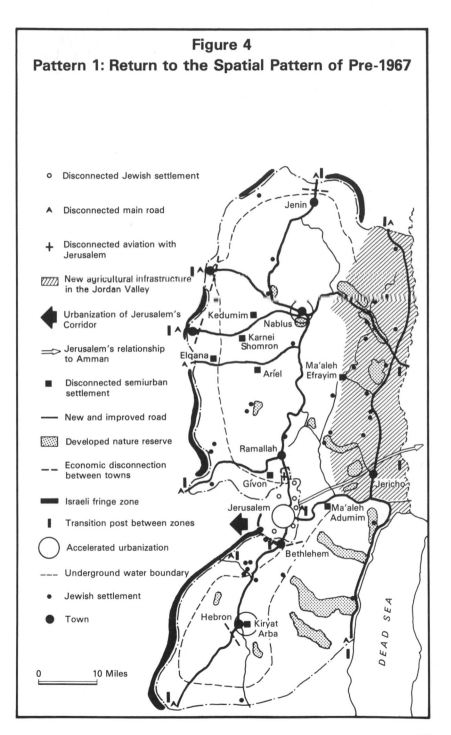

Figure 4
Pattern 1: Return to the Spatial Pattern of Pre-1967

○ Disconnected Jewish settlement

∧ Disconnected main road

+ Disconnected aviation with Jerusalem

▨ New agricultural infrastructure in the Jordan Valley

◀ Urbanization of Jerusalem's Corridor

⇒ Jerusalem's relationship to Amman

■ Disconnected semiurban settlement

— New and improved road

▨ Developed nature reserve

- - Economic disconnection between towns

▬ Israeli fringe zone

❙ Transition post between zones

◯ Accelerated urbanization

- - - Underground water boundary

• Jewish settlement

● Town

0   10 Miles

Jenin

Kedumim ■   Nablus

Karnei
Shomron ■

Elqana ■

■ Aríel   Ma'aleh
                 Efrayim

Ramallah

Gívon

Jerusalem   ■ Ma'aleh
                 Adumim

Jericho

Bethlehem

Hebron   ■ Kiryat
              Arba

DEAD SEA

31

operate the air routes between 'Atarot and other parts of the country. A considerable portion of the present airspace will be lost to Israeli civil and military aviation.

• Israel will leave in Judea and Samaria a greatly improved infrastructure of traffic arteries, such as the Jerusalem-Ramallah road, the Bet Horon road, the Jerusalem–Dead Sea road, the road from Jericho to En Gedi, and the Jordan Valley road, in addition to the widening and improvement of many other roads carried out in the course of the last few years.

• At Ma'aleh Adumim the infrastructure of a large industrial zone will remain, and it is doubtful whether the Arabs will be able to utilize it efficiently.

• In the Jordan Valley there will remain an extremely advanced agricultural infrastructure, with newly prepared soil, a new network of irrigation pipes, and fields of hitherto unknown crops.

• As in the past, Jerusalem will have to turn in the only direction left to her, namely to the west, and to prepare the corridor for the urban development that will be required in the capital. The lack of a sufficiently wide infrastructure will necessarily bring about the curtailment of building activity in the city.

• The partition between the two sections of Jerusalem will strengthen the ties between the Old City and Amman. East and West Jerusalem will develop in opposite directions, with a consequent waste of planned land uses.

• The interruption of the economic interrelationship which has developed between pairs of towns on both sides of the armistice line, such as Kefar Sava–Kalkilya, Natanya–Tulkarm, 'Afula–Jenin, Jerusalem–Bethlehem, Beersheba–Hebron, etc., would be a loss to the Jewish population as far as the employment of Arab workers from the occupied territories and mutual relations are concerned.

• There will be a renewal of frontier settlement along the armistice line, together with the attendant security installations. This will lead to an increase in population of areas and settlements on both sides of the frontier, with a consequent rise in tension, both in security and agricultural matters.

• If mutual relations are to be established between both sides of the armistice line, new entrance and exit points or frontier checkpoints will be required opposite Bet Shean, Tulkarm, Kalkilya, Jerusalem, Latrun, and east of Nablus.

• There would be an accelerated growth of Nablus and Hebron, the urban centers of influence in Samaria and Judea, respectively.

• Israel would lose control over the groundwater resources of Judea and Samaria, which are an undivided part of the country's groundwater system. Such control is necessary for regulating pumping and for utilizing the water in the coastal plain.

• If the present Jewish population of Judea and Samaria should be forced to vacate their homes, the problem would arise of settling about 12,000 persons in towns and villages within the armistice line.

Pattern 2: Return to the Pre-1967 Spatial Pattern, Excluding East Jerusalem. It is possible that East and West Jerusalem will continue to be united and form, as is the case today, a single municipal, economic, and administrative unit while the remaining parts of Judea and Samaria would return to the situation existing before 1967. The consequences of such an alternative (see figure 5) will be:

• Development of both sections of Jerusalem, Jewish and Arab, which has been held up in recent years owing to the political uncertainty, will be accelerated. In particular, there will be more Jewish building in the areas that were annexed to Jerusalem after 1967.

• Jerusalem would gradually strive to achieve a metropolitan structure, which will be expressed by strengthening the Jerusalem-Shu'fat-Ramallah axis, by completing the building up of the hills to the south, by extending in the direction of Bethlehem, Beit Jala, and Beit Sahur, and by filling up the as yet unbuilt areas in the city itself.

• The physical and economic growth of Jerusalem may cause changes in the settlement pattern over a wide area surrounding the city, such as the rapid urbanization of villages and the building of new Arab satellite towns. There will also be changes in the uses of agricultural land near Jerusalem and an accelerated creeping urbanization.

• There would be a growth in size and population of the Arab villages between Ramallah in the north and the Etzion Block in the south because of the increased economic strength of Jerusalem. As a result, the balance between the Jewish population of Jerusalem and the Arab population of the surroundings will be in danger of being upset.

• The increase of investments in Greater Jerusalem will arrest the urban flow to the Jerusalem Corridor. The possibility of allocating more area in the city proper for building purposes would prevent the conversion of the villages in the corridor into semiurban settlements.

• The growing importance of East Jerusalem as part of Greater Jerusalem would reduce the importance of Hebron and Nablus as district centers. Economic and social activity will naturally be concentrated in the largest and most populous center, which is Jerusalem.

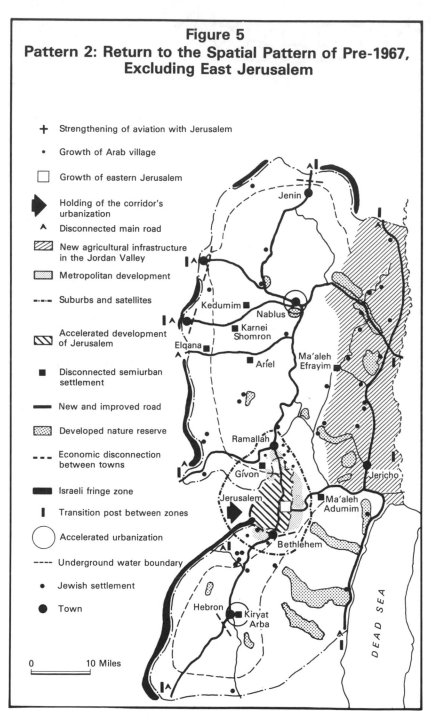

Figure 5
Pattern 2: Return to the Spatial Pattern of Pre-1967, Excluding East Jerusalem

+ Strengthening of aviation with Jerusalem

• Growth of Arab village

☐ Growth of eastern Jerusalem

Holding of the corridor's urbanization

∧ Disconnected main road

New agricultural infrastructure in the Jordan Valley

Metropolitan development

Suburbs and satellites

Accelerated development of Jerusalem

■ Disconnected semiurban settlement

New and improved road

Developed nature reserve

Economic disconnection between towns

Israeli fringe zone

▌ Transition post between zones

◯ Accelerated urbanization

Underground water boundary

• Jewish settlement

● Town

0   10 Miles

Jenin

Kedumim ■

Nablus

Karnei
Shomron ■

Elqana
∧   ■ Ariel

Ma'aleh
Efrayim ■

Ramallah

Givon

Jerusalem

Ma'aleh
Adumim ■

Jericho

Bethlehem

DEAD SEA

Hebron ● Kiryat
Arba

34

• If permitted, a rapid rise in the Arab population of East Jerusalem can be expected, contrary to the past, when other Arab towns also offered advantages. This rise would be due to the growing economic activity in Jerusalem, which would be accompanied by a rise in the standard of living.

• The more stable conditions in Greater Jerusalem and the granting of special status to Christian and Muslim holy sites will increase the flow of tourists from overseas and from the neighboring countries and will widen the scope of reconstruction, restoration and conservation work in the city.

Pattern 3: Return to the Pre-1967 Spatial Pattern, Excluding East Jerusalem, with Minimal Border Revisions. Adding minimal border revisions along the armistice line to pattern 2 will maintain the operational unity of road transport and agriculture and will prevent the displacement of a number of settlements and sites which are important from a security point of view. The following are recommended revisions (also see figure 6):

• The required border revisions will affect the Latrun enclave, the area west of Tulkarm, Battir village, the area near Ramot, and East 'Atarot. What used to be a no-man's-land between double armistice lines will have to be abolished.

• The border revision at the Latrun enclave is necessary for maintaining normal road services between Jerusalem and the coastal plain and in order not to interfere with the Jerusalem–Tel Aviv freeway.

• West of Tulkarm it will be necessary to annex a medium-sized area of land in order to permit the undisturbed operation of freight trains using the Lod–Haifa railroad.

• West of Battir in the Jerusalem Corridor the railroad right-of-way must be widened in order to secure the regular rail service to the capital.

• The northwestern part of the Jerusalem municipal boundary will have to be modified so as to include the almost completed Ramot quarter within the municipal area of the city.

• The municipal boundary will also have to be changed east of 'Atarot in order to enable the enlargement of the airfield and its conversion into an international airport.

Pattern 4: Return to the Pre-1967 Spatial Pattern, Excluding East Jerusalem and the Jordan Valley, with Minimal Border Revisions. It is very possible that the Jordan Valley, which was only sparsely settled in the past and since 1967 has undergone an intensive develop-

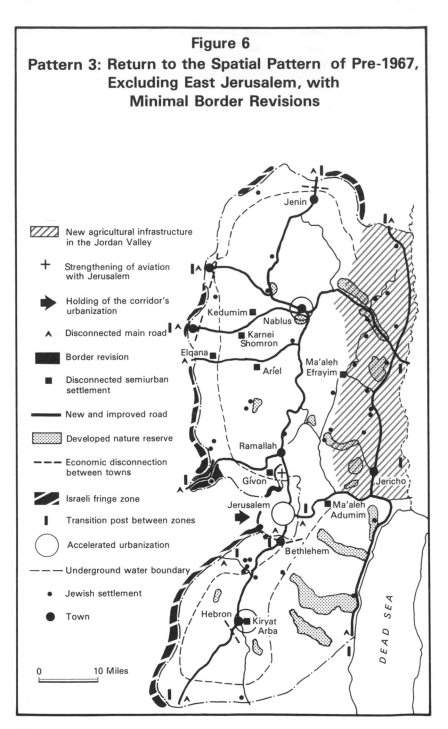

Figure 6
Pattern 3: Return to the Spatial Pattern of Pre-1967, Excluding East Jerusalem, with Minimal Border Revisions

New agricultural infrastructure in the Jordan Valley

Strengthening of aviation with Jerusalem

Holding of the corridor's urbanization

Disconnected main road

Border revision

Disconnected semiurban settlement

New and improved road

Developed nature reserve

Economic disconnection between towns

Israeli fringe zone

Transition post between zones

Accelerated urbanization

Underground water boundary

Jewish settlement

Town

Jenin

Kedumim

Nablus

Karnei Shomron

Elqana

Ariel

Ma'aleh Efrayim

Ramallah

Givon

Jericho

Jerusalem

Ma'aleh Adumim

Bethlehem

Hebron

Kiryat Arba

DEAD SEA

0   10 Miles

ment process, both as regards population and agriculture, will constitute a special and important element within the autonomy framework. This is the part of Judea and Samaria which has had the greatest influx of Jewish settlers (see figure 7) and where there have been the largest investments. The inclusion of the Jordan Valley in the area of Israeli sovereignty will raise the following problems:

• A continuous physical link between the Jordan Valley and the rest of the State of Israel will have to be provided, if not by territorial additions, then at least by special traffic arteries in the direction of Bet Shean in the north and Jerusalem in the southwest, in addition to one or two latitudinal axes which will cross Samaria and connect the Jordan Valley with the coastal plain.

• It will be necessary to provide traffic corridors to and from the valley, as well as entrance and exit points for the Jewish and Arab inhabitants. It will also be necessary to ensure the interregional traffic between the Transjordan and Judea and Samaria, using the Jordan bridges and the corridors leading to them.

• There will be an increasingly intensive Jewish settlement in the valley, necessitating massive investments, both for securing the Jordanian border and for achieving the greatest possible productivity in this area, where all territorial disputes will have been settled.

• It is to be expected that Jericho will grow in size and population, as a result of its new role as a transit town between the Jordan Valley and Jerusalem and the State of Israel, in addition to its position on the main route between both sides of the Jordan. It is therefore possible that, apart from tourism, Jericho will also attract industries and services connected with agriculture.

• There will probably be some thickening of border settlement, mainly to the east, south, and west. This will consist of defense installations, military camps, and various types of military agricultural settlements.

• Israeli sovereignty over the Jordan Valley will make possible the establishment of a number of urban settlements between Jericho and Bet Shean, thus creating an urban continuity from north to south.

• It may be assumed that the Jordan Valley will be most intensively exploited, for agricultural, engineering, and other kinds of installations which are particularly suited to this region.

Pattern 5: Division of the Region between Jews and Arabs, Excluding East Jerusalem and the Jordan Valley, with Minimal Border Revisions.
There exists the possibility that, with the exclusion of East Jerusalem and after minimal changes along the armistice line, the whole of

Figure 7
Pattern 4: Return to the Spatial Pattern of Pre-1967, Excluding East Jerusalem and the Jordan Valley, with Minimal Border Revisions

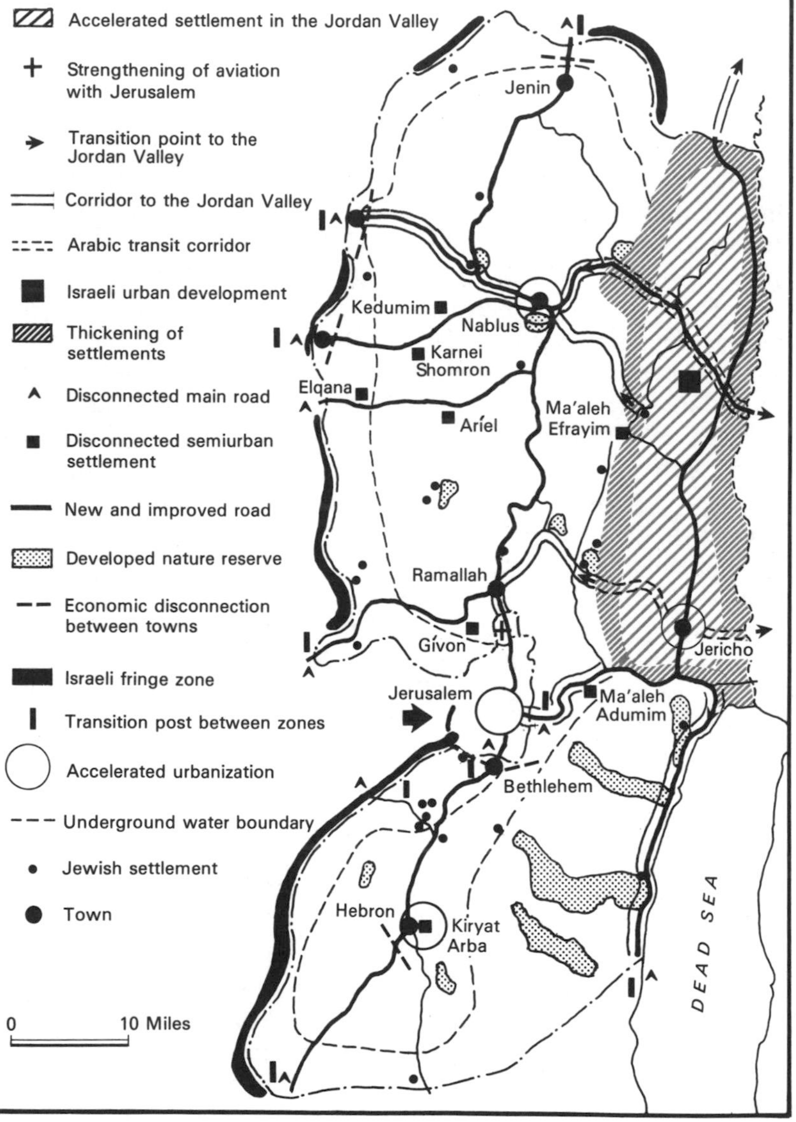

Legend:

- ▨ Accelerated settlement in the Jordan Valley
- ✛ Strengthening of aviation with Jerusalem
- ➤ Transition point to the Jordan Valley
- ═ Corridor to the Jordan Valley
- ⁼⁼⁼ Arabic transit corridor
- ■ Israeli urban development
- ▨ Thickening of settlements
- ⋀ Disconnected main road
- ■ Disconnected semiurban settlement
- ▬ New and improved road
- ▨ Developed nature reserve
- ⁻⁻ Economic disconnection between towns
- ▬ Israeli fringe zone
- ❙ Transition post between zones
- ◯ Accelerated urbanization
- ⁻⁻⁻ Underground water boundary
- • Jewish settlement
- ● Town

Map labels: Jenin, Kedumim, Nablus, Karnei Shomron, Elqana, Ariel, Ma'aleh Efrayim, Ramallah, Givon, Jerusalem, Ma'aleh Adumim, Jericho, Bethlehem, Hebron, Kiryat Arba, DEAD SEA

0   10 Miles

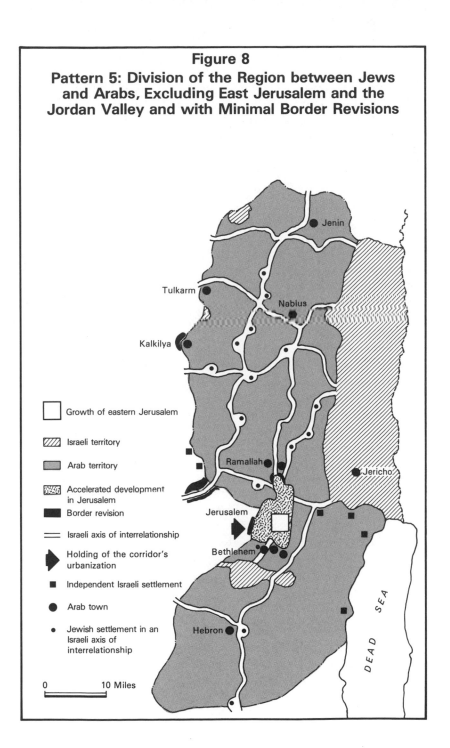

Figure 8
Pattern 5: Division of the Region between Jews and Arabs, Excluding East Jerusalem and the Jordan Valley and with Minimal Border Revisions

Jenin

Tulkarm

Nablus

Kalkilya

Growth of eastern Jerusalem

Israeli territory

Arab territory

Accelerated development in Jerusalem

Border revision

Israeli axis of interrelationship

Holding of the corridor's urbanization

Independent Israeli settlement

Arab town

Jewish settlement in an Israeli axis of interrelationship

Ramallah

Jericho

Jerusalem

Bethlehem

DEAD SEA

Hebron

0   10 Miles

Judea and Samaria will be partitioned between Jews and Arabs, with each party exercising sovereign rights over the territory and the population of its area (see figure 8). In this case it will be necessary to define the areas with predominantly Jewish or Arab population, the transit points between the two areas, the relationship between them, and the axes of interrelation necessary for safeguarding the territorial interests of each side. The plausible solutions are as follows:

• The whole area north of Bethel up to the armistice line would be allocated to the Arabs, with the exclusion of the Rehan and Sal'it enclaves and the whole of the Jordan Valley.

• The greater part of the Hebron Mountains and the Judean Desert would be allocated to the Arabs.

• The whole of the Etzion Block, including all existing and proposed settlements between Hafurit in the west and Teqo'a in the east, would form part of the Jewish area.

• The whole of the Jordan Valley, within the boundaries of the agricultural and regional settlement plans, from the Bet Shean valley in the north to Jericho in the south, would be one continuous Jewish area.

• Wherever there are existing Jewish settlements within areas that for the purposes of autonomy have been defined as Arab, they would be independent enclaves or a part of axes of a certain defined width.

• There would be an axis of Jewish settlements in the Samaria Mountains, in the general direction of Jerusalem-Shiloh-Nablus.

• There is a need for a western longitudinal axis, in the direction of Jerusalem-Ariel-Nablus-Dotan Valley.

• There would have to be a number of transverse Jewish settlement axes from Baq'a el Garbiya to the Jordan Valley, from Kafr Qasem to Ma'aleh Efrayim, from the Modi'im region to Giv'on, from Hafurit to Teqo'a, and from Lakhish to Kiryat Arba.

• There would have to be a Jewish longitudinal axis from Jerusalem to Kiryat Arba, and from there to Arad, in order to ensure the link between existing Jewish towns without having to cross the mountain backbone.

• Axes of communication would also be required between Jerusalem and Ma'aleh Adumim, between Jerusalem and Giv'on in the north, and between Jerusalem and the Etzion Block in the south.

Pattern 6: Enforcement of Israeli Sovereignty over the Entire Region of Judea and Samaria. If we accept the premise that the whole of Judea and Samaria will remain under Israeli sovereignty, that the armistice line will cease to have any significance, and that the Jordan River will be the only national boundary to the east (see figure 9), we can expect the following main physical consequences in the area:

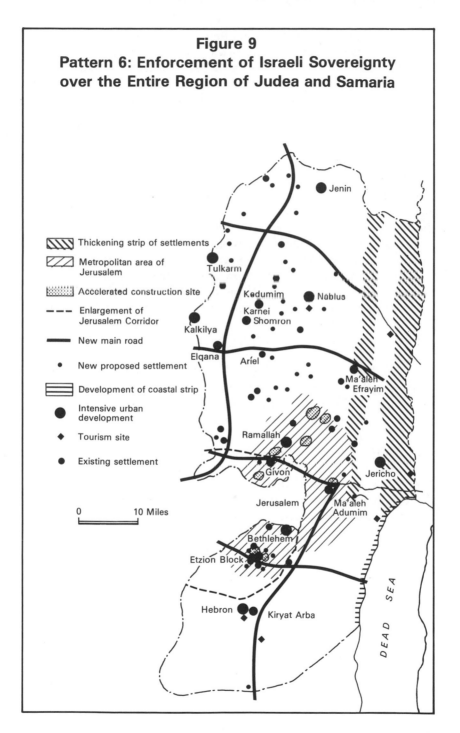

Figure 9
Pattern 6: Enforcement of Israeli Sovereignty over the Entire Region of Judea and Samaria

Thickening strip of settlements

Metropolitan area of Jerusalem

Accelerated construction site

Enlargement of Jerusalem Corridor

New main road

New proposed settlement

Development of coastal strip

Intensive urban development

Tourism site

Existing settlement

0   10 Miles

Jenin

Tulkarm

Kedumim

Karnei Shomron

Nablus

Kalkilya

Elqana

Ariel

Ma'aleh Efrayim

Ramallah

Givon

Jericho

Jerusalem

Ma'aleh Adumim

Bethlehem

Etzion Block

Hebron

Kiryat Arba

DEAD SEA

41

- There would be intensive building of installations and of settlements along the Jordan Valley near the Jordanian frontier, and on the eastern slopes of the Samaria Mountains, in order to secure the area against the Arab states to the east.
- The metropolitan area of Jerusalem would spread beyond the ring of rural settlements which encircle the city at a radius of 5–10 km (3–6 miles).
- Arab building in Jerusalem would lessen, while Israeli building would increase, both in the city itself and in the outskirts.
- Settlement in the Jerusalem Corridor would expand north- and southward. There would be a development of agricultural settlement between the former armistice line and the Bet Horon road to the north and the Bet Govrin–Hebron road to the south.
- New north-south and east-west traffic arteries would improve communications between Judea and Samaria and the State of Israel.
- There would be an increase in the number of settlements in all parts of the region. New settlements would be established in the southern part of the Jordan Valley, the Etzion Block on the Hafurit–Teqo'a axis would be extended, more settlements would be built in the Samaria Mountains, and the periphery of Jerusalem would be developed.
- The Dead Sea littoral would benefit from greater investment in tourism and bathing-beach improvements. The nature reserves on the slopes of the Judean Mountains would be expanded and form part of the Dead Sea shore development.
- Selected localities in the region would be the subject of intensive urban development. The most important among these are the Etzion Block, Ma'aleh Adumim, Giv'on, Ari'el, and Karnei Shomron.
- It is to be assumed that the new urban and rural settlements in the region would form a hierarchy distinct from that of the Arab sector. It would be based on Jerusalem as the primary town, on a system of medium-sized satellite towns, and on an additional system of medium-sized towns over all of Judea and Samaria.
- There would be intensive development of tourist sites in Judea and Samaria, including archaeological and historical sites, parks, and nature reserves.

Conclusions: Advantages and Disadvantages in the Choice of Spatial Patterns

The six patterns presented here offer political leaders various alternatives for the future of Judea and Samaria and emphasize four basic elements:

- the extent of Israeli spatial autonomy
- the extent to which facts established in the past will be accepted
- the possibility of increasing the Jewish population of the region
- the status of Jerusalem

It is clear that patterns 1 and 6 represent extreme and opposing situations, namely, either a return to the pre-1967 situation, in which Israel's spatial autonomy would be almost nonexistent, or full spatial control, in which Israel's autonomy would approach a maximum.

A more detailed examination of patterns 2–5 may, however, lead to other solutions which emphasize other elements in various combinations within the spatial framework of autonomy. Readiness to accept a medium status for Jerusalem and to forgo all other options leads to pattern 2. A medium status for Jerusalem, combined with the possibility of a medium-sized population increase in the region, leads to pattern 3. A demand for medium spatial control over the Judea and Samaria region, combined with at least some measure of keeping the status quo and a medium-sized status and population increase in Jerusalem, leads to pattern 4. Finally, a large degree of spatial autonomy, maximum possibilities for population increase and the strengthening of Jerusalem, as against only a medium measure of keeping the status quo, leads to pattern 5.

It should be added that in each of these patterns significance should be attached to the physical elements it contains, such as agricultural areas, roads, settlements, interrelationship axes, water resources, industrial areas, etc.

An overall perspective of Judea and Samaria from a spatial point of view, and an examination of the various alternatives, can be of help when it comes to reaching political decisions regarding the implementation of autonomy and the establishment of a satisfactory mutual relationship between Jews and Arabs in this region.

2

The Israeli Settlements in
Judea and Samaria: Legal Aspects

Moshe Drori

In 1967, shortly after the Six Day War, Israeli settlements began to appear in the area of Judea and Samaria.[1] At first, former residents of the Etzion Block—a group of Jewish settlements that fell to the Jordanians in 1948—returned with their children to reoccupy the sites of their villages.[2] They were followed by other settlers who came to the Jordan Valley, Kiryat Arba near Hebron, and to other settlements in the area of Judea and Samaria. Since its inception and up to the present, Israeli settlement has been a subject of discussion and debate in various international forums, but closer inspection reveals that though slogans abound, methodical and substantive discussion of the subject is lacking.

Following a short review of the legal status of Judea and Samaria, this chapter examines the legal background of the establishment of settlements, with respect both to the land upon which the settlements are built and to their status under international law. It turns then to the question of how the settlements were regulated from the point of view of Israeli municipal law. A particularly important issue here is how the Israeli authorities coped with the tension entailed in establishing settlements in an area whose territorial law is a mixture of Turkish, British Mandatory, Jordanian, and military law, when the intention of the settlers—as well as that of the

[1] This paper deals with Israeli settlement only in Judea and Samaria, not in East Jerusalem and in the Old City. On the status of Jerusalem and Israel's rights there (including the right to Jewish settlement), see Y. Z. Blum, *The Juridical Status of Jerusalem*, Jerusalem Papers on Peace Problems (Hebrew University of Jerusalem, 1974).

[2] A concise English description of the beginning of Israeli settlement in Judea and Samaria after the Six Day War can be found in A. Gerson, *Israel, the West Bank and International Law* (London: Frank Cass, 1978), pp. 136 ff.

State of Israel—was that they would be considered Israelis, to whom Israeli law applies.

Another section of this chapter discusses the organizational and municipal structure of the settlements and the powers conferred upon the municipal bodies. By examining the personal status of the settlers, I will attempt to show how everyday, concrete problems such as taxation and national insurance (social security), etc., were solved. The final section considers the relationship between the Israeli settlers and the Israeli judiciary, the question of whether Israeli courts have jurisdiction over settlers' affairs, and if so, under what conditions. The chapter concludes with a legislative proposal and with possible legal solutions relating to the Israeli settlers in Judea and Samaria and their links with Israel.

The Legal Status of Judea and Samaria

On June 5, 1967, Jordan attacked Israel, despite Israel's message to Jordan that "Israel will not attack any state which refrains from attacking it."[3] After three days of fighting, the area of Judea and Samaria was taken by the Israel Defense Forces (IDF), and it has since been administered by a military government. Formal expression has been given to this situation in a proclamation issued by the IDF commander in the area.[4]

Diverse opinions exist on the question of the status of the area. Is it an "occupied area" or one with a special status? Does the Geneva Convention apply to Israel's presence there, or is it sufficient if Israel complies only with the "humanitarian" part of the convention?[5] I will summarize those opinions briefly.

Three Views of the Area's Status. International law in the sphere of warfare and the administration of occupied areas has two objectives: to ensure the welfare of the local population; and to preserve the

[3] Abba Eban, Israel's foreign minister, in: General Assembly, *Official Records*, 1526th meeting, June 19, 1967, p. 9; Blum, *Juridical Status of Jerusalem*, p. 19, n. 54. Mr. Eban's version of the message was confirmed by General Old Bull, then chief of staff of the UN Truce Supervision Organization.

[4] See the Proclamation concerning the Institution of Government by the IDF (Proclamation No. 1), in *Collection of Proclamations, Orders and Appointments of the I.D.F. Command in the West Bank Area* (hereinafter CPOA), no. 1, p. 3; Proclamation concerning Law and Administration (West Bank Area), no. 2 (1967), *CPOA*, no. 1, pp. 3-4.

[5] Geneva Convention Relative to the Protection of Civilian Persons in Time of War, August 12, 1949, *Kitvei Amana* [Israel Treaty Documents], vol. 1, no. 30 (1949), p. 559.

situation in an occupied area as it was, as a "trust" for the original sovereign, who might return after the occupation.[6] The first question to be asked, however, is whether Judea and Samaria belong to the previous ruler—Jordan.

Jordan occupied Judea and Samaria unlawfully in 1948,[7] and the annexation of the West Bank to Jordan in 1950 was basically contrary to international law. The annexation was not recognized by the United States, the Soviet Union, or the Arab states, nor by any except Pakistan and the United Kingdom (de facto).[8] Thus, according to one view, Jordan had, at most, the status of an occupying power. Since Jordan was never sovereign in the area, the first opinion points up the problem of the "missing reversioner." Since the Six Day War was a war of self-defense on Israel's part and Jordan was the aggressor, in the absence of any other state possessing better title, Israel's conquest of the area during that war gave it the best title.[9] Israel, therefore, is bound to comply only with the humanitarian part of the law of warfare and not with the rules intended to protect the interests of the previous regime.[10] In this view, the Geneva Convention does not apply to the occupation of Judea and Samaria, since this is not a case of one state's occupying part of another.

Another view has been expressed to the effect that, even

[6] Y. Z. Blum, "The Missing Reversioner: Reflections on the Status of Judea and Samaria," *Israel Law Review* (hereinafter *Is.L.R.*), vol. 3 (1968), pp. 293-94; J. Stone, *No Peace, No War in the Middle East: Legal Problems of the First Year* (Sydney: Maitland Publications for the International Law Association, Australian Branch, 1969), pp. 39-40. And see also article 47 of the Geneva Convention, prohibiting interference with previous government institutions and the interpretation of this article in J. S. Pictet, *Commentary on the IV Geneva Convention Relative to the Protection of Civilian Persons in Times of War* (Geneva: International Committee for the Red Cross, 1958), pp. 273-74.

[7] Blum, "The Missing Reversioner," pp. 283-88; Stone, *No Peace, No War,* p. 39; M. Shamgar, "The Observance of International Law in the Administered Territories," *Israel Yearbook on Human Rights* (hereinafter *Is.Y.H.R.*), vol. 1 (1971), pp. 264-66; Blum, *Juridical Status of Jerusalem,* pp. 8 ff.

[8] Blum, "The Missing Reversioner," pp. 289-91; Stone, *No Peace, No War,* p. 39; Shamgar, "Observance of International Law," pp. 264-66. Only Pakistan and the United Kingdom (the latter with a reservation regarding East Jerusalem) had recognized the annexation of the West Bank to Jordan. See also, Lorch in Symposium, *Is.Y.H.R.,* vol. 1 (1971), p. 67.

[9] Blum, "The Missing Reversioner," pp. 293-94; Stone, "No Peace, No War"; Shamgar, "Observance of International Law," p. 266; Schwebel, "What Weight to Conquest?" *American Journal of International Law,* vol. 64 (1970), p. 344.

[10] In a recent decision of the Israeli High Court, this view was adopted, based on Blum's and Shamgar's articles, cited in the preceding note. See H.C. 61/80, *Haetzni v. State of Israel et al.* (1980) *P.D. (Piskei Din* [Law Report of the Israeli Supreme Court]) 34(3) 595 (hereinafter the *Haetzni* case).

assuming that Jordan was never sovereign in Judea and Samaria, Israel must nevertheless comply with the Geneva Convention and other rules relating to occupied territories. This is because such rules apply not only to the occupation of an area which had previously been under some other sovereign, but to any occupation whatsoever. Israel is bound by the convention because it is the acknowledged military occupier of Judea and Samaria.[11]

Finally, A. Gerson has proposed that Israel be regarded as a trustee administering the area for the local population which constitutes the true sovereign there.[12] Israel is not bound, according to this view, to retain the existing law and government institutions, since there is no need to maintain the status quo in order to facilitate the return of the previous ruler—Jordan—to the area. Rather, Israel's top priority must be the interests of the local population.

I will attempt to assess Israel's actions in the area in the light of the above three views (even though, according to Professor Stone, to view Israel's activities in the light of the assumption that Israel is an occupier causes a measure of injustice to Israel). In fact, Israel maintains a military government in Judea and Samaria and does act according to the humanitarian sections of the Geneva Convention. Furthermore, whenever the validity of an order of the military government has been the subject of discussion in the Israeli High Court of Justice, the government has acceded to the court's deciding the question according to the principles of customary international law and, in particular, the Hague Conventions of 1907. The representative of the State Attorney's Department has stated that he is not seeking any decision to the effect that the conventions apply to Judea and Samaria, but that in fact the area commander does act in conformity with the conventions, and the State Attorney's Department is willing to have the High Court of Justice examine the legality

---

[11] See article 2 of the convention; see also, Lorch in Symposium. From the words of M. Greenspan, in Symposium, *Is.Y.H.R.*, vol. 1 (1971), pp. 370, 371, it may be concluded that he also supports this view. See also, S. M. Boyd, "The Applicability of International Law to the Occupied Territories," *Is.Y.H.R.*, vol. 1 (1971), pp. 258-61; Boyd in Symposium, *Is.Y.H.R.*, vol. 1 (1971), pp. 367-68, 370-73. He has a different interpretation of article 2 of the Geneva Convention. Most of the countries of the world, the Red Cross, and the UN Security Council and General Assembly hold the view that the Geneva Convention *does* apply to Israel's occupation of Judea and Samaria. See Boyd, "Applicability of International Law," p. 259.

[12] A. Gerson, "Trustee-Occupant: The Legal Status of Israel's Presence in the West Bank," *Harvard International Law Journal*, vol. 14 (1973), pp. 1-49, and Gerson, *Israel, the West Bank*.

of the order(s) of the area commander in the light of those conventions.[13]

Since the Likud party came to power in 1977, an even more indeterminate situation has developed. The government, and in particular the prime minister, consider Judea and Samaria part of Israel. In practice, however, the military government operates according to legal principles that are based on the supposition that the area is being administered as occupied territory. I will examine the consequences of this inconsistency at a later stage, while discussing lands in the area and their use for Israeli settlements.

Lands and the Israeli Settlements

Judea and Samaria together cover some 5,780 square kilometers. The process of land registration was begun in Judea and Samaria before the Six Day War, but by 1967 only about half the land had been registered and classified. For the other half, the Land Registry bears no records of rights of ownership, and uncertainty arises as to ownership of each and every parcel of land.

Some of the land is owned by private persons, residents of Judea and Samaria who are actually present in the area. Other parts are registered in the names of "absentees"—private persons who do not reside in the area. In the latter case, the land passes into the possession of the commissioner for abandoned property (private property), whose function is analogous to that of a custodian: to preserve and attend to the property until such time as its owners should return. He does not acquire ownership, and if he leases the land, he must deposit the rents in the name of the owner, pending his return.[14] Almost 430,000 dunams (a dunam is approximately one-fourth of an acre) of land in the area belong to absentee owners.

Another category of land is commonly called "state lands." It must be stressed, however, that these are not lands belonging to the

[13] This line was adopted in the first petition that was filed with the High Court of Justice concerning the validity of an order of the area commander: H.C. 337/71, *The Christian Association for the Holy Places* v. *The Minister of Defense et al.* (1971) P.D. 26(1) 574. See M. Drori, *The Legislation in the Area of Judea and Samaria* (Hebrew University of Jerusalem, 1975; in Hebrew), pp. 79 ff.

A certain change could be discerned in the approach of the Supreme Court in the *Haetzni* case, cited in note 10. There the *petitioner*, not the state, demanded that the High Court decide the legal status of the area. The state adhered to its position that the High Court was not the proper forum for deciding Israel's status in the area. The state's position was that judicial review would be based on the assumption that Israel upholds the conventions applying to occupied territory.

[14] See Drori, *Legislation*, p. 192, for a discussion of the custodianship of absentees' property.

State of Israel, but rather to the state that previously controlled the area, that is, Jordan. They are registered in the Land Registration Office in the name of the king of Jordan or of the British high commissioner who preceded him. These lands spread over 700,000 dunams (one-eighth of the entire area of Judea and Samaria).

Remaining unregistered property could fall into one of two categories: (1) private lands belonging to residents or absentee owners lacking proof of ownership, to which the laws of prescription and the laws of possession apply (these laws are a patchwork of Ottoman, Mandatory, and Jordanian laws, which few have mastered); and (2) lands belonging to no one, which some say means that they are to be administered by the de facto ruler in the area, which is the Israeli military government. Even according to this view, however, the military government does not have greater rights over ownerless property than it does over "state lands" registered in the Land Registry in the name of Jordan.

Governmental Property or "State Lands." The starting point of international law in relation to occupied territories is that the conquering power occupies the area only until it is returned to its former sovereign or any other element determined by the peace agreement that terminates the war that resulted in the occupation. During its occupancy, the occupying power is obliged to restore order to the area and to preserve the status quo that existed on the eve of conquest, in order to facilitate the handing back of the area. These principles are subject to the requirements of military need, public order, and the welfare of the population, which may impel the occupying power to amend the existing law and change the status quo in the area.[15]

It is against this background that we may understand the principles relating to state lands.[16] Ownership of the property that was registered in the name of the king of Jordan has not been transferred to the Israeli government because the Israeli government is not a successor to the Jordanian king or government. On the other hand, lands registered in the name of the high commissioner of the British Mandate which are within the "Green Line" (the accepted designation of the 1949 armistice line) now belong to the State of Israel because Israel is the legal successor to the Mandate.

The military government is only the administrator of the governmental lands previously owned by Jordan, as stipulated in regu-

---

15 See article 43, "Regulations respecting the Law and Customs of War on Land," Annex to the Hague Conventions, 1970; Drori, *Legislation*, pp. 49 ff.

16 Yoram Dinstein, "The International Law of Belligerent Occupation and Human Rights," *Is.Y.H.R.*, vol. 8 (1978), pp. 104, 127 ff., esp. 129-30.

lation 55 of the Hague Convention of 1907. As such, it is required to preserve these lands and has *usufructus* (the right to enjoy their "fruits") regarding them. The military government may set up army bases and such other similar installments as are necessary on government lands, but it may not sell these lands to anyone for the simple reason that it does not own them. Therefore, the settlers now living on government lands are not the owners either. They merely have permission from the temporary administrator of the lands (the commissioner for government property) to stay on the lands, and only for as long as the lands are administered by the commissioner—that is, as long as the occupation continues.[17] Upon termination of the occupation, the commissioner will be obliged to return the lands to their registered owner—the king of Jordan—unless a peace agreement between Israel and Jordan should stipulate otherwise.

Private Property. The international conventions categorically prohibit the confiscation of private property, permitting only temporary seizure of such property when necessitated by military requirements.[18] The result is twofold. First, the lands are seized only for as long as required for military purposes or until the occupation is terminated, whichever date is earlier (although a peace agreement may provide otherwise). With reference to this legal position, Judge Witkon of the Israel Supreme Court said in the *Bet El* case that "the petitioners were never divested of their ownership." Second, seizure is permitted for military purposes only. This condition has been reviewed by the High Court of Justice, which is empowered to decide on the sincerity of the military argument. In the *Bet El* case, the court was convinced by the affidavit of General Orli, the coordinator of activities in the territories, of the military necessity for the Bet El and Bekaot B settlements.[19] In the *Elon Moreh* case, the High Court of Justice specified that military necessity must be the dominant consideration, and not just a consideration secondary to political motives. The court here was convinced that the Elon Moreh settlement was initiated on the political level, following demonstrations by Gush Emunim supporters, and that the military consideration was

[17] This point was emphasized in the decisions in the *Bet El* and *Elon Moreh* cases. See *Oyev et al.* v. *Minister of Defense et al.* (1978) *P.D.* 33(3) 111 (hereinafter the *Bet El* case); *Dawikat et al.* v. *The Government of Israel et al.* (1979) *P.D.* 34(1) 1 (hereinafter the *Elon Moreh* case). A summary of the *Elon Moreh* case has been translated into English and published in *Is.L.R.*, vol. 15 (1980), pp. 131-36.

[18] Hague Convention, articles 46 and 52; Dinstein, "International Law of Belligerent Occupation," pp. 134 ff. *Bet El* case, pp. 129 ff.

[19] *Bet El* case, pp. 117 F-G, 119, 124 ff., 132 ff.

only secondary. The court therefore decided that the seizure of lands there was illegal.[20]

When land is seized, the owners are not compensated for its value, as they remain the owners and have the right of ownership. The military government offers them yearly payments for use of the land, but most of the owners have refused to accept such payments.

After the area commander has seized the lands which he is convinced are necessary for "vital and immediate military requirements," to use the words of the preamble to the seizure order (as quoted in the *Bet El* case),[21] he may allow settlers to move onto those lands. Once again, however, the commander may grant the settlers only that which he has himself—just as he is not the owner, nor are the settlers owners; and just as he seized the land temporarily, so is their presence limited to the duration of his administration. The question arises, How then is it possible to establish a permanent settlement on land that was seized for temporary use? This question was called a "weighty one" by Justice Moshe Landau, then acting president of the Supreme Court of Israel (now president of the court), who answered it in the *Bet El* case by adopting the argument of the state's attorney:

> [T]he civilian settlement may exist in that area for as long as IDF possesses that land by virtue of a seizure order. This possession may one day be terminated as a result of international negotiations, which are likely to end in a new arrangement that will acquire validity according to International Law, and will determine the fate of this settlement and all the other settlements that have been established in the Administered territories.[22]

In the *Elon Moreh* case, the High Court of Justice decided that under the law, it is not permissible to establish a permanent settlement with the intention that it remain after the termination of the occupation, "for the Military Government cannot create facts in its area for military purposes with the prior intention that they persist after the end of the Military Government in that area, when it is as yet unknown what will be the future of the area after the end of the Military Government."[23]

---

20 *Elon Moreh* case, pp. 8 ff. and esp. pp. 19-20.
21 *Bet El* case, p. 116 C.
22 *Bet El* case, p. 131 B-C.
23 *Elon Moreh* case, p. 22 B.

Other Property Categories. When a former resident has left the area, his property is administered by the custodian for abandoned property. The custodian has leased considerable portions of these lands to agricultural settlements for the purpose of cultivation, particularly in the Jordan Valley (this began before 1977 when the Labor government was in power). The legal position here is that when the absentee owner returns, he will be entitled to reclaim his land, in addition to all the "fruits" it bore over the years ("fruits" refers to the rent paid by the settlements to the custodian).[24] This category of land will become more problematic upon the return of those who became refugees in 1967, as provided by the Camp David agreements.

Another category of property consists of those lands that were owned by Jews prior to 1948, particularly in the Etzion Block and in Hebron, and which are still registered in Jewish names in the Land Registry. More than 32,000 dunams of land fall into this category.[25] The rights of the Jews still persist, and the legal changes in the area from British Mandate to Jordanian annexation and then to Israeli military government have not affected those rights, subject to certain reservations. Some of the lands owned by Jews (particularly houses and shops in Hebron) were acquired by the Jordanian custodian for Jewish property, and were administered by the Jordanian government in the years of its control over Judea and Samaria. The rights of this custodian devolved upon the Israeli commissioner for governmental property but not upon the original Jewish landowners. The Jordanian law discriminated against Jews, and hence may be considered void.[26] The situation here is complicated, however, by the political fear that a precedent will be created. This gives rise to a demand for symmetry with respect to Arab property in Israel which is administered by the Israeli custodian for absentee property.

Since 1967, Jews have also been purchasing land in Judea and Samaria. About 73,000 dunams have been acquired by the Heymanuta Company, which is affiliated with the World Zionist Organization, and has been registered in the name of that company. Land has also been purchased by individual Israelis but has not yet been registered in their names.[27]

[24] See section 13 of Order no. 58 (as amended in Order no. 273), Drori, *Legislation*, p. 192, n. 43.

[25] A. Shalev, *The Autonomy: Problems and Solutions* (Tel Aviv University, 1979; in Hebrew), p. 118.

[26] On the power of the military government to cancel discriminatory legislation of the occupied state, see Drori, *Legislation*, pp. 121-22.

[27] Shalev, *Autonomy*; Gerson, *Israel, the West Bank*, describes the debate in Israel before the Yom Kippur War on the issue of the purchase of land by Israeli persons and companies in the area.

Expropriation, Seizure, and Closure. We have seen that the military government may not, according to international law, expropriate lands from private persons and deprive the original owners of their ownership rights. (There are cases of expropriation under Jordanian law, but these were effected for civilian matters concerning the local population, such as roads and markets.) Seizure constitutes effective possession of the land without interfering with ownership rights, and is permitted, according to Israel High Court decisions, only for vital military purposes, the necessity of which may be reviewed by the High Court of Justice.

Closure for a limited period is permitted for military purposes such as maneuvers and training. Much land has been closed for maneuvers, rifle ranges, etc., and the government allows the residents to cultivate these lands when no military activities are being conducted. In several cases, including Kiryat Arba, closure has constituted the first step toward seizure of the land for settlement.[28]

The Land Dilemma and a Possible Solution. The combination of the legal principles outlined here and the political principles advocated by the Likud government results in a dilemma for that government. Politically, the Likud regards Judea and Samaria as part of the Land of Israel, a central target for settlement, but the legal instruments employed by the government are aimed exclusively at freezing the situation in the territories as it was in 1967. The prime minister's great awareness of and respect for the law only complicates the matter further (though no less could be expected of him). In the past, Mr. Begin justified his position by the fact that he acted upon the counsel of respected jurists, and that the policy of settlement was approved by five Supreme Court justices in the case of Bet El. But scrutiny of the court's decision and of the quotations cited above reveal that Begin's assessment that the court upheld the policy of settlement is questionable: all that was decided in the *Bet El* case was that it is in fact permitted to *seize* lands *temporarily* when immediate and vital military considerations so require. The building of settlements on these lands is legal only when the settlements are vital for military purposes and are built *primarily* for those purposes. The *Elon Moreh* case demonstrated that it is not easy to convince the court of the military necessity for the settlements, and that if the court is not convinced, it will declare the seizure order void. The army and settlers will then have to evacuate the private property in question. The legal instruments that exist at present are thus not

---

[28] See *Hilo et al.* v. *The Government of Israel et al.* (1972) P.D. 27(2) 169.

suited to—or may even work against—the policy of the government of Israel, which is to expand the Israeli settlements in Judea and Samaria.

Some ideas for a solution may be fielded, although they require further thought. It is clear that the most natural course is to apply Israeli law to Judea and Samaria—that is, to annex them. In this way, the political approach would conform to the legal approach expounded by Professor Blum.[29] This course (apart from the political problems involved in its application) was closed to the government by the Camp David agreements, according to which Israel agreed to grant autonomy to the area for a period of five years, at the end of which four parties would decide on its fate: Israel, Egypt, Jordan, and the representatives of the Palestinians, each one endowed with the power of veto. Unilateral annexation by Israel at this stage would not be in keeping with this agreement.

A different solution to the problem would be Knesset legislation providing that certain lands be expropriated for the purpose of settlements or empowering a body appointed by the Knesset to carry out expropriations. In both cases full compensation would be paid to the owners. In this case, the High Court of Justice would be bound by the law of the Knesset and would not be able to invalidate such confiscations, even though they do not conform to the law of warfare if it applies to Judea and Samaria. Such a step, however, would be considered a violation of international law in international forums. From an international point of view, the Knesset is bound by international law, and the international community sees Judea and Samaria as occupied territories.

A more modest course of action would be to apply the Jordanian law of 1953 concerning expropriation of property for public purposes. The underlying idea here is that if land may be expropriated in Israel in order to build roads, markets, and new suburbs, and if in Judea and Samaria expropriation for the welfare of the local population is legal, why should there be discrimination against Israeli settlements? Furthermore, Israeli settlers were recognized by the court as part of the population in the area.[30] Expropriation should be legal for that purpose too, and full title of ownership would be transferred to the state after it pays full compensation to the owners of the land.

[29] Blum emphasizes that Israel has the *right* to apply Israeli law to the whole area of Judea and Samaria, and that applying Israeli law to East Jerusalem alone was the result of purely political considerations. From a legal point of view, Israel could and can do the same in the whole area of Judea and Samaria. Blum, *Juridical Status of Jerusalem*, p. 23.

[30] *The Electricity Company for the District of Jerusalem Ltd.* v. *Minister of Defense et al.* (1972) *P.D.* 27 (1) 124, 138 F; Drori, *Legislation*, pp. 84-85.

If it is absolutely vital to establish a settlement on private lands, and the solution of expropriation according to the two alternatives mentioned above is not adopted, settlement is permissible only if it is initiated on the military level. Hence, the army should suggest settlement sites that are necessary for security purposes. If the political authorities accept these recommendations and decide that for military (not political) reasons the settlement should be established, then the seizure order would be valid even according to the *Elon Moreh* judgment.

The most simple course from a legal point of view is for Israeli buyers (the Heymenuta Company or individuals) to purchase privately owned lands. This method has no legal defect and no questions arise as to ownership. Therefore, the decision to allow Israelis to purchase lands, which amounts to an abrogation of the prohibition imposed by Jordanian law on the purchase of land by Jews or foreigners,[31] would prevent conflict over the expropriation or seizure of private lands. It is to be hoped that this method succeeds and that the Arabs agree to sell their land despite the Jordanian government's imposition of the death penalty by law on anyone who does so.

Furthermore, the way is still open for Israel to establish settlements on government lands, in which case the owners—that is, Jordan—could not, in court at least, demand the evacuation of the settlers. Here, too, however, the existence of the settlement is certain only as long as there is a military government, and its fate will be decided finally after the five-year autonomy period.

Israeli Settlements and International Law

It has been asserted that the establishment of Israeli settlements in the administered territories is in violation of international law.[32] In international customary law, however, including the 1907 Hague Convention, there is nothing that prohibits nationals of the state having effective control of a territory from moving into and taking up residence in that territory. There is, however, the problem of private property discussed above.

It has been claimed that article 49 of the Geneva Convention, "On the Protection of Civilians in Time of War," is pertinent. As

---

[31] Gerson, *Israel, the West Bank*, ignored this fact of Jordanian law, and therefore his commentary and analysis are somewhat incomplete and misleading to the uninformed reader.

[32] An example of this assertion is found in UN Security Council Resolution 446, May 22, 1979, and 465, March 1, 1980.

we saw above, there is serious doubt about the application of the convention to the area, and Israel reaffirms its position that the convention is not applicable and that Israel is not a belligerent occupant in any part of the former Palestine Mandate. Nevertheless, it should be pointed out in this respect that even under article 49, the establishment of settlements is not forbidden.[33]

From the overall reading of article 49 of the Geneva Convention it is evident that the purpose of this article is to protect the local population from deportation and displacement.[34] Paragraph 6 must be read in light of the general purpose of the article. It thus becomes apparent that the movement of population into the territory under control is prohibited only to the extent that it involves the displacement of the local population.

This conclusion is given expression by the leading writers on the subject. Oppenheim-Lauterpacht states:

> The occupying power must not deport or transfer parts of its own civilian population into the territory occupied by him—a prohibition intended to cover cases of the occupant

[33] The Supreme Court of Israel did not deal with this problem, because it was convinced that article 49 of the Geneva Convention is not part of customary international law. It considered article 49 constitutive, that is, applicable only among the parties who signed it; thus it cannot be used before municipal courts. See the *Bet El* case, pp. 119 ff., 127 ff.

[34] Article 49 of the Geneva Convention, concerning deportation, transfers, and evacuations, reads as follows:

> Individual or mass forcible transfers, as well as deportations of protected persons from occupied territory to the territory of the Occupying Power or to that of any other country, occupied or not, are prohibited, regardless of their motive.
>
> Nevertheless, the Occupying Power may undertake total or partial evacuation of a given area if the security of the population or imperative military reasons so demand. Such evacuations may not involve the displacement of protected persons outside the bounds of the occupied territory except when for material reasons it is impossible to avoid such displacement. Persons thus evacuated shall be transferred back to their homes as soon as hostilities in the area in question have ceased.
>
> The Occupying Power undertaking such transfers or evacuations shall ensure, to the greatest practicable extent, that proper accommodation is provided to receive the protected persons, that the removals are effected in satisfactory conditions of hygiene, health, safety and nutrition, and that members of the same family are not separated.
>
> The Protecting Power shall be informed of any transfers and evacuations as soon as they have taken place.
>
> The Occupying Power shall not detain protected persons in an area particularly exposed to the dangers of war unless the security of the population or imperative military reasons so demand.
>
> The Occupying Power shall not deport or transfer parts of its own civilian population into the territory it occupies.

bringing in its nationals for the purpose of displacing the population of the occupied territory.[35]

Article 49 must be understood against the background of World War II. It was aimed in part against such horrors as the barbarous extermination camps in occupied Europe to which Jews and others were taken by the Nazis, and in part against the displacement of the local population with a view to making room for the German invaders.[36]

Bearing in mind both the provisions of the article and its legislative history, it is clear that the situation envisaged by article 49 does not apply to the Jewish settlements in question. No Arab inhabitants have been displaced by Jewish settlements or by these peaceful villages and townships. It should also be pointed out that close scrutiny of the precise language of article 49, paragraph 6, reveals that it refers to state actions by which the government in control transfers parts of its population to the territory concerned. This cannot be construed to cover the voluntary movement of individuals. As is well known, the Israeli pioneers who have established the settlements in the area have done so not as a result of state transfer but on their own volition and as an expression of their personal choice.

The Legal Issue of the Israeli Settlements

Israeli settlement in Judea and Samaria gives rise to the problem of conflict between territorial law and personal law. In the area of Judea and Samaria, the law is made up of two components: the first, the local law that was in force until the Six Day War (which itself contains Ottoman, Mandatory, and Jordanian elements); the second, orders and regulations enacted after 1967 by the Israeli military authorities.[37] Such law is of territorial application, and it is binding on all who live in the area of Judea and Samaria, Israelis and Arabs alike.

On the other hand, much of Israeli legislation applies only within the borders of the State of Israel, and not to an Israeli resident or citizen residing outside those borders. This gives rise to a situation whereby the Israeli settlers in Judea and Samaria are subject to the

---

[35] Oppenheim-Lauterpacht, *International Law*, 7th ed., vol. 2, p. 452.

[36] Cf. Pictet, *Commentary on the IV Geneva Convention*, p. 283.

[37] Drori, *Legislation*, and M. Drori, "The Legal System in Judea and Samaria: A Review of the Previous Decade with a Glance at the Future," *Is.Y.H.R.*, vol. 8 (1978), p. 144.

legal system in force in the territories, while most of the laws of the State of Israel do not apply to them.

The attempts to resolve this problematic state of affairs have been few, superficial, and incidental, providing no solution or guidelines, even though those who made the attempts during all those years possessed legislative powers both in Israel and in Judea and Samaria. I shall attempt to assess the present legal situation on the basis of this legal starting point and propose or hint at a number of possible solutions or arrangements. The analysis will be neither exhaustive nor complete, for the issues are numerous and complex. I have therefore selected a number of important points that illustrate the problems and their solutions.

The Municipal-Organizational Framework of Israeli Settlement

One of the most fundamental questions involved in Israeli settlement in the occupied areas in general, and in Judea and Samaria in particular, is that of the municipal-organizational status of the settlements. I will discuss the various types of settlements separately.

Agricultural Settlements. With respect to the few agricultural settlements (kibbutzim, cooperative settlements, and workers' settlements)—as opposed to the regional councils discussed later—the problem is relatively simple: these settlements are incorporated in accordance with Israeli law as cooperative agricultural associations in the framework of the settlement movements. On this basis every settlement constitutes a legal entity (though only under Israeli law, not under the law in force in Judea and Samaria), competent to contract an agreement, to conduct negotiations, to purchase, to sell, to open a bank account, etc.[38] The rules for accepting and expelling members are laid down in the settlements' articles of association, and each member commits himself to abide by those rules. From a strict legal point of view, a complete solution to the problem of enforcement is not achieved in this manner. For example, which legal organ will execute the decisions of the society (or the decisions of the registrar of associations who serves as the arbitrator and judge in disputes among members of the society[39]): will it be the Israeli courts and executive authorities or those in the area of Judea and Samaria,

[38] See the Cooperative Societies Ordinance, no. 50 (1933) esp. section 21; Drayton, ed., *Laws of Palestine*, vol. 1, chap. 24, p. 360.

[39] Cooperative Societies Ordinance, no. 50, section 52; and Cooperative Societies (Arbitration of Disputes) Regulations (1972); *K.T.* (*Kovetz Hatakanot* [Subsidiary Legislation in Israel]), 1972, no. 2818, p. 746.

either directly or by enforcing a decision of the Israeli authorities? The absence of any satisfactory solution to this question can seriously impair the stability of the settlements, enabling anyone who so desires to evade payment of dues to the settlement committee, as well as undermining the committee's authority over members of the settlement, including the substantial difficulty in expelling a member who does not conform to the articles of association.

From a liberal world outlook this may be a blessing, but when compared with the situation in a similar settlement within the borders of the State of Israel, this difference is of great significance. For the purpose of solving the problem of expelling a member, one may have recourse to private law, under which a settler remains in the settlement on sufferance of the World Zionist Organization, which leases the land from the military government authorities.[40] Should the settlement wish to expel a member, it can turn to the World Zionist Organization, which will inform the settler that he is no longer permitted to remain on the land (a contract with a person on sufferance may be terminated unilaterally), and the settler will then leave the settlement. In the absence of a judicial authority, even the enforcement of an evacuation order is no simple matter, as we shall presently see.

Community Settlements. The situation is different with respect to urban or semiurban community settlements, such as the Allon Shvut Regional Center or the urban community settlements established by Gush Emunim. Indeed, attempts have been made to establish the community settlements as cooperative societies, but the pluralistic nature of an urban settlement is barely reconcilable with the structure of a cooperative agricultural society. For example, could a resident of a religious community settlement who sends his son to a secular school be considered to be violating the rules of the articles of association, and therefore be ousted from the settlement? Could a resident of a community settlement sell his house to anyone he pleases, or could the settlement committee impose a veto upon a certain potential purchaser, and if so, what considerations are valid (religion, political belief, age, size and structure of family, etc.)? Could the members of a community settlement organize a group of parents and demand that only one school of a certain type be established in the settlement? Is it possible for an "oppressed minority" in the settlement to have recourse to an Israeli court? Usually, the articles of association of community settlements provide that the Israeli courts are competent

---

[40] After seizing the land, the military government leases it to the World Zionist Organization, which assists in developing the settlements.

to settle disputes among members. In the absence of such a provision and in those settlements which have no articles of association anchored in the existence of a cooperative society under Israeli law, it is most doubtful whether an Israeli court has jurisdiction over a civil dispute between two Israeli settlers in the area of Judea and Samaria. If there is nothing linking the dispute with Israel (such as the place of the dispute or place of plaintiff's residence), then the Israeli court has no jurisdiction.[41]

Regional Councils. Thus far, we have seen that the organizational structure of the settlements is regulated by private law. The settlers organized themselves into a cooperative society, which is of great significance: the initiative must come from the settlers and the element of coercion is not clear. With respect to the provision of services for the settlements, there is a need for an apparatus of enforcement, and legislative validation is necessary for the decisions of such a body to acquire force. For this purpose in Israel, regional councils are set up by the minister for the interior by virtue of Israeli law.[42] During the first years of Israeli settlement in Judea and Samaria, an arrangement existed whereby every group of settlements in Judea and Samaria was "adopted" by a nearby regional council in Israel. (The regional council of Mateh Yehudah, for example, adopted the settlements of the Judean district, the regional council of Emek Bet Shan adopted the settlements in the Jordan Valley, and the settlements in the area of the Dead Sea were adopted by the Tamar Council.) The adopted councils served mainly to channel the funds from the Ministry of the Interior to the settlements in Judea and Samaria, although the councils not infrequently assisted the settlements with advice and training and at times offered them municipal services. Obviously, this was not the ideal solution, but it was effective in practice during the first twelve years of Israeli administration in Judea and Samaria.

Six days before the signing of a peace treaty between Israel and Egypt and approximately half a year after the Camp David agreements, the area commander for Judea and Samaria promulgated an order establishing four regional councils in Judea and Samaria: the Jordan Valley Regional Council, the Bet El Regional Council, the Samaria Regional Council, and the Etzion Regional Council (see

---

[41] Recently the former president of the Supreme Court, Dr. J. Sussmann, ruled that the district court in Jerusalem was not capable of dealing with disputes between residents of Kiryat Arba. The court could only turn to the legislature, amend the law, or refer the plaintiff to the local court in Hebron. See C.A. 301/77 *Mansurrah* v. *Cohen* (1977), *P.D.* 32(3) 405.

[42] Local Councils (Regional Councils) Order (1958), *K.T.* 1958, no. 797, p. 1259.

table 1).[43] This order provides that the Israeli settlements will be administered within the framework of regional councils according to rules to be determined. These rules are in fact copies of Israeli legislation regarding local councils, with the necessary modifications.[44] This is not the place to discuss the details of the various arrangements, some of which will be considered at a later stage. It is pertinent, however, to remark that the establishment of this legal body could constitute a turning point in the development of a stronger and more comprehensive bond with Israeli law, and these regional councils may serve as the channel through which the Israeli settlements draw upon the Israeli law and administration.

Urban Settlements. Urban settlements, too, have been set up in Judea and Samaria. Under current plans, these towns are to be populated by thousands of residents and, in the future, by tens of thousands. Consequently, the cooperative-society solution is not applicable to them, nor is a superstructure along the lines of a regional council. What is needed is an authorized municipal body, empowered to collect taxes, to regulate and supervise the licensing of businesses, planning, and building, etc., and mainly to exercise legal authority over every resident of every settlement.

The problem first arose in Kiryat Arba, which borders on Hebron. Admittedly, Jordanian legislation in the municipal sphere is relatively well developed and modern. It is difficult, however, to view Kiryat Arba as being integrated into the framework of Jordanian law, according to which the minister of the interior appoints mayors, and the elections for city councils are conducted according to rules set down in Jordanian law including, inter alia, an economic franchise as a prior condition of participation in the elections. (A further provision in the Jordanian law limiting the right of women to vote was repealed by the military government in 1976, before the second municipal elections on the West Bank).[45] As opposed to this, the Israeli minister for

---

[43] Order concerning the Administration of Regional Councils (Judea and Samaria), no. 783, March 20, 1979, and the Regulations of the Regional Councils (Judea and Samaria), same date, and the amendment of the regulations (no. 3) dated June 15, 1981, which added a fifth council—Megilot.

[44] For legislation in the area that is based on Israeli legislation, see Drori, *Legislation*, esp. pp. 94-97.

[45] See all of the following by M. Drori: "Legal Aspects of the Relationship between the Central Government and the Local Government in Judea and Samaria," *Ir Ve ezor* [City and region], vol. 2, no. 3 (1975), pp. 57-69; "Municipal Elections in Judea and Samaria," *Is.L.R.*, vol. 9 (1974), pp. 97-116; "Second Municipal Elections in Judea and Samaria under Israeli Administration: Legislative Changes," *Is.L.R.*, vol. 12 (1977), pp. 526-40; *Local Government, Elections*
(Note continues on page 63)

TABLE 1
Jewish Settlements in Judea and Samaria and Their Municipal Status

---

Local Councils in Judea and Samaria

Kiryat Arba	Ariel
Ma'ale Adumim	Ma'ale Ephraim
Elkana	

Settlements Composing the Regional Councils

Jordan Valley Region Council

Mehola	Fazael
Ro'i	Tomer
Bekaot	Gilgal
Tamara	Netiv Hagdud
Argaman	Naaran
Mehora	Yitav
Masuah	Shlom Zion Regional Center
Gittit	

Bet El Regional Council

Ofra	Mitzpe Yericho
Bet El	Shilo
Neve Zuf	Mattityahu
Givon	Kfar Ruth
Bet Horon	Kfar Adumim
Mevo Horon	

Samaria Regional Council

Sanor (Bet Homot)	Karnei Shomron
Shomron	Tapuah
Kedumim	

Gush Etzion Regional Council

Har Gilo	Kfar Etzion
Rosh Tzurim	Migdal Oz
Elazar	Tekoah
Allon Shvut	Efrat

Megilot Regional Council

Almog	Mitzpe Shalem
Kaliya	Vered Yericho

SOURCE: Author.

the interior may not set up a municipality in Kiryat Arba by virtue of the Israeli Municipalities Ordinance,[46] because Kiryat Arba lies outside the territorial boundaries of the State of Israel.

The solution that has been reached is as follows: the area commander for Judea and Samaria promulgated an order which included the main provisions of Israeli municipal legislation. The order stipulated that Kiryat Arba would be administered by a body called the Kiryat Administration, which posesses powers basically similar to those of a local council in Israel.[47] The order contains an interesting innovation, however: the Kiryat Arba Administration comprises not only five elected representatives of the settlers but also one person appointed by the authorities. This person is in fact the mayor (in the order, his title is "Administrator of the Affairs of the Kirya"), and he possesses the right of veto over all the administration's decisions. At first, the appointee was an army officer, but later a person recommended by the minister for the interior was appointed. Thus, we are faced with a curtailed form of democracy: the settlers were given the right to participate in the determination of their future, but the body that was set up, in which an outsider possesses the power of veto, "contaminates the atmosphere," and many complaints have been voiced against the system. The Kiryat Arba Administration is unlike any local authority in Israel, or even any local authority in Judea and Samaria: it is a sui generis body. In any case, it is noteworthy that in recent years, a variegated system of bylaws of the administration on various matters, such as municipal rates, business licensing, etc., has begun to develop.[48]

Ma'ale Adumim, another urban settlement in the area, close to Jerusalem on the way to Jericho, also acquired a separate status. An order promulgated by the area commander set up a local council in the settlement.[49] The order is similar in principle to the one promul-

---

and Democracy in Judea and Samaria: Legal Aspects (Jerusalem: Jerusalem Institute for Federal Studies and Bar-Ilan University, Institute of Local Government, 1980).

[46] Municipalities Ordinance (New Version), Laws of Israel, no. 8, 197.

[47] See the Order concerning the Administration of Kiryat Arba, Judea, and Samaria, no. 561 (1974), CPOA, no. 34, p. 1384.

[48] Recently, however, a local council—similar to that of Ma'ale Adumim—has been established for Kiryat Arba without outside veto. See Order concerning Administration of Local Councils (Judea and Samaria), no. 892, March 1, 1981.

[49] Order concerning the Administration of Ma'ale Adumim (Judea and Samaria), no. 788 (1978), March 27, 1979, and the Code of Ma'ale Adumim, 1978, of the same date. It is noteworthy that this order was signed a day after the peace treaty with Egypt, which was signed on March 26, 1979. At present Ma'ale Adumim, like Kiryat Arba, Elkana, Ariel, and Ma'ale Ephraim, is dealt with under Order No. 892 (see note 48).

gated for Kiryat Arba, with one important difference: the whole council is elected by and selected from the local settlers. The reason for the difference is that Kiryat Arba is a very sensitive spot owing to its proximity to Hebron, which views at least part of the area of Kiryat Arba as territory falling within its municipal boundaries. This being the case, the military government and the Israeli government saw fit to create a supervisory body so that a representative of the central authority would be able to "keep a finger on the pulse" of the area and minimize tension with Hebron. The situation is different with respect to Ma'ale Adumim, located on the outskirts of the Judean Desert on desolate land supporting no local population. The absence of any risk of conflict with local Arab residents led, it seems, to the decision to grant the settlers of Ma'ale Adumim complete freedom to elect their local council as has always been the practice in Israel.

There is no special arrangement concerning the other settlements that are supposed to become towns or cities (such as Ariel in the heart of Samaria). These settlements are at present incorporated into the framework of regional councils including not only the agricultural settlements but the community settlements as well. One may suppose that as the urban settlements develop, their municipal status will also change, and they will adopt local councils and possibly become municipalities.[50]

The Powers of the Municipal Authorities

The setting up of a municipal framework is not in itself sufficient. It is important to examine the functions and the powers given to those various local authorities. It is not my present intention to describe or analyze all those powers in detail, but rather to mention various legal aspects of some of the powers conferred on these bodies.

Jurisdictional Boundaries. The jurisdictional boundaries of every municipal authority determine the territorial framework within which that authority will operate. Within the municipal area, the bylaws will apply, taxes will be paid, building permits will be issued, etc.

In the present case, the importance of the jurisdictional boundaries is much greater. Whereas in Israel the territorial division between the various municipal authorities is mainly a function of purely local interests, in Judea and Samaria the determination of the boundaries of the Israeli municipal authorities involves a clear political aspect; within those boundaries, only Israel's authorities will operate, and those areas will be under de facto Israeli control.

[50] At this writing, these settlements have local councils (see notes 48 and 49).

It must be stressed that we are concerned here with the problem of the boundaries of the municipal body (the regional or local councils), and that the determination of the municipal boundaries is relevant only on the level of public law, and in particular with respect to the application of the municipal bylaws. It does not affect any matters of private law, the most important of which is ownership of land. It is true that in most cases the municipal area is identical to the area seized for military purposes or government lands; nevertheless, cases may arise in which the municipal boundaries will extend farther, encompassing the lands of local residents.

From the point of view of consistent legal thought and also from the point of view of legal policy, there is nothing wrong with such a divergence. Whereas in Israel the regional councils cover contiguous territory encompassing the defined settlements, in Judea and Samaria the area commander chose another course: the area of most of the regional councils equals the total of the defined area of every settlement, without territorial contiguity and with no provision that the traffic arteries between the settlements are to be included in the area of the regional council. With respect to services such as education, health, and garbage collection, there may be no reason why the powers of the regional council cannot apply only to the settlements and not to the areas joining them. The difference between this order and the accepted system in Israel, however, will cause difficulties in the functioning of the councils, and it may also give rise to a feeling of discrimination on the part of the settlers.

Furthermore, were the boundaries of the regional councils to include all the settlements as well as the areas joining them, these boundaries would be suitable for the future, too. Today, in contrast, the regional council has powers exercisable only within the present confines of the settlement, and any extension of the area of a settlement requires a change in the boundaries of the regional council. The solution to this problem is to include within the borders of the settlement not only the area presently in use but also any whose use is planned in the future. This seems to be the case with respect to most of the settlements, as evidenced by the maps marking their boundaries.

In the Jordan Valley, the situation is otherwise. The whole valley, excluding the Arab settlements, is included in the jurisdictional boundaries of the council. Thus there is territorial contiguity between the settlements, and the roads, too, are included in the jurisdictional boundaries of the council.

The Scope of Power. The local authorities possess powers similar to those of local authorities in Israel, since the constituting order is based on parallel Israeli legislation. Because of the special status of the municipal authorities, however, and the fact that they constitute an Israeli "island" in Judea and Samaria, there is room to consider extending the powers of these local authorities so that they may serve as channels through which the Israeli government authorities can operate in Judea and Samaria. As such, the local authorities should be given added powers in matters of education, health (and especially in the light of the enactment of the Health Insurance Law in Israel), and the like. A careful examination of each of the powers and their transfer to municipal settlements is beyond the scope of this paper; I will restrict myself to indicating this course, which merits detailed development and analysis.

Municipal Courts. The orders constituting the municipal authorities did not change the judicial system in Judea and Samaria, which is based primarily on the local courts.[51] A judicial instance ought to be established, competent to judge violators of bylaws of the Israeli municipal authorities (such as building violations, running of unlicensed businesses, etc.), similar to the urban courts in Israel and those recently established in Judea and Samaria.[52] The powers of such a court should be extended beyond purely municipal affairs to cover civil matters concerning the municipalities as well, such as non-payment of taxes. Similarly, thought should be given to the possibility of conferring upon this court wider jurisdiction in both civil and criminal matters not related to local authorities (this, however, should be regulated in the framework of a comprehensive solution to the question of the relationship between the settlers and the Israeli judicial system). In any case, should the court be an urban one, the enforcement of its rulings should rest with an execution office (either an independent office or a subsidiary of the execution office in Israel), and there should be provision for recourse to Israeli authorities (such as by giving an Israeli prison power to keep a prisoner who has been

---

[51] On local courts in the area, see Drori, *Legislation*, pp. 118-21.

[52] Municipal Courts Ordinance, no. 18 (1928), Drayton, ed., *Laws of Palestine*, vol. 2, chap. 97, p. 1015, and Order concerning the Establishment of Municipal Courts (Judea and Samaria), no. 631 (1976), *CPOA*, no. 36, p. 60. See Drori, "Legal System in Judea and Samaria."

Yet, in Order no. 892 (note 48), chapter 16, municipal courts were established: the judge in this court is a magistrate judge from Jerusalem, and appeals will be heard by three judges from the district court of Jerusalem. The jurisdiction of the municipal courts is limited to bylaws and building violations.

judged in the urban court). The establishment of this judicial forum is a natural complement to the orders constituting the municipal authorities.

Planning and Building. Planning and building, together with the licensing it involves, is a subject of utmost importance, for it is in fact the lifeblood of Israeli settlement.

The Jordanian Cities, Town and Buildings Planning Law (no. 79 of 1966) has territorial application in the area of Judea and Samaria. The law was not really applied prior to the Six Day War, but it was applied by the military government, which appointed the planning bodies in accordance with it. An order of the area commander set up the Supreme Planning Council comprising six Israeli staff officers, and it was on this council that the powers of the regional committee and the Supreme Planning Council were conferred by law.[53] The powers of the local committees were conferred upon the municipalities in the cities and upon local bodies in the towns (the town planning council includes three Arab government clerks—the engineer of the Planning Bureau, the engineer of the Department of Public Works, and the regional doctor).

Apart from the city areas over which the urban planning committees have authority, there are also towns under the authority of town planning councils. It should be mentioned that the regions of planning do not necessarily coincide with the boundaries of municipal jurisdictions. An urban planning area may extend farther than the boundaries of municipal jurisdiction. A later order amending that mentioned above laid down that there would be certain planning areas in which special planning committees would be set up. This order may be invoked with respect to Israeli settlement, and thus authority in matters of planning and building in these areas will not lie with the local committees.[54]

To date, this order, as well as others constituting the municipal authorities, have not been invoked, and Israeli settlers consequently

[53] Order concerning City, Town, and Building Planning Law (Judea and Samaria), no. 418 (1971), *CPOA*, no. 27, p. 1000. See Drori, "Legal Aspects of Relationship," p. 68, and see the recent High Court of Justice ruling per M. Shamgar, in H.C. 145/80, *Al-Masulia et al.* v. *Minister of Defense et al.* (1981) *P.D.* 35(2) 285.

[54] Order concerning City, Town, and Building Law (Amendment) (Judea and Samaria), no. 604 (1975), *CPOA*, no. 36. To complete the picture, it should be pointed out that in a number of settlements, steering committees were formed, with the participation of representatives of the government offices concerned with the development of settlement (such as the Ministry of Housing and Building, the Ministry of Industry and Trade, etc.). Representatives of the settlers participate in these steering committees. Although they have great pull, the steering committees have as yet to acquire a recognized legal status.

are not partners—at least from a statutory point of view—in the planning of the settlements in which they live. To close the circle, it is necessary to complete the regulation of planning and building by granting powers to Israeli settlers in the sphere of planning, preparing town plans, and licensing with respect to the settlements in which they live.[55]

Elections. The orders constituting the municipal bodies were promulgated with a view to eventual democratic elections. At the first stage, provision was made for an appointed council; at the next stage, democratic elections would be held, their rules, identical to the rules governing the elections in Israel, to be determined in those same orders. There were to be direct elections for the local council, the mayor and its members, and elections for representatives of each settlement as members of the regional council.

It is unnecessary to dwell on the justice and the logic of these provisions, which correctly reflect the fact that these settlements are indeed like Israeli settlements for all intents and purposes. If the intention is to realize this equality fully, it is worth considering the provision in the order promulgated by the commander stating that elections are to be held for the councils in Judea and Samaria on the same day as the elections for the local authorities in Israel, and that with respect to the local councils in Judea and Samaria (Ma'ale Adumim, Kiryat Arba, Ma'ale Ephraim, Ariel, and Elkana) there would be direct elections for the mayors.

The Personal Status of the Israeli Settlers

Were we to adhere to the precise literal meaning of the law, we would reach some rather interesting conclusions concerning the Israelis who live in Judea and Samaria. They are not residents of Israel, and therefore Israeli laws applying to residents will not apply to them. Thus, for example, section 24 of the Population Registry Law of 1965 states that "a resident who is in Israel and who has reached the age of 16 years may acquire an identity card," but a resident of Judea and Samaria does not fall into this category.[56] The Israelis among them (who constitute the decisive majority), however, are entitled to receive identity cards because the law also

[55] During 1980-1981, gradually the areas where there was settlement were declared "special zones" and thus under the jurisdiction of special planning committees, which are the local and regional councils.

[56] *S.H.* (*Sefer Ha Hukim* [Principal Legislation in Israeli]), 1965/5725, no. 466, p. 270.

applies to Israeli citizens who are not residents of Israel.[57] Now, even if in the past these people received identity cards when they were living within the boundaries of the "Green Line," it is nevertheless not at all clear whether, from a legal point of view, it is possible to write on their identity cards that their present address is a settlement in Judea and Samaria in which they live. The Population Registry Regulations (Registration of Address) of 1974 lists a *numerus clausus* of settlements specified in the first appendix to the Municipalities Ordinance and to the Local and Regional Councils Order, and also a list included in the regulations themselves: only those settlements may be listed as addresses in the Population Registry and on identity cards.[58] The absence from the regulations of a list of settlements from the area of Judea and Samaria means that the registration clerk is not permitted to mark down those settlements as addresses. We know that in practice the residents of the territories appear in the Israeli Population Registry and the settlements in which they actually live are listed as their addresses, but it is possible that should the matter ever come before the courts, the arrangement will be found to be illegal. The chance that the matter will arise before the High Court of Justice is, however, very small: an Israeli resident of Judea and Samaria will not bring the matter, and should a person who opposes Israeli settlement in the area wish to file a petition in the court, he will have no *locus standi*, for he is "interfering in a matter which does not concern him," and his petition will not be heard.

The fact that the settlers in Judea and Samaria are not Israeli residents has many legal ramifications. For example, section 42 of the Bar Association Law of 1961 states that one of the qualifying conditions for a lawyer is that he be a resident of Israel.[59] Should he cease to be a resident, his membership in the association will expire by virtue of that law. And indeed, there have been cases in which lawyers left Israel, settled outside the country, and were disbarred.[60] Needless to say, there is a great difference between a lawyer who left Israel to settle in London, for example, and one who settled in Judea and Samaria as a pioneer. From a formal, legalistic point of view, however, neither lawyer is an Israeli resident, and their fate should be identical. Moreover, if we were to ask any Israeli settler in the area where his domicile is, he would undoubtedly say that

[57] Section 1(c) of the law states: "The provisions of this Law which confer rights upon a resident or impose duties upon him, or which concern a resident, will also apply to an Israeli citizen who is not a resident."

[58] *K.T.* 1974/5734, no. 3189, p. 1384.

[59] *S.H.* 1967/5721, no. 347, p. 178.

[60] H.C. 242/65, *Weill* v. *Israel Bar Association* (1965) *P.D.* 20(1) 276.

his life is centered in Judea and Samaria rather than Jerusalem or Tel Aviv, where he lived previously (even though he may still have an apartment or an office there). The fact that the Israeli settlers are not residents of Israel is of great importance, especially with respect to the jurisdiction of the courts, and in particular that of the rabbinical courts, which have jurisdiction over Israeli residents, as we shall see below.

The laws of the agricultural marketing boards do not apply to the settlers either, even though in practice the marketing boards treat the settlers of Judea and Samaria like all other farmers within the State of Israel.[61] There are many more such legal situations which require legislative solutions.

The Judiciary and Israeli Settlement

The most problematic matter, raising basic questions of sovereignty, is that of the competence of the courts to handle matters involving the Israeli settlers in Judea and Samaria.

The courts, under Israeli law, sit in judgment only in Israel and not outside its borders. This fact is supported by general principles of the territorial jurisdiction of the courts and may be deduced from the Courts Law of 1957.[62] It was crystallized in the attorney general's directives to the government, which state, "A court shall never sit outside the borders of the State."[63] It is thus clear that an Israeli court cannot sit in Judea and Samaria, and we must therefore examine whether an Israeli court sitting in Israel is competent to judge the matters of Israeli settlers in Judea and Samaria.

The subject is a very complex one, to which the rules of private international law, as "imported" to Israel via English law by means of section 46 of the Palestine Order in Council of 1922, apply.[64] These rules are supplemented by Israeli legislative acts, both general laws which are to be interpreted with due consideration for the special situation pertaining in the territories, and laws and regulations specially enacted after 1967 for the purpose of ordering the problem, but which touched on only certain parts of it. The discussion henceforth is not intended to deal with all the issues arising but hints at the main ones among them.

[61] See, for example, the Council for the Production and Marketing of Ground Nuts Law (1959), *S.H.* 1959/5719, no. 277, p. 76; Council for the Production and Marketing of Vegetables (1959), *S.H.* 1959/5719, no. 292, p. 222.

[62] *S.H.* 1957/5717, no. 233, p. 148.

[63] *Directives of the Attorney General*, no. 21.151, November 1, 1968.

[64] Drayton, ed., *Laws of Palestine*, vol. 3, p. 2569.

Civil Law. According to the Israeli legal system, Judea and Samaria is an area in which a different system of law applies, and apparently, therefore, a plantiff wishing to serve court documents upon a defendant must apply to the court for a permit to send documents beyond the boundaries of the court's jurisdiction, by virtue of regulation 467 of the Civil Procedure Regulations of 1963.[65] In 1969, however, the Civil Procedure (Service of Documents to the Administered Territories) Regulations were enacted, laying down certain procedures for this matter.[66] These regulations provide that the service of documents in the territories is effected in the same way as in Israel (either by mail or by hand), and that every document must be accompanied by an Arabic translation certified by a lawyer as being correct.

A few years ago, Justice Sussmann, then deputy president of the Supreme Court, ruled that by virtue of the 1969 regulations, a court permit is unnecessary for the purpose of serving documents under regulation 467: an Arabic translation and the usual service are sufficient in order for the Israeli court to acquire jurisdiction.[67] Even though this ruling was criticized in legal literature,[68] it nevertheless is binding in Israel, and its meaning is clear: except for the translation (it is difficult to understand the necessity for such translation when the parties are Israelis; in practice this requirement is not strictly followed in most cases), the same law applies in Israel and in the territories with respect to the service of court documents.

As for local jurisdiction, the 1969 regulations do, it is true, provide a positive answer to the question of whether an Israeli court is at all competent to hear an action, but the question of which local court—in Jerusalem, Tel Aviv, or Haifa—is competent remains. If the bond according to Civil Procedure Regulation (for example, if the place of damage or the place of obligation) was Israel, then there is no problem. If, however, no such bond exists, then in the absence of any local jurisdiction, formally there is no jurisdiction at all.[69]

This is not the whole picture, however; if the civil matter is foreseeable, the sides can agree in advance on the court which is to

[65] K.T. 5723, no. 1477, 1869.

[66] K.T. 5730, no. 2482, 458.

[67] B.R.A. [Code of list of trials] 55/71, Al Kir and Sons, Gaza v. Van der Horst Hofrin Roterdan et al. (1971), P.D. 25(2) 13.

[68] See B. Bracha, "The Service of Court Documents in the Administered Territories," Mishpatim, vol. 4 (1972/5732), p. 119. And see Z. Inbar, "The Competence of Courts in Israel to Hear Actions against a Resident of the Administered Territories," Hapraklit, vol. 28 (1972/5732), p. 11.

[69] See the recent Supreme Court decision in C.A. 301/77 Mansurrah v. Cohen (1977), P.D. 32(3) 405. Also see note 41.

have jurisdiction. Thus, for example, if the parties draw up a contract of sale, of partnership, or a work agreement or if they decide to set up a settlement society as explained above, they may include in the contract, or in the articles of association, a clause to the effect that an Israeli court will be competent to deal with the matter. The court will then acquire jurisdiction. Similarly, one may, in a contract, specify the law which is to apply. If, however, nothing is specified in the contract, or if the cause of action was a civil wrong, the question then arises, Which law will be applied in an Israeli court? We are faced with a problem of private international law concerning the question of which law of which country should be applied in a case involving a foreign element, that is, an element of the legal system of another country. It should be stressed that from this perspective Judea and Samaria are like any other foreign state, with all the ramifications.

This, however, is not the end of the road. How should a plaintiff, armed with a decision in his favor, execute the decision? To answer this question the Order concerning Legal Aid was promulgated in Judea and Samaria, and it states that an Israeli decision can be executed by the execution office in the area as if it were a decision of a West Bank court.[70] This solution is effective with respect to defendants who are Arabs, and not infrequently large sums of money awarded in an Israeli court have been collected by means of the execution office in Judea and Samaria. A special order has recently been promulgated by virtue of which an award may be enforced by the Israeli Execution Office (in Netanya) if the defendant is an Israeli.[71] There is Israeli legislation allowing for the enforcement in Israel of a judgment given by a local court in Judea and Samaria.[72]

Labor Courts. The same principles and regulations described with respect to civil courts and the service of court documents are applicable in the labor courts.[73] (Here, too, the problem of which substantive law—Israeli or West Bank labor law—arises; but this question is beyond the scope of this paper.) The problem of local

[70] Order concerning Legal Aid (Judea and Samaria), no. 348 (1969), *CPOA*, no. 20, p. 694. This order must be viewed against the background of legislation regulating the relationship between Israel and Judea and Samaria. See Drori, *Legislation*, p. 202, n. 110.

[71] Order concerning Legal Aid, Amendment no. 3 (1977), *CPOA*, no. 41, p. 132.

[72] Emergency Order (Areas Administered by the IDF—Legal Aid), no. 2 (1976), *K.T.* 5736, no. 3524, p. 1670. This order was promulgated by virtue of regulation 7 of the regulations cited in n. 79 in this chapter.

[73] Labor Court (Service of Documents in the Occupied Territories) Regulations, 1969, *K.T.* 5730, no. 2482, p. 460.

jurisdiction is as difficult in this branch of law as in civil law, for the determining factor is the employee's place of work or the employer's place of business. If both are located in Judea and Samaria, there will be no local jurisdiction. It must also be mentioned that if one of the parties is the National Insurance Institute, then under regulation 2(6) and 2(7) of the Labor Courts (Procedure) Regulations of 1969,[74] local jurisdiction lies with the court in the plaintiff's place of residence. If the plaintiff lives in Judea and Samaria, which court will have jurisdiction?

Rabbinical Courts. The subject of the competence of rabbinical courts has raised many questions throughout the years since the enactment of the Rabbinical Courts Jurisdiction (Marriage and Divorce) Law of 1953.[75] Recently, the Supreme Court has ruled that the meaning of section 1 of the law, which states that "Jurisdiction in matters of marriage and divorce of Jews in Israel who are citizens or residents will lie exclusively with the rabbinical courts," is that both parties must be either Israeli citizens or residents, and they must be in Israel.[76] Although the settlers in Judea and Samaria are not residents of Israel, most of them are Israeli citizens, and therefore that part of the law is fulfilled. But the new requirement instituted in the *Chen* case—that both parties be in Israel—is not satisfied in the case of the Israeli settlers in Judea and Samaria.[77] Consequently, married couples in Judea and Samaria will be left without a court that is competent to judge their affairs; neither the Israeli court nor any court in Judea and Samaria has jurisdiction (in contrast to civil cases, in which the local court in Judea and Samaria has jurisdiction). Here, too, a partial solution lies in the two sides' mutually agreeing upon a court, but any person with even a little experience in family law knows that in most of the cases the conflict between the parties is so bitter that the chance of securing mutual agreement on the question of jurisdiction is minimal. In any case, it is quite clear that the party who is doubtful of the outcome of the case will be advised by his counsel to argue lack of jurisdiction and thereby to frustrate the intention of the other party to draw him into a legal battle.

Regarding substantive law, the obligation to conduct the wedding ceremony according to Jewish law (*halakhah*) applies only in

[74] K.T. 5729, no. 2440, p. 2088.

[75] S.H. 5713, no. 134, p. 165.

[76] H.C. 297/77, Chen v. *Regional Rabbinical Court of Haifa* (1978), P.D. 31(3) 679. And see M. Shava, "Conditions of Jurisdiction of the Rabbinical Court in Matters of Marriage and Divorce," *Hapraklit*, vol. 32 (1978/5738), p. 39.

[77] Cf. Shava, "Conditions of Jurisdiction," pp. 61-62.

Israel, by virtue of section 2 of the above law, and does not apply in Judea and Samaria. The proposed amendment whereby Israeli law would have personal application would be of help in solving these problems.

Criminal Law. Criminal offenses committed in the administered territories, including Judea and Samaria, are triable before either of two types of courts: the local courts, which have continued to operate since 1967, or military courts, set up by order of the area commander, which have concurrent jurisdiction.[78] In addition to the military courts in Judea and Samaria, the Israeli courts are competent to try Israelis and Israelis living in Judea and Samaria for crimes committed in the territories, as if the crimes had been committed in Israel. The competent court is that whose area of jurisdiction is closest to the place where the offense was committed.[79]

The High Court of Justice. There are many cases in which the High Court of Justice has been petitioned on matters concerning the administered territories. The petitions touch on every aspect of life, including labor matters, electricity, municipal elections, deportation, review of the military and the local courts, the legality of the settlements, the evacuation of the Rafah Approach, etc. Elsewhere I have dwelt on the question of the competence of the High Court to hear matters in which the military government is a party. Even though the military government operates beyond the borders of the State of Israel, it is an authority operating by virtue of law.[80] In most cases, it is the Arabs of Judea and Samaria who file petitions with the High Court, but it is nevertheless clear that that court has jurisdiction to hear the petitions of Israeli settlers as well.[81]

Taxation

The subject of taxation in occupied territories in general, and in the territories administered by the IDF in particular, involves a combination of international law and the specific law of the occupied state. The particular economic situation in the zone is also a relevant factor.

[78] Drori, *Legislation*, pp. 118 ff., 126 ff., and esp. 160 ff. See M. Drori, "Concurrent Criminal Jurisdiction in the Administered Territories," *Hapraklit*, vol. 32 (1979/5739), p. 386.

[79] See the Law Extending the Force of Emergency Regulations (Judea and Samaria, Gaza Strip, Ramat Hagolan, Sinai and Southern Sinai—Criminal Jurisdiction and Legal Aid), 1967, *S.H.* 1968/5728, no. 517, p. 20.

[80] Drori, *Legislation*, pp. 74-90; Drori, "Legal System in Judea and Samaria," pp. 156-59.

[81] See, for example, the *Haetzni* case.

What follows is a general summary of taxation of the Arab inhabitants of the administered territories.[82]

Direct taxation was not adjusted to Israeli standards, so income tax in Judea and Samaria is much lower than in Israel. Moreover, the changes made in local laws were mainly concerned with converting sums of money from dinars to Israeli lirot,[83] even though this entailed a slight increase in the amounts collected.

This is not the case in relation to indirect taxation. Owing to the close connection with Israel and the intermingling of the two economies, indirect taxation had to be standardized in order to avoid fraud, evasion, and unfair competition. Under international law, however, it is not easy to enact legislation to this effect. Local laws were not simply repealed and replaced by Israeli law, but rather the existing framework was retained, and the Israeli rates of taxation, as well as the Israeli purchase tax, were introduced within that framework.[84] Value added tax, too, was introduced under the title of "additional excise tax" and was incorporated into the local excise law.[85]

Income Tax. Under the generally accepted norms of tax law—the principle of the territorial application of taxes—the income of Israelis living in Judea and Samaria ought to have been taxed under Jordanian law, for such income was "derived, received or obtained" in Judea and Samaria, and not in Israel. In practice, however, the taxation authorities of the military government did not collect the Jordanian taxes from Israeli citizens living in Judea and Samaria. Companies

---

[82] See R. Lapidoth, "Public International Law Rules concerning Taxation in Occupied Territories," *The Israeli Tax Review*, vol. 10 (1968), p. 111; D. Shefi, "Taxation in the Administered Territories," *Is.Y.H.R.* 290 (1971); M. Hertzberg, "Legislation concerning Indirect Taxation in the Administered Territories, *The Israeli Tax Review*, vol. 20 (1971), p. 347; see also, Drori, "Legal System in Judea and Samaria," pp. 165-66.

[83] See the Order concerning the Law of Income Tax (Amendment) (Judea and Samaria), no. 636 (1976), *CPOA*, no. 38, p. 118.

[84] Hertzberg, "Legislation concerning Indirect Taxation," pp. 348-50; Lapidoth, "Public International Law."

[85] Order concerning Law of Excise on Certain Products (Amendment no. 2) (Judea and Samaria), no. 658 (1976), *CPOA*, no. 38, p. 182; Kuttner remarks that the imposing of the value-added tax "falls within the orbit of art. 49 of the Geneva Convention." See Kuttner, "Israel and the West Bank—Aspects of the Law of Belligerent Occupation," *Is.Y.H.R.*, vol. 7 (1977), p. 185. It is noteworthy that the updating of customs rates is carried out by an officer of the customs staff by virtue of the powers of his office, and changes are publicized in customs houses, chambers of commerce, and local municipalities. See section 3(c)(3), Order concerning Customs' Tariff (West Bank), no. 103 (1967), *CPOA*, no. 6, p. 231; Instruction concerning Publication of Customs' Tariff (Judea and Samaria) (1968), *CPOA* Supplement no. 4, p. 391.

and associations that were registered in Israel usually paid their taxes directly in Israel, whereas Israelis whose sources of income were in the administered territories in effect paid no income tax.

In 1978 the picture changed. The Knesset amended the Israeli Income Tax Ordinance, adding section 3A, which states: "The income of an Israeli citizen which was produced, obtained or received in the territories will be regarded as income produced, obtained or received in Israel."[86] This act created the situation whereby the Israeli legislature regards Israelis who work in Judea and Samaria as similar to Israelis working in Israel, and as such, they are subject to Israeli taxation, by virtue of Israeli law, and according to the rates pertaining in Israel.[87] The motive behind the amendment is obvious, and it was expressed by the then deputy finance minister, Y. Flumin, when he tabled the draft bill in the Knesset: "It is proposed to add to that income which is regarded as produced in Israel the income of Israeli citizens which has its source in territories under Israeli control. The amendment comes *to prevent these territories from becoming tax havens* for Israeli citizens.[88]

Value Added Tax. A number of the substantive provisions of the Israeli Value Added Tax Law were enacted by the military government in an order imposing an additional excise on residents of Judea and Samaria. This tax, however, although its rate is similar to the Israeli value added tax, is collected by the taxation authorities of the military government, and it differs in nature from the tax payable under the Israeli law. By virtue of a law of the Knesset, the Israeli Value Added Tax Law was extended to apply to Israelis living in Judea and Samaria. The legislative technique was similar to that used to extend the application of the Income Tax Ordinance.

The government put forward the proposal to apply the value

---

[86] Income Tax Ordinance (Amendment) Law, no. 32 (1978), *S.H.* 5738, no. 910, p. 216. The amendment added section 3A to the ordinance. A "citizen" is both a physical person and a company in Israel—section 3A(a) of the just-mentioned law. The same section defines a "region" as Judea and Samaria, the Gaza Strip, the Golan Heights, Sinai and southern Sinai.

[87] The application of the Jordanian tax did not expire, however, because the income had its source in Judea and Samaria. Therefore, section 3A(a) provided that if that person paid taxes to the taxation authorities in the area of Judea and Samaria, he would be exempt from the Israeli tax up to the amount that he had already paid. The reason for this is clear: the coffers are the same, and double taxation is unfair. Nor is there any need for a convention on double taxation, for both taxation authorities are in fact subject to the same legislator.

[88] See *Divrei Haknesset* [The minutes of the Knesset], vol. 82 (1978/5738), p. 2346 (emphasis added).

added tax to Israelis living in the territories[89] soon after the proposal concerning income tax. The motive for extending the application of the value added tax, however, is not only the negative one of not wanting to create a tax haven in Judea and Samaria, but from an economic point of view, there is no separation between Israel and the Administered Territories. It is important that the same law should apply to a businessman in the Territories who is an Israeli citizen and to a businessman in Israel.[90]

With respect to value added tax, unlike income tax, recourse was not had to the formulation of a fiction—"the income will be regarded as . . ."; rather, it was explicitly stated that the law applies also to transactions effected in the area by Israeli citizens.[91]

Land Appreciation Tax. In Israel a special tax, the land appreciation tax, applies to profits derived from the sale of land. The rate of tax depends on the period of time which has elapsed between the purchase and the sale, with a certain allowance being made for inflation, and on whether the land is a plot or business asset or a home.[92]

In the summer of 1980, the Land Appreciation Tax Law was changed with respect to homes, becoming more liberal on many points, so that in most cases, a seller will now be exempt on the sale of his home, and only a person owning more than one apartment (or other residence) who sells within four years of having made a previous sale will pay tax.[93] Accompanying this amendment was another, initiated by the Finance Committee of the Knesset, which did not appear in the draft amendment. It states: "For the purpose of this Law, the same law applies to the sale of the home of an Israeli citizen in the territories and the sale of a home in Israel."[94]

The aim of this amendment was to prevent a situation wherein the Israelis living in Judea and Samaria who own two apartments— one in Israel and one in the territories—could sell them without paying tax. Judea and Samaria are no different from Israel for this purpose, and only if a person falls within the exempt category specified by the

---

[89] Value Added Tax (Amendment) Bill (1978), *H.H. (Hatza'ot Hok* [Legislative Bills in Israel]), 1978/5738, p. 126, at p. 134 (sec. 28).

[90] Ibid., p. 135.

[91] Section 144A of the Value Added Tax Law, as added in s.40 of the Value Added Tax (Amendment no. 3) Law (1979), *S.H.* 5739, no. 927, 52, at 59.

[92] Land Appreciation Tax Law (1963), *S.H.* 5723, no. 405, p. 156.

[93] Land Appreciation Tax (Amendment no. 8) Law (1980), *S.H.* 5740, no. 975, p. 144.

[94] See *Divrei Haknesset* (9th Knesset), Stenogramic Protocol, Session no. 451, July 7, 1980, pp. 8-10, per M.K. S. Lorencz, chairman of the Finance Committee.

law—that is, one sale every four years or more—will he be able to sell his apartments without paying tax.

In this way, the land appreciation tax was applied to apartments in Judea and Samaria, whereas for other property to which the law applies, such as plots of land, business assets, etc., the Land Appreciation Tax Law will not apply, and an Israeli who profited from the sale of such property in Judea and Samaria will be exempt from the land appreciation tax.[95] It must be assumed that the law was amended partly as a result of the public criticism aimed at some of the settlers in Judea and Samaria who in addition to their homes in Israel own another home in Judea and Samaria which the government helped finance and build. The imposition of tax on the sale of both the homes was intended to create parity between such an Israeli and one who has two homes inside the "Green Line."

National Insurance. In the State of Israel the payments made to national insurance are of great importance; in quite a number of cases, they constitute an additional form of taxation payable by the citizen. Are the Israelis living in Judea and Samaria obliged to make contributions to national insurance, and are they entitled to avail themselves of its services? Prima facie, the Israelis in the area are not residents of Israel, and as such, the law—or at least large parts of it that specifically apply to Israeli residents—does not bind them.[96] Contrary to this, if the Israeli is a worker whose income is subject to income tax, it is possible that he will be liable for national insurance payments.[97] There is a special branch of national insurance which undoubtedly applies to Israelis living in Judea and Samaria, that is, payments for reserve duty, for these payments are made to everyone who serves, by law, in reserve duty, irrespective of his place of residence.[98] In practice, the Israelis living in Judea and Samaria do pay dues to the National Insurance Institute, and they avail themselves of the services of the institute.

[95] It is possible that this profit will be regarded as capital gains, which will be liable to capital gains tax by virtue of section 3A of the ordinance.
[96] National Insurance Law (Consolidated Version), 1968, S.H. 5728, no. 530, 168. See, for example, section 7, which states that an "insured person" for the purposes of super annuation and insurance of dependents is a resident of Israel who has reached the age of eighteen years. This definition is also employed for maternity insurance (section 92). See also, sections 90B (insurance for accident victims), 104 (child insurance), 127A (unemployment insurance), and 127 (21) (disability insurance).
[97] Cf. section 164 of the National Insurance Law.
[98] See section 127(68) ff.

Summary and Solutions

The problems described above attest that, to date, the State of Israel has neglected the Israeli settlers in Judea and Samaria, leaving them with no "juridical father." Only a few of the problems have been tackled in legislation, and even this legislation does not provide complete solutions.

One possible response would be to apply Israeli law and administration to those territories in which Israeli settlement is concentrated, as has been done in East Jerusalem.[99] This is a very convenient course from both a practical and a legal point of view, but its political drawbacks are obvious. It is not in accordance with the Camp David agreements, which provide that the final status of Judea and Samaria will be determined five years after the introduction of autonomy into the area.

A second possible course would be for the Knesset to enact a central piece of legislation (and should the need arise, specific acts addressed to specific problems) to the following effect:

Israeli law and administration will apply to the citizens of the State of Israel or to whosoever is registered in the Israeli Population Register and is living permanently in Judea and Samaria. Such persons will be regarded as residents of Israel for the purposes of all laws.

This formulation is somewhat reminiscent of the law enacted in 1967, by virtue of which Jerusalem was unified,[100] but there is a fundamental difference between the two. The 1967 law applied Israeli law to a certain *territory* (East Jerusalem), whereas my proposal is that Israeli law should continue to apply to Israeli *persons*.

Such legislation would settle a debt of honor owed to pioneers who were encouraged by Israel to settle in Judea and Samaria. It would prove that Israel regards them as having rights and duties equal to those of all Israelis, and that the government will render them support even when the umbrella of autonomy is spread over them. Such legislation would be comprehensible to the world community. It could be justified as the obligation of the state to care for its citizens who are situated in an area in which Jordanian law currently applies in principle, and who in the future will be subject to the autonomy authorities.

[99] On this point, see in detail Blum, *The Juridical Status of Jerusalem*.
[100] Section 11B of the Law and Administration Ordinance (1948), as added in 1967, *S.H.* 727, no. 499, 74.

I am aware that legal theoreticians and historians will criticize this approach, saying: "You are suggesting a return to the regime of capitulations of the nineteenth century, and are substituting personal law for territorial law. How can we regress so in the twentieth century?" My answer is that this is indeed not a perfect solution, but it is a solution suited to the current situation in which thousands of Israelis are living in Judea and Samaria. It is preferable to constant speculation about the theoretical legal problems that arise in the application of any solution. Moreover, the special situation pertaining in the territories has several international precedents;[101] my proposed legislation concerning the Israelis living in Judea and Samaria would simply add another precedent to the list.

[101] See, for example, R. Mushkat, "The Geneva Convention of 1949 in the Light of the Military Occupation of Territories Held by Israel—Some Observations," *International Problems*, vol. 12, no. 3-4(24) (October 1973), p. 29.

3

Water Resources in Judea, Samaria, and the Gaza Strip

J. Schwarz

The areas of Judea and Samaria and the Gaza Strip delineated by the 1949 armistice lines (see figure 1), were separated politically and economically from Israel in the period 1948–1967, and their future is at present being negotiated. One of the major problems in cutting these areas off from the other parts of the country is that of water resources. The problem relates, on the one hand, to supplying the water demand of these areas from the limited local resources and, on the other hand, to deterioration of water resources in other parts of the country in the case of overexploitation of the local resources. This chapter depicts the general geography of the areas and contains a detailed description of the water resources that supply or are influenced by them. It concludes by noting that the future outlook for the water economy of the two areas depends on large-scale development and the investment of capital and know-how to close the gap between scarce resources and continuously increasing demand.

Geographic Background

Judea and Samaria and the Gaza Strip are climatically and hydrologically interconnected with the other regions of Israel, and their water resources must be studied in the framework of the overall hydrology of the country.

Israel is longitudinally divided into three topographic units running roughly north-south: the coastal plain along the Mediterranean in the west, a hilly region in the center, and the Jordan Rift Valley in the east (see figures 1 and 2). The coastal plain is about 15 km wide in the central part of the country (north of Tel Aviv) and 20 km wide

---

NOTE: This chapter was prepared in May 1980.

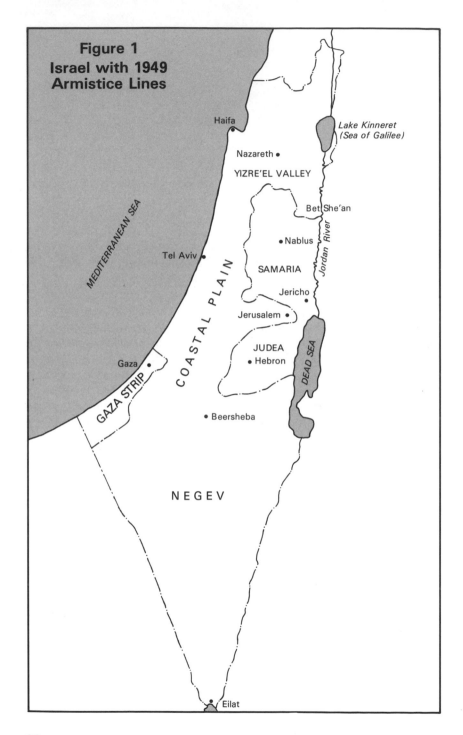

Figure 1
Israel with 1949
Armistice Lines

MEDITERRANEAN SEA

Haifa

Lake Kinneret
(Sea of Galilee)

Nazareth

YIZRE'EL VALLEY

Bet She'an

Nablus

Tel Aviv

COASTAL PLAIN

SAMARIA

Jordan River

Jericho

Jerusalem

JUDEA

Gaza

Hebron

DEAD SEA

GAZA STRIP

Beersheba

N E G E V

Eilat

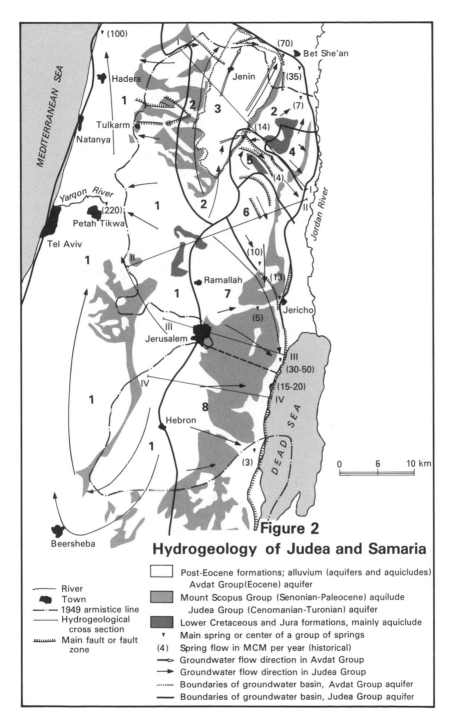

Figure 2
Hydrogeology of Judea and Samaria

River
Town
1949 armistice line
Hydrogeological cross section
Main fault or fault zone

Post-Eocene formations; alluvium (aquifers and aquicludes) Avdat Group(Eocene) aquifer
Mount Scopus Group (Senonian-Paleocene) aquilude Judea Group (Cenomanian-Turonian) aquifer
Lower Cretaceous and Jura formations, mainly aquiclude
▼ Main spring or center of a group of springs
(4) Spring flow in MCM per year (historical)
➡ Groundwater flow direction in Avdat Group
→ Groundwater flow direction in Judea Group
.... Boundaries of groundwater basin, Avdat Group aquifer
— Boundaries of groundwater basin, Judea Group aquifer

farther south at the latitude of Jerusalem. Its elevation is about 50 meters above mean sea level (MSL), with a line of sand dunes and sandstone hills along the seashore and lower-lying heavier soils farther inland.

The transition from the coastal plain to the central mountains is sharp in the northern part of the country. South of the Jerusalem latitude the transition occurs through an interim area of low foothills. Judea and Samaria are located mainly in the central hill area—the Judean and Samarian mountains—between the Yizre'el Valley in the north and the Beersheba Valley in the south, but it also includes a section of the Jordan Valley between Bet She'an Valley in the north and the Dead Sea in the south, and small areas in the coastal plain near Tulkarm and Kalkilya. The Gaza Strip is situated in the southern part of the coastal plain.

Judea and Samaria lie astride the main watershed between the Mediterranean Sea and the Jordan River, chiefly on the western side of the watershed, at elevations approaching 800 meters above MSL. Along the central ridge are a few small plains, from which the slopes drop down to the west and east in terraces. The overall slope on the eastern side of the watershed is three times as steep as on the western side. The western slope south of Jerusalem is characterized by two terraces, followed by a hilly area composed of chalky Eocene limestone. North of Jerusalem, the western slope down to the coastal plain has one terrace. On the eastern slope, the southern section has five to six terraces down to the Jordan Valley, and the northern section two or three. Of the eastern terraces, only the first is inhabited today; the entire slope beyond that is part of the Judean Desert.

Dry watercourses ("wadis") starting from the watershed cut the mountain zone into a series of blocks, like ribs extending from a spine. South of Hebron one such wadi cuts right across the mountain ridge, dividing it in two. In the northern section, the Dotan Valley—a branch of the Yizre'el Valley—penetrates the western Samaria mountains near Jenin and separates them from the Gilboa Range.

The Jordan Valley is located on the eastern boundary of the country. It is the northernmost part of the Syrio-African Rift Valley. In the Neogene and early Pleistocene period it was a plateau connecting Lake Kinneret (Sea of Galilee) with the Dead Sea; the base of the valley is composed of marl layers originating from that period. Mainly along the western margin of the valley, silt brought down during floods has accumulated. The valley gets progressively wider from north to south. It has two terraces—the flood plain of the Jordan River, called Zhor in Arabic, and the rest of the valley, called Ghor.

Israel lies between the low-rainfall region of Egypt to the south and southwest and the high-rainfall area of Lebanon to the north. It thus constitutes a transition region from a subtropical arid to a subtropical wet climate and as such has an unusually wide range of rainfalls for a country of its size. The southern part of the country is arid, with less than 30 mm of rain per year, while the north receives as much as 700–1,100 mm per year. The western slopes of Judea and Samaria have an annual rainfall of 500–700 mm, the eastern slopes 100–500 mm, and the Gaza Strip 200–400 mm.

There is a distinct rainy season, occurring in winter, mainly from November to May, with maximum rainfall in January. There are large deviations from this pattern, however, the winters sometimes being dry at the beginning and wet later on, or vice versa, or with a dry spell in the middle. There is also a considerable deviation from the average rainfall from year to year and for longer periods. Analysis of the rainfall records of the Jerusalem rain-gauging station over 115 years (1861–1862 to 1975–1976) showed seven distinct periods, three of them wet, two average, and two dry. The wettest period was from 1877–1878 to 1905–1906, with an average rainfall 15 percent higher than the overall average. The driest was from 1923–1924 to 1935–1936, with an average rainfall about 27 percent lower than the overall average. Another dry period, less severe, was from 1945–1946 to 1962–1963.

There is an abundance of sunshine, with an average radiation of 5,000–7,500 kcal/m^2 per day on a horizontal area in summer. Potential evaporation is high: typical values are 1,900 mm per year in the Gaza Strip, and in Judea and Samaria 1,900 mm in the western part and 2,600 mm around Jericho in the Jordan Valley.

In the higher parts of Judea and Samaria, rain-fed agriculture is possible. In the Jordan Valley, the Gaza Strip, the coastal plain, and all the southern parts of Israel, only irrigated agriculture is possible. Irrigation water requirements for typical modern agriculture amount to 1,000–1,500 mm per year in the Jordan Valley and 500–700 mm per year in the Gaza Strip.

As a result of the climatic, topographic, and geological conditions, surface water is scarce. The only surface-water source is the Jordan River and its tributaries, which can meet only about a third of the country's water requirements. As a result, groundwater constitutes the major source. The main aquifers of Israel, draining to the west, are the Coastal Plain Aquifer and the Judea Group (Cenomanian-Turonian) Yarqon-Tanninim Aquifer of central Israel. Some smaller aquifers also drain to the east.

Water Sources of Judea and Samaria

The physical structure of Judea and Samaria determines to a large extent the location and character of the water sources—as well as the population distribution.

Rainfall is the origin of the water sources. Part of it percolates into the ground and replenishes the aquiferous formations, which finally discharge by springs. Part flows as surface runoff and drains to watercourses as flash floods. A major part of the rainfall returns directly to the atmosphere by evaporation. The following are the components of the hydrological cycle in Judea and Samaria.

Rainfall, Evaporation, and Runoff. The climate of the area is influenced by its physical structure and its proximity to the sea. Rainfall is confined to the winter months (mainly November to May), and is mainly related to the mountainous lay of the land owing to the west-to-east topographic rise from the plain to the ridges, followed by the sharp descent to the Jordan Valley beyond. The long-term average rainfall record for the period 1931–1960 shows the following trends. The highest average rainfall of 700 mm per year occurs at the locations of highest elevation—a pocket around Shechem (Nablus) and one just south of it, another north of Ramallah, and a fourth southwest of Bethlehem. The western slopes have an average of 500–600 mm per year, and on the steep eastern slopes the average drops sharply from 450 mm near the watershed to 150 mm per year around Jericho. In addition to this trend of increasing and then decreasing rainfall from west to east, there is a decreasing trend from north to south, particularly along the Jordan Valley, where the rainfall drops in the south to 100 mm along the shores of the Dead Sea.

Annual evaporation in Judea and Samaria averages between 1,900 mm per year on the western slopes of the watershed to 2,600 mm per year on the shores of the Dead Sea. The highest monthly average is in July, with 8 mm per day on the western slopes and 11 mm per day in the Jordan Valley.

The surface runoff in Judea and Samaria is composed of flash floods and springs. Owing to the karstic nature—the high solubility of the rock in water creates underground features such as caverns, sinkholes, and "lost" rivers—of most of the outcrops in the upper part of the catchment basins floodwater runoff is minimal—usually not more than 1 or 2 percent of the rainfall. According to various estimates, the floodwater runoff in the area averages between 30 and 50 MCM (million cubic meters) per year, of which 20 MCM flows west of the watershed and the rest flows eastward. Springs drain the groundwater basins, as will be discussed later. It is estimated

86

that the total discharge of the springs which issue within Judea and Samaria is 75–115 MCM per year, of which the bulk flows eastward and about 5 MCM flows westward. Altogether the surface runoff in Judea and Samaria thus averages 105–165 MCM per year, of which about 25 MCM flows westward.

The Aquifier System. The system of aquifers (water-bearing rock formations) in the Judea and Samaria region comprises several rock formations from Lower Cretaceous to Recent age, which include limestone, dolomite, and marl formations. In limited areas it comprises clastic rocks—sandstones, conglomerates, and clays. In the inner valleys, there are alluvial and other deposits of Neogene and Pleistocene age. In the Jordan Valley east of the hilly block, there are mainly continental deposits of Neogene to Recent age.

The various formations generally occur in a series of aquifers and aquicludes (impermeable geological formations), as follows:

- Kurnub Group aquiclude, of Albian age. The section is mainly marl with some limestone horizons, and the thickness is up to 300 m.
- Judea Group (also known as Ajlun Series) aquifer, of Cenomanian and Turonian age. The section is dolomite and limestone, with interim chalk and marl formations. The formation thickness is 400–900 m, but only part of it is below the water table.
- Mt. Scopus Group (also known as Belqa Series) aquiclude, of Senonian-Paleocene age. The section is of chalk and marl, and the thickness 150–250 m.
- Aquifer-aquitard of the Avdat Subgroup of the Mt. Scopus Group (also known as Jenin Subseries of the Belqa Series), of Eocene age. The section consists of chalk and limestone, with a thickness of 200–500 m. This layer may form an aquitard (a semipermeable geological formation), according to the proportion of chalk in the rock. In the large Nablus-Jenin syncline, however, this section forms the major aquifer.
- Local aquifers and aquicludes of Neogene and Pleistocene age (Beida and younger formations). Conglomerates, marls, clays, and sands of thicknesses from a few meters to hundreds of meters are found in the Jordan Valley.

The Judea Group aquifer is the major one, having the largest outcrop area and the largest replenishment. It outcrops along the entire length of the hilly backbone in the center of the country. Along the upper ridge only its lower portion exists, overlying the Kurnub Group aquiclude, while along the margins of the hills, the aquifer is usually confined beneath the Mt. Scopus aquiclude. The aquifer descends steeply westward below the coastal plain, and in several areas one can distinguish a clear subdivision into two subaquifers with different water levels.

The Avdat Group aquifer exists in some synclines (trough or V-shaped rock downfolds) along the margins of the hilly block and in the large Nablus-Jenin syncline in the center of the hilly region in northern Samaria. It is composed of chalky and limestone layers, differing in aquiferous properties from place to place. It overlies the Mt. Scopus Group aquiclude.

The Neogene-Pleistocene aquifers are composed mainly of layers a few tens of meters thick, and they are important only in the Bet She'an Valley and in the southern part of the Jordan Valley around Auja and Jericho.

Groundwater Basins. The hilly backbone of Judea and Samaria, which coincides with the anticlinal (tent or arch-shaped rock upfolds) structures of the center of the country, constitutes the natural re-plenishment area of several of the largest underground reservoirs of the country. Rainfall over the hill outcrops percolates into the rocks of the various aquiferous units and spreads as underground flow in all directions (see figure 2).

The axes of the main anticlines also determine the main water-sheds dividing the underground flow to the west (toward the coastal plain), to the east (toward the Jordan Valley), and to the northeast (toward the Yizre'el Valley and Bet She'an). Accordingly, the systems of aquifers related to Judea and Samaria can be divided into several basins:

- West: Although its natural discharge is via two separate spring systems and although some faults cut across it from east to west, the whole western drainage basin is considered as one unit, namely the Yarqon-Tanninim basin (number 1 in figure 2). It discharges into the coastal plain.
- Northeast: This drainage basin is subdivided into two overlying aquifers, both discharging mainly in the Bet She'an and Yizre'el valleys: the Samaria basin (number 2 in figure 2) draining the Judea Group aquifer, and the Nablus-Jenin basin (number 3) draining the Avdat Group aquifer.
- East: The eastern basins drain into the Jordan Valley. They include five almost separate catchment areas: Buquei'a–Wadi Malih (number 4); Fari'ah (number 5); Auja-Fasavil (number 6); Ramallah-Jerusalem (number 7); the Judean Desert (number 8).

Natural Outlets and Springs. The majority of the flow outlets of these aquifers are springs issuing at the foot of the hilly region—starting from the slopes of the Gilboa and the Bet She'an Valley in the northeast, along the Jordan Valley and the shore of the Dead Sea in the east, and up to Rosh Ha'ayin (the Yarqon springs) and the Carmel slopes (the Tanninim springs) in the coastal plain in the west.

A change of composition in the Yarqon-Tanninim basin—from carbonaceous dolomite limestone and chalk formations to argilaceous (clayey) formations in the coastal area, where it is covered by hundreds of meters of overlying clayey Neogene formations—creates an impervious hydrologic barrier which prevents groundwater from draining into the Mediterranean Sea and forces the flow to the Rosh Ha'ayin springs near Petah Tikwa and to the Tanninim springs north of Hadera. These springs are the principal points of natural outflow of the aquifer system in the western drainage basin. Impervious fill layers in the Yizre'el, Bet She'an, and Jordan valleys create similar phenomena there, so that the springs along the northern and eastern margin of the hills constitute the principal points of outflow of the northeastern and eastern drainage basins.

The springs draining the various groundwater basins are:

- The natural drainage outlets of the Yarqon-Tanninim basin are the Yarqon springs near Petah Tikwa in the central part of the country (discharge originally 235 MCM per year, salinity 150–200 ppm [parts per million] chloride) and the more northerly Tanninim springs, north of Hadera (discharge originally 100 MCM per year, salinity 600–1,000 ppm chloride). As a result of the drastic drop in the water table, most of this water no longer issues spontaneously and must today be pumped. The Yarqon spring waters are mainly pumped from wells located from the Lod plain south of Petah Tikwa as far as Beersheba in the south. The Tanninim waters are pumped from wells in the Sharon plain (coastal plain between Petah Tikwa and Hadera). By this replacement of the natural spring flow by pumpage, it is possible to achieve better regulation of water utilization between summer and winter and between wet and dry years.
- The natural drainage outlets of the Samaria basin are chiefly the springs in the Bet She'an Valley—four major springs and some twenty small springs—which in the past had a discharge of 40–45 MCM per year. Today they yield only about 10 MCM per year, the rest of the water being pumped from wells in the Gilboa–Bet She'an area. Salinity ranges between 80 and 800 ppm chloride. An additional 20 MCM per year leaks from the

Samaria basin to the Nablus-Jenin basin (see below) and drains to the springs of that basin.

- The natural drainage outlets of the Nablus-Jenin basin are two groups of springs. The Gilboa springs, seven in number, lie along the margin of the Bet She'an Valley, with a discharge of 70–80 MCM per year and salinity ranging from 250 to 1,100 ppm chloride. (This quantity includes the 20 MCM per year which leaks, as mentioned above, from the Samaria basin.) The Wadi Fariah springs near Nablus, eight in number, have a discharge of about 18 MCM per year and salinity 20–40 ppm chloride.

- The drainage outlets of the Buqei'a–Wadi Malih basin are the springs of Wadi Malih, with a discharge of 0.6 MCM per year and salinity 120–600 ppm chloride.

- The Fariah basin drains to three springs, with a total discharge of 4 MCM per year and salinity 50–60 ppm chloride.

- The Auja-Fasayil basin drains partly into the Auja spring (10 MCM per year, salinity 30 ppm chloride) and into small springs in Fasayil and Ein Samiya. Auja spring has no buffer underground storage, and so its discharge varies from zero in dry years to 25 MCM per year in wet years. A major part of the water from the basin drains southward into the Feshkha springs in the next basin.

- The Ramallah-Jerusalem basin drains into the Jericho springs (three springs with total discharge of 13 MCM per year and salinity 28–40 ppm chloride), the springs of Wadi Qilt (5 MCM per year, salinity 22–30 ppm chloride), and the Gihon spring in Jerusalem. In addition, some 30–50 MCM per year drains into the Feshkha springs (salinity 1,000–5,000 ppm chloride) on the shores of the Dead Sea.

- The Judean Desert basin drains mainly into the shores of the Dead Sea—some 15–20 MCM per year into the Ghuwer and Turaiba springs and an additional 3 MCM per year into the Ein Gedi springs. A few small springs near Hebron yield some 0.3 MCM per year from this basin.

The natural replenishment of all the aquifers in the central hilly block between the Mediterranean Sea and the Jordan River is estimated from the total natural discharge of these springs and some small direct percolation into the Jordan River to be 580 MCM per year, comprising western drainage of 335 ± 10 MCM, northeastern drainage of 140 ± 10 MCM, and eastern drainage of 105 ± 20 MCM. The natural outlets for the greatest part of the western and northeastern drainage (455 MCM) is through three major groups of springs: the Yarqon springs in the coastal plain (235 MCM), the Tanninim springs in the coastal plain (100 MCM), and the Bet She'an–Harod springs in the Bet She'an Valley (120 MCM).

Utilization and Management of Water Resources in Judea and Samaria

The hill region of Judea and Samaria has throughout history suffered from a lack of flowing water. Crops have been dependent on rainfall, while rainwater has had to be collected and stored in cisterns for drinking purposes. A small number of wells and springs, fed by small perched groundwater horizons—that is, groundwater collected above impermeable lenses above the major water table of the aquifer—were utilized in the central mountains. These sources, such as the Gihon spring near Jerusalem and Jacob's Well in Samaria, have been well known since biblical times. In spite of this scarcity of water, a population which numbered hundreds of thousands, or even millions, lived in the hilly region and flourished. Life was based on rain-fed agriculture. Only for the End of Days was flowing water throughout the year promised for Jerusalem (Zech. 14:8). Today the water consumption within Judea and Samaria is estimated at 113 MCM per year. Of this quantity, about 10 MCM per year is pumped directly from the Jordan River; the rest comes from groundwater exploitation, which is divided approximately evenly between pumping from wells and utilization of freshwater springs. A little more than half this amount is drawn from the eastern basin, and the balance from the western basin (20 MCM per year) and the northeastern basin (25 MCM per year).

The rainfall from the hilly region draining eastward and feeding the springs of the Jordan Valley brought, according to the biblical record, plentiful water to the area, and "all the plain of Jordan . . . was well watered everywhere" (Gen. 13:10). Toward the west, the large quantities of water draining from the western basin of the central hills to the coastal plain caused swamps in the area between the Yarqon and Tanninim springs, and that area was therefore largely uninhabited; only sizable drainage works made possible the existence of a handful of settlements there. At the end of the last century the pioneering Settlement Movement succeeded in overcoming the drainage problems in the coastal plain and bringing about the development and the full and effective utilization of the springs and other groundwater sources. Today these water sources, including those fed from the western underground basin of the central hills, are insufficient to meet the water demand of the dense population in the coastal plain.

In the first decades of the present century similar full development of unutilized spring flows and swampy lands occurred in the Yizre'el and Bet She'an valleys at the outlets of the northeastern basins.

A comparison between the total present utilization and the estimated natural replenishment of the western and the two northeastern basins indicates that groundwater is mined at a rate of 30–40 MCM per year in the western basin and 10 MCM per year in the two northeastern basins. This overutilization had led to a drop in the water table at a rate of 0.3–0.4 m per year in the Yarqon-Tanninim basin and about 2 m per year in the Judea Group aquifer of the northeastern basin.

Salinity Hazards. The concentration of chloride ions is the common indicator for the salinity of aquifers. This concentration is a function of the flow regime and of the distribution of the sources of salinity.

The chloride concentrations in the aquifers in the natural replenishment regions near the watershed are in the range of 25–40 ppm in Samaria and the Jerusalem hills; they reach 60–80 ppm in the Hebron hills. These concentrations originate from washout of airborne salts by rainfall, and their levels reflect the different ratios between evaporation and infiltration in the two locations.

From the regions of natural replenishment, groundwater flows toward the drainage outlets under confined or semiconfined conditions created by overlying aquitardic formations. The natural replenishment of the aquitardic formations is very small, and the salinity of the water confined in these layers is therefore as high as several thousand ppm. The leakage from these layers to the Judea Group aquifers is negligible from the aspect of water balance, but it is very significant as far as the salt balance is concerned, causing a distinct increase in salinity along the streamlines of groundwater flow. The intensity of the leakage increases with the utilization of the water resources of the principal aquifers, owing to the drop in the water table.

The amount of dissolved solids in the rainwater accounts for only 10 percent of the chloride concentration in the groundwater. The remainder probably originates from ionic diffusion of dissolved solids from brines in the lower Cretaceous and lower layers. In these layers, which underlie the entire aquifer complex of Judea and Samaria and extend beyond it, there are ancient calcium chloride brines whose salinity equals or exceeds that of seawater.

Other possible sources of salinity are lateral diffusion along the impervious boundaries of the various aquifers, particularly possible diffusion of seawater from the Mediterranean Sea along the western margin of the Yarqon-Tanninim basin and of brines along the Jordan Valley and the Dead Sea shore. Some hypotheses attribute the principal source of salinity to present seawater intrusion.

As a result of the combined effect of the flow regime, the distribution of sources of salinity, and their relative intensity, the groundwater aquifers are surrounded along most of their boundaries—both in the horizontal plane and in the vertical plane—by saline water bodies. These constitute a grave potential danger to the intensified utilization of groundwater, since there exists a delicate hydrodynamic balance between the fresh and saline water bodies. This balance is maintained as long as the water table remains above the so-called red line. Any lowering of the water table below this line would upset the balance. The principal hazards, as foreseen for the Yarqon-Tanninim basin, are illustrated in figure 3, and may be summed up as follows:

- Massive intrusion of seawater or of water from brine bodies close to the Tanninim outlet
- A lateral shift of the saline water bodies situated in the aquifer along its western and southern margins toward the centers of pumpage
- Intensification of the leakage from brackish aquitards which overlie the upper aquifer
- Rising of saline water bodies under part of the pumping fields

In principle, similar hazards would be expected in the other over-exploited basins.

Already today, with the groundwater level still above the red line, the natural equilibrium has been upset to some extent, leading to a "creeping" increase in chloride concentrations. A typical rate of salinization in the Yarqon-Tanninim basin is on the order of 1–2 ppm chloride per year. There are, however, several salinity foci where the increase is 10 ppm chloride per year and more.

Groundwater Management. The drop in the water table in the western basin is causing an increase in groundwater salinity which is typically on the order of 1–2 ppm chloride per year. Continued over-pumpage is likely to cause saline water intrusion to the main pumpage areas of the aquifers, particularly in the plains adjoining Judea and Samaria. In the early 1960s Israel moved to prevent any further depletion of the aquifers by introducing a stringent control system in these plains and starting a large-scale artificial recharge program in the

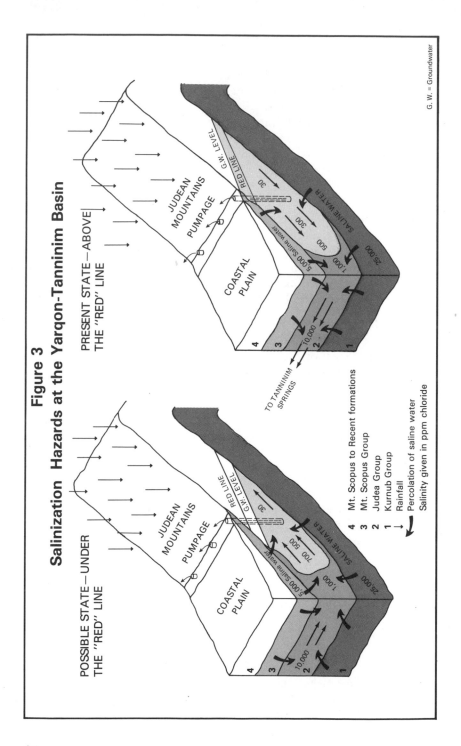

Figure 3

Salinization Hazards at the Yarqon-Tanninim Basin

G. W. = Groundwater

western basin with water imported from Lake Kinneret. These measures stabilized the water table at a level within the minimum possible range above the red line. To maintain this margin of safety in the western and northeastern basins, pumpage from wells should be frozen at the present levels, or even reduced, and artificial recharge should be increased. In the eastern basins, there is still room for increasing pumpage, partly at the expense of the discharge from springs which are at present not fully utilized.

Water Resources of the Gaza Strip

The Gaza Strip extends over an area of about 360 km^2 in the southern part of the coastal plain of Israel. It is 40 km long and about 9 km wide. A ridge of sand dunes with elevations of up to 40 m above MSL extends along the coast. East of these dunes, the soils are heavier and consist mostly of clayey sand to silt and sometimes even loess.

Rainfall occurs only in winter (mainly November to May). The mean annual rainfall ranges from 220 mm per year in the southern part of the Gaza Strip to 370 mm per year in the northern part, with an overall average of 275 mm per year. The mean annual evaporation is 1,800–1,900 mm per year. Since the moisture balance of the soil is negative throughout the summer, agriculture—which is the main local source of income of the population—is, by and large, irrigated.

There are no surface-water resources in the Gaza Strip. One dry watercourse—Nahal Besor—traverses the region, carrying water about ten days annually. All the water flows to the sea at present, but there are plans to capture the floodwater in the upper part of the 3,500 km^2 catchment basin.

The only water resource of the Gaza Strip is groundwater, which occurs in the sand and sandstone aquifers underlying the entire area at a depth of 10–50 m below ground surface. The groundwater is replenished both by direct rainwater infiltration, particularly in the sand dunes along the coast, and by underground flow entering from the east. Rainwater replenishment is estimated at 40 MCM per year and underground flow from the east at 10–20 MCM per year. At present, groundwater is also replenished by return flow from irrigation and cesspools. This amount is estimated at 20–30 MCM per year, but it is expected that increased efficiencies of irrigation and intensified water-saving measures will reduce this to 10–15 MCM per year.

Before intensive groundwater utilization began, the inflow to the area drained away through the aquiferous layers that stretch out to the continental shelf of the Mediterranean Sea. The high water table and this seaward direction of groundwater flow prevented the intrusion of seawater into the Gaza Strip aquifers. It may be assumed that also in the future a seaward outflow of not less than 20 MCM per year will be required to keep seawater intrusion into the aquifers within tolerable limits.

The long-term utilizable groundwater resources of the Gaza Strip are thus estimated at about 40 MCM per year. In addition to this, one-time reserves of about 20 MCM per year may be mined for a period of about ten years.

Hydrogeology of the Gaza Strip. Information on the hydrogeology of the Gaza Strip is limited and has been collected only in recent years. Nevertheless, the data available from the small number of observation wells drilled give some indication of its geological structure.

The Gaza Strip aquifer consists of a number of subaquifers composed mainly of sand, sandstone, and pebbles of Pleistocenian age. In places, the subaquifers overlie each other and are separated by impervious and semipervious clay layers (see figure 4). The uppermost aquifer (designated A in figure 4) lies mainly under the seabed, and extends only a few hundred meters inland—up to 2 km from the shoreline. The lower the subaquifer, the farther it extends inland from the coast; the lowest one (C) extends up to 5 km inland. The total thickness of the aquiferous layers varies from 10 m on the eastern boundary to 120 m near the coast.

The eastern end of the aquiferous complex extends beyond the boundary of the Gaza Strip. In this region, however, the aquifers are thin and saline, thus limiting the utilization of the groundwater. Only in the northeastern corner of the complex—in the Nir Am region, which is outside of the Gaza Strip—is the groundwater fresh, and it has been fully utilized since the 1940s when it constituted the major water resource of the Negev. A scrutiny of the Gaza Strip groundwater contour maps indicates that the levels slope downward toward the west. Thus, the dominant direction of underground flow is from east to west.

As a result of pumping, the water table has dropped throughout the region. In the vicinity of Beit Lahiya, situated north of Gaza, and in the area west of Deir el Balah in the center of the strip, the water table has dropped to approximately sea level near the coast. In Jabaliya, located north of Gaza, as well as south of Gaza near Deir el Balah, the water table has dropped to about 1 m below MSL at a distance of 1–2 km from the coast. In the eastern part of the Gaza Strip, the water table is at an elevation of 2–4 m above MSL. These generally low water table levels will inevitably result in seawater

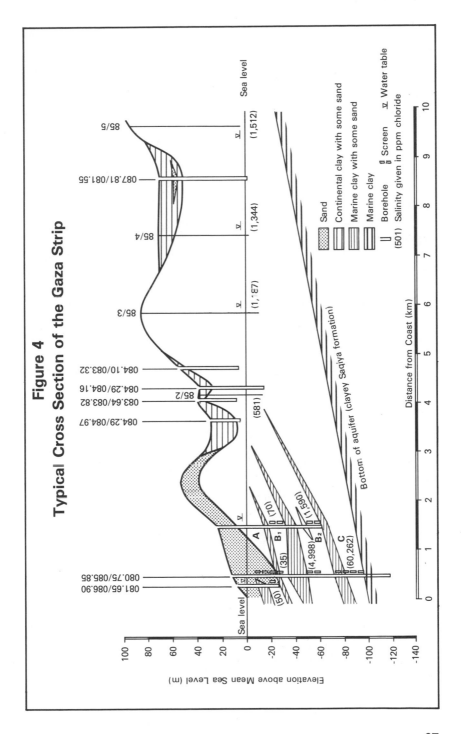

Figure 4
Typical Cross Section of the Gaza Strip

intrusion into the aquifers up to a distance of 1.5 km or more from the coast.

Salinity. Information on the salinity of the aquifers has been obtained by taking water samples from a number of selected wells and correlating their salinity with the meager geohydrological information available (see figure 4). It appears that salinity increases from the upper toward the lower subaquifers, and increases in each subaquifer in the seaward direction, approaching in most cases (except for the uppermost subaquifers) the salinity of seawater or even exceeding it.

The source of the salinity of groundwater in the Gaza Strip is primarily the groundwater entering from the east. In the region opposite the town of Gaza and south of it, inflow salinity ranges in most places from 600 to 1,300 ppm chloride. In a small section north of Nahal Besor, inflow salinity exceeds 2,000 ppm chloride. Seawater intrusion from the west also contributes. Between these two sources of salinity, there is relatively fresh water inflow in the center of the region, originating in rainfall percolating directly into the soil, mostly in the sand dune region along the coast.

As noted, salinity increases with depth. This is probably due to the stratification of the aquiferous structure as well as to the flow regime. In the past, highly saline water flowing in from the east in the lower subaquifers drained seaward. At the present lowered level of the water table this no longer happens, and the deeper saline water mixes and is pumped up along with the less saline water lying in the shallower layers. The groundwater table contour map indicates that only in the upper part of the aquifer and in the vicinity of the sea is there still flow of groundwater (largely fresh) toward the sea.

The boreholes in the eastern part of the Gaza Strip, which penetrate the deep subaquifers, have the highest salinity, while those in the western part, which penetrate the upper subaquifers, have in many cases lower salinity. There are other trends in addition, however, as shown in the salinity map in figure 5. As a result of higher rainfall, the salinity in the northern part of the region is much lower than in the southern part. In the boreholes near the coast north of Gaza, salinity is 50 ppm chloride, between Gaza and Deir el Balah it ranges from 200 to 1,000 ppm chloride, while south of Deir el Balah relatively fresh water of 100 ppm chloride is again encountered. The center of the region shows similar trends: north of Gaza salinity ranges from 200 to 400 ppm chloride, between Gaza and Khan Yunis it ranges from 600 to 1,000 ppm chloride, and south of Khan Yunis, it ranges from 200 to 400 ppm chloride.

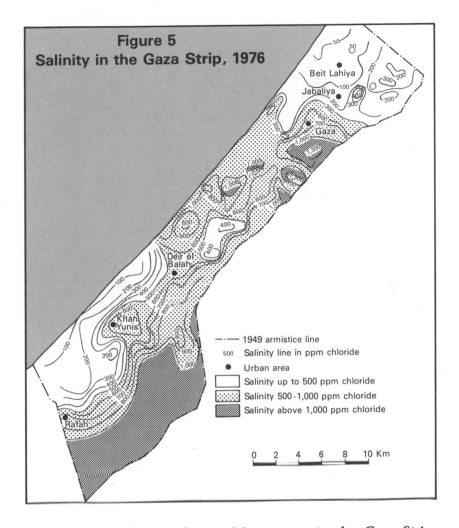

Figure 5
Salinity in the Gaza Strip, 1976

—·— 1949 armistice line
500 Salinity line in ppm chloride
●   Urban area
     Salinity up to 500 ppm chloride
     Salinity 500-1,000 ppm chloride
     Salinity above 1,000 ppm chloride

0 2 4 6 8 10 Km

Consumption and Groundwater Management in the Gaza Strip.
Water consumption in the Gaza Strip is estimated at 100 MCM per
year, of which 90 percent is used for irrigation. The entire amount
is pumped by about 1,600 wells.

The utilizable replenishment in the area has been estimated, as
already mentioned, at about 40–50 MCM per year, and permissible
mining of one-time reserves is estimated at about 20 MCM per year
for ten years. Thus, present overexploitation amounts to about 30–60
MCM per year. This has lowered the water table in the course of
the last five years by 0.5–2.5 m. The salinity of the pumped water
has increased in this period by 20–200 ppm chloride. A recent study
shows that if pumping continues at the present rate, the water table
will drop 1.0–3.5 m below the present levels in the next decade, and
in the same period the salinity will increase by 30–300 ppm chloride.

99

The hydrological conditions in the Gaza Strip indicate that groundwater pumping should be curtailed by 30–60 percent. Because reserves of groundwater still exist, this decision may perhaps be postponed for a few years, but as long as the overexploitation continues, seawater intrusion will increase and so will the inflow of saline waters from the east and from aquifers below the zone of utilization. The damage that will be caused to groundwater storage—and to groundwater users, who are scattered all over the Gaza Strip—will be beyond repair.

The authorities in the area, recognizing the severity of the situation, have limited and controlled groundwater utilization. It is clear, however, that an additional water source will be required in the near future to supply the needs of the Gaza Strip.

Outlook for the Future and Conclusions

The scarcity of water in the region between the Mediterranean Sea and the Jordan River has resulted in a situation where all the major groundwater aquifers are already fully exploited. In the Gaza Strip and in the western and northeastern basins of Judea and Samaria, the groundwater aquifers are already overexploited. Exploitation of water resources must end in Judea and Samaria and decrease in the Gaza Strip. According to present forecasts of demographic and economic development, there will be a water deficit by the end of the century of 200–400 MCM per year in these two areas.

Cutting Judea and Samaria off from the rest of the country may result in the mismanagement of groundwater resources. Increasing groundwater pumpage will draw the water table below the red line and cause the irreversible salination of the aquifers in the plains adjoining Judea and Samaria. This process may be ameliorated by decreasing groundwater pumping and water supply. This (indirect) transfer of water from other parts of the country to Judea and Samaria will result in heavy economic and social damages to the prior users of the aquifers in both the territories and Israel and is opposed to accepted modern national or international water laws.

There is no solution in sight for the water deficiency problem from the natural water resources of the area. The problem can be alleviated somewhat by the full utilization of the eastern drainage basins and reclamation of sewage flows, but the eventual solution must be sought in the import of water from external, still unutilized resources, and in brackish and seawater desalination on a large scale. Closing the gap between limited water resources and growing needs will, therefore, require large-scale development and huge investments of capital and know-how.

PART TWO

The Economy, Government, and Social Services

4

Local Government in the Administered Territories

Sasson Levi

Since its establishment in 1967, the Israeli military government in the administered territories has maintained a close and continuous relationship with the network of local governments existing there. This relationship has shaped the character of local government in general in the territories and of the individual municipalities. The nature of the relationship was determined in part by the Israeli political authorities and in part by the restrictions of international treaties, law, and custom.

The decision by the Israeli government to consider the areas conquered during the Six Day War as "occupied territories" was basically political. It is reasonable to assume that this decision was weighed and examined from various perspectives, including the requirements of international law and the rights and obligations the Israeli government would assume as a result of "occupation."

In fact, the Israeli government adopted three separate decisions, each with a different significance.[1] The first was to extend Israeli law to the eastern portion of greater Jerusalem, thereby bringing it under Israeli authority permanently. Although this decision was criticized by various countries and international bodies, the Israeli government ignored their criticism and recognized this area as a part of the capital city of the State of Israel.[2]

This decision applied to the territory itself, whereas its residents were given the option to choose Israeli or Jordanian citizenship. At

---

[1] I. Dinstein, "Zion Was Redeemed with International Law" (in Hebrew), *Hapraklit*, vol. 27, p. 316, and "And It Was Not Redeemed" (in Hebrew), *Hapraklit*, vol. 27, p. 519.

[2] Y. Blum, "East Jerusalem Is Not an Occupied Territory" (in Hebrew), *Hapraklit*, vol. 28, p. 183.

the same time, they were declared citizens of Jerusalem, with rights to vote and to be elected to the city council and other institutions. It should be noted that Israeli law generally allows permanent residents of a municipality who are not citizens of Israel to vote in municipal elections and hold local office.

The second decision applied to the other territories occupied by the Israel Defense Forces (IDF), including Judea, Samaria, and the Gaza Strip. These territories were to be held under Israeli administrative rule, a decision that placed them under the jurisdiction of the laws of war, including the Hague convention of 1907 and the Geneva convention of 1949.

The third section of the Hague convention, and particularly article 43 of that section, deals with the status and relationship of a sovereign state with another sovereign state over whose territory it rules as a result of an existing sate of war between them.[3] This article was interpreted by the Israeli High Court of Justice in an appeal brought before it. According to this interpretation, in a state of war between two sovereign states, when the forces of one control the territory of the other, the sovereign powers of the latter are suspended and are transferred to the state that is in physical control of the territory. At the same time, the controlling forces have to uphold the existing laws in the territory, apart from special cases of preventive action.[4]

The third decision applied to the Golan Heights. In essence, this territory was also defined as "occupied." The absence, however, of even the slightest sign of governmental or legal arrangements there or of any bureaucratic systems to maintain such arrangements led the Israeli government to its decision to apply Israeli law in that area. This was not accomplished directly, but rather by means of legislative measures published by the military commander. Thus, the status of the Golan Heights remained that of an "occupied" area while being governed by Israeli laws.

The policy of the Israeli government toward the administered territories called for normalizing the daily lives of the inhabitants and maintaining a network of relationships between them and the Israeli military government. This government had been forced on the local residents; they neither desired nor had ever foreseen the possibility of living under Israeli rule. The network of relationships was based on a minimum of interference in the internal problems of the

[3] See article 43, "Regulations Respecting the Law and Customs of War on Land," Annex to the Hague Conventions, 1970.
[4] High Court of Justice 337/71.

population on the part of the military government and the civil administration functioning alongside it. In this way, the range and points of potential friction between the military government and the population were limited.

Governmental and Legal Arrangements

Following the Six Day War, the commanders of the Israeli forces in Judea, Samaria, and the Gaza Strip—each in his own district— issued Proclamation 2, dealing with governmental and legal arrangements in the territories.[5] According to this proclamation, the laws existing in the territories prior to the transfer of government to the IDF were declared valid provided that they were not in contradiction with the stated proclamation, nor with any legislation issued by the military commander, whether by him or in his name. Thus, validity was granted to the laws and ordinances enacted by Egypt in the Gaza Strip and by Jordan in Judea and Samaria.

With regard to Gaza, the Egyptian army had entered the area and seized control of it after May 15, 1948. The Egyptian government never claimed sovereignty over the area, however, and never acted as if it had. The situation in Judea and Samaria was very different. The Jordanian army (Arab Legion) had been introduced into the area during the later days of the British Mandate by order of the British high commissioner. Upon the conclusion of the Mandate, the legion remained in control of the bulk of the area by order of the Jordanian government. After the 1948–1949 war between Israel and its Arab neighbors, de facto partition of western Palestine had come about.

Internal political manipulations within the local population, accompanied by pressure and coercion exerted by the Jordanian army, led to the decision by some five hundred notables of the area to ask the Jordanian ruler to annex them to his country and to make them Jordanian citizens. The granting of this request by the Jordanian authorities transformed the West Bank region into a part of the Hashemite Kingdom of Jordan. Jordanian government and law were extended to the region, and the population received full Jordanian citizenship.

The validity of these arrangements has been questioned under a number of points of international law and custom. The annexation contravened the decision of the UN General Assembly of November

[5] Chief Military Command, *Orders and Proclamations, Judea and Samaria* (in Hebrew), 1968-1972, 1975.

29, 1947; the local population never accepted or desired this annexation; the notables who requested it did not represent the people and were not authorized to speak in behalf of the people; and, because of the coercion involved, the process of annexation had no validity as a voluntary act. Moreover, such a process requires the recognition of other states, but, aside from Pakistan, which recognized the annexation de jure, and Britain, which recognized it de facto, no other country granted the annexation recognition. Even the Arab League and its member states were opposed to it.

The Legislative Basis

The system of local government in Judea and Samaria and in the Gaza Strip is governed by two sets of laws: the municipalities law and the rural council law. These two laws, in both regions, are based on the laws of the British Mandate period. They were applied only partially, however, in the Gaza Strip, where elections to the urban and rural councils have never been held. Instead, all the council members were appointed by the Egyptian general commander and later by the Israeli military commander. In Judea and Samaria, in contrast, the municipalities law was fully applied, and the law governing rural councils is in the process of being implemented, though gradually and cautiously.

The Jordanian Municipalities Law

The municipalities law[6] grants the right to vote to every male born in the city or registered as a resident of the city on the condition that he pay at least one Jordanian dinar yearly in property or business tax. This tax restriction differentiated—and discriminated—among the citizens of the city on the basis of their right to vote and to be elected. As a result of this situation, someone who paid 200 dinars in taxes, for example, could obtain for himself, his friends, his family, or anyone he wished 200 votes by recording the names of 200 people in the voter registry as taxpayers. In fact, this condition of the law gave the wealthy landowning families the political power to run for the elected offices in the city council. The greater the property on which the family paid taxes, the greater its power to ensure for itself elected offices and control over the city council.

[6] Chief Military Command, *The Jordanian Municipalities Law—Selection of Jordanian Laws* (in Hebrew), 1973.

Privileges in the Law. According to the municipalities law, the central government could appoint two members to the city council, in addition to those elected in the general elections. Similarly, the government possessed the exclusive authority to appoint the mayor of the city, on the condition that he be a member of the council. In this way, the central government could create a local political balance congenial to it. By limiting the right to vote to a certain type of taxpayer, and thus confining electoral power to property owners and to people possessing a certain status in society, the government could prevent other local political forces from reaching elected positions. The appointment of two members by the government, and the possibility of simultaneously appointing one of them to the position of mayor, gave the central government the ability to control the heads of the landowning families in each municipality and limit their political power.

The city council of Hebron serves as a good example. The Jordanian government preferred the el-Jabari family over the other families in the area. The electoral power of the el-Jabari family in the city was weak, however, and its chances to acquire a majority of the elected positions were nil. To save himself from an electoral defeat, the head of the el-Jabari family decided not to run for office. At the same time, he ensured himself the office of mayor, since, upon the conclusion of the tally, the announcement of those candidates who had won seats on the city council, and the confirmation of their election, two orders were issued: the appointment of el-Jabari to the council and his appointment to the office of mayor. The extent and manner of this interference by the central government was an expression of the degree of mutual support and cooperation between these two institutionalized bodies.

According to Jordanian law, the status of the district commissioner was no different from his status during the British Mandate period. He was, in fact, the ruling administrative-operative authority in the municipality and the coordinator of the relations between the central government in Amman and the local authorities. This control by the district commissioner was established by law and in effect restricted the maneuverability of each municipality in various fields, including the scope of possible budgetary manipulations. The budget was one of the means by which the central government exercised control over the city councils.

Budgetary Resources. A certain percentage of income from gasoline sales throughout Jordan was deducted by law to finance the municipalities, giving them a significant segment of their regular budgets.

The way in which this income was divided among the municipalities was subject to the administrative discretion of the minister responsible for the municipalities. This is one of the means by which the central government exercises control.

For financing development projects, the Jordanian government placed a special fund at the disposal of the municipalities on easy terms. Here, too, the granting of loans was subject to approval by the district commissioner and on the ministerial level—an approval which was based on the considerations and interests of these authorities as well as on the relationships existing between them and the city council in each municipality.

The Administrative System of Control. The district commissioner had a variety of prerogatory powers which gave him considerable influence within each municipality, even in matters of manpower, grading, and ranks. In addition, each municipality was required to submit a current report of the council meetings, the stages of implementation of projects, and the outlay of funds. These reports kept the district commissioner informed of everything happening within the local authority on one hand, and on the other, granted him the authority to inspect and control these activities.

In the absence of regional arrangements for various service infrastructures, such as water, electricity, and intermunicipal coordination, such projects were carried out by each municipality independently. The lack of such arrangements resulted in the total disintegration of specific services and in a lack of elementary coordination between suppliers and consumers. This in fact released the central government from the burden of responsibility but also created a very poor level of service delivery from both a qualitative and a quantitative point of view. Such a situation placed the obligation and the responsibility for the provision of these services in the hands of the municipalities themselves. The city councils possessed their own foci of internal powers. Success in the fulfillment of these obligations allowed the council to accumulate more power and thus to enhance its chances of being reelected in the future. At the same time, the council could direct development in the direction it desired.

The municipalities possessed the authority by law to deal with matters of additional social and communal services, such as school construction, welfare, and so on. Yet their dependence on the central government for the income to implement such projects could decisively affect all their activities.

Retrospectively, therefore, the municipal system in Judea and Samaria can be seen as a clearly bureaucratic system, in which the elected authority had no defined base or spheres of activity. It was dependent on the central government, which could interfere in the electoral process, alter the local political balance of power, influence priorities in the functioning of each municipal authority, and cause its success or failure in the fulfillment of its role according to central government interests and considerations.

The Israeli Military Government

With the entry of the Israeli army into the region and the issuing of Proclamation 2, the military commander became the legislative authority. He could enact any law, cancel or suspend an existing law, or make legislative changes, all in accordance with the restrictions and provisions of the laws of war in general and of article 43 of the Hague convention in particular. The military commander was also placed at the head of the executive authority within each administrative region of the military government.

Contributing Factors. The suspension of the powers of the Jordanian government and their transfer to the hands of the commander of the Israeli forces severed, in theory and in practice, the network of reciprocal authority relationships between the municipalities in the region and the Jordanian government. Another network of relations developed in place of the previous one, but without the authoritative-coercive element—namely, the Jordanian government's ability to force its decisions and desires on a mayor or city council. In place of this, there developed another network of relations based on the element of persuasion, with positive incentives, such as financial grants and loans, as well as the granting of other powers in exchange for recognition and the maintenance of functional contacts with the central government in Amman.

The removal of the Jordanian bureaucratic system from the region, with all its authoritative and manipulatory powers, and its replacement by an Israeli bureaucratic system with a different character and interests, freed the mayors and the councilmen from Jordanian pressure and coercion. They were indeed faced with Israeli demands, but these were of an entirely different nature.

Local personalities who had been closely tied to the Jordanian government system, such as members of the Jordanian parliament and high officials in the Jordanian establishment, disappeared from the region. With their departure, the system of reciprocal influence lost its effectiveness. The involvement of these persons in all areas of life in the region, including relationships between the individual citizens and the various authorities, had been significant. This change created new patterns and new conditions that had no precedent in the region. In fact, the mayors and councilmen now became the recognized, authoritative, and unrivaled local political force.

The policy of the Israeli government was to avoid interfering in the internal affairs of the local population, to allow them to determine their own relationships, and to recognize the municipalities and the elected institutions as the exclusive authoritative-formal bodies representing the residents of the cities and towns. This policy, together with the development of a new network of relationships between the individual citizens and the Israeli military governments, the range of matters in which the mayors could intervene on behalf of the citizens before the military commander, the military government's recognition of the mayor as the elected head and chief officer within his city, and the military commander's discretion in dealing with the mayors and city councilmen—all these served to bring about a total change in the character and image of the city council in general and of the mayor in particular. The mayor became an authoritative power to whom all began to turn for advice or favors; the city council became an independent body possessing independent powers and the ability to act within the scope of its authority unhindered and without control by a higher governmental system, as long as this government was not interested in exercising the prerogatory powers which it possessed by law.

The prosperity and social welfare that resulted from the opening of the doors of the State of Israel to the inhabitants of the territories and the opportunity given to them to work in Israel and to earn higher wages than those paid in the territories or in other Arab countries created problems and centers of conflict within each municipality. The crux of the problem lay in the vital services which the residents demanded for themselves and which were within the municipalities' jurisdiction—including electricity, water, sewage, internal road networks, sidewalks, sanitation, and other municipal services. The absence of a minimal infrastructure in almost all the municipalities made it very difficult to cope with these demands.

Very large investments were needed to finance these projects, but the municipal councils in general and the mayors in particular were unwilling to increase the tax burden. For national-ideological reasons, they did not want the development of such systems to appear as an achievement of the Israeli military government as opposed to the failure of the previous Jordanian government. The military government, on the other hand, demonstrated its willingness to aid the municipalities financially or otherwise in carrying out the projects with the voluntary agreement of the councils and the mayors, on condition that they were able to finance their share of each project in realistic and practical ways. This combination of factors led to a slow and gradual development of municipal service infrastructures in the majority of the municipalities in Judea and Samaria. Nevertheless, had the mayors and municipal councils acted according to other principles and not according to supposedly nationalistic ideologies, the results would have been much more impressive.

A typical example of this is the problem of the electricity supply in Hebron, Nablus, Tulkarm, and Kalkilya. These cities each had municipally owned power plans for supplying electricity. The output of these power plants did not meet existing needs, however, much less additional consumer demands. The generators in these plants were outdated, and their replacement required extensive financial outlays which the municipalities could not afford. The cost of electricity supplied by these power plants was, and still is, much higher than the electricity rates in Israel. In other words, most of these plants constituted a heavy financial burden on the municipalities through the losses involved in the maintenance of an old and improvised network which lacked any fundamental planning base.

Nevertheless, the municipalities were strongly opposed to the proposal of the Israeli military government that they be directly linked to the Israel Electric Company, which would supply electric current to all the municipalities at the going rate for large consumers in Israel, even though the military government would have borne the cost of the laying of the huge voltage lines up to the outskirts of each city. The Nablus municipality was vehemently opposed to the idea, refusing to link up with the Israel Electric Company, and preferred to purchase additional generators abroad rather than become dependent upon the Israeli company. Its reasons for this were purely political and contrary to any economic considerations of profitability. Because of a lack of financial resources, the municipalities of Hebron, Tulkarm, and Kalkilya were forced, against their will, to link up with the Israel Electric Company. The profits of these municipalities from supplying their consumers increased immeasurably in contrast to the earlier losses, while the Nablus municipality, which laid out huge sums for the purchase of generators, continues to suffer losses, and its new generators still do not meet the needs of the people.

The problem of water supply is no less acute. There is, in fact, no special problem of availability. When each municipality must locate and drill its own wells, lay pipelines, and operate a water system, however, the result is that the majority of the urban population suffers from irregular water supply and the municipalities cannot increase output to meet demands. In many cases the urban population continues to live without water pipes in their homes and must supply themselves with water from private wells or cisterns.

The case of the three Christian cities—Bethlehem, Beit Sahur, and Beit Jala—is instructive. There was a general consensus among them on the need to set up a joint water system: they share the same water source and are territorially contiguous with the projected pipelines crossing the lands of all three municipalities. The need for joint administration, however, and the issue of the division of profits among them, should there by any, delayed the establishment of the plant for years. Finally, with the military government acting as mediator, a formula was found permitting the establishment of a system, to no small extent thanks to the military government's participation in the cost as a positive incentive to the formation of the partnership among the three municipalities.

Budgets. In effect, the military government maintained Jordanian regulations in budgetary matters with regard to both revenues and expenditures. It distinguished between regular budgets and special budgets for project financing. The regular budgets were generally funded through the income from the municipalities' gasoline taxes, which the military government collected and passed on to each municipality, and sometimes through grants-in-aid by the military government to specific municipalities. Development budgets are financed from various 'sources, including surpluses from the regular budgets and local fund raising by the municipalities, or from sources outside the region, primarily contributions or grants given by various bodies and institutions, including Arab governments and even various terrorist organizations.

Loose control by the military government over these sources of income, the ability of the municipality to arrange payment for implementing projects in such a way that the contracting and other expenses are paid in Amman, the reduction of the cost of the projects by half, with that portion paid outside Judea and Samaria not appearing in the agreed cost—all these have led to unavoidable difficulty in estimating the scope of the actual budgets of the municipalities and in showing the increase in their proportions.

Electing the Municipal Authorities. Among the other measures the military government took in the region after the 1967 war was an order extending the term of office of the municipal councils until further notice. This in effect suspended the provision of the municipalities law calling for elections to the municipal councils once every five years. On the basis of this order, the municipal councils in Judea and Samaria continued to function under the military government.

In the latter half of 1971, the decision was made by the Israeli government to hold municipal elections in Judea and Samaria. This decision reflected a number of considerations centering on maintaining an orderly military government in the territories. It also constituted part of the policy of maximizing normalization in the day-to-day life of the local population, as well as in relations between the population and the Israeli institutional-governmental system.

The decision of the Israeli government was interpreted according to the same policy of noninvolvement and noninterference in the life of the people except as involvement or interference might be necessary to inhibit terrorist action and political subversion. Therefore, the military government had to maintain almost total neutrality toward the electoral contests while at the same time ensuring that they were conducted according to law.

It was apparent to all that the Jordanian municipalities law discriminated against a large portion of the urban population while allowing a minority to control the municipal council and the elected institutions in each city and town. The political echelons of the Israeli administration decided to hold elections without amending the law—to minimize interference with established arrangements. At the same time, a juridical experiment was made to reinterpret several of its provisions, including the provision whereby voter registration was conditional upon the payment of certain taxes. This restriction was broadly interpreted to mean that any payment of fees to the municipal treasury, such as fees for service delivery, led to the right to be included in the voter registry.

The question of the candidacy of government employees for elected positions was treated in a similar manner. The Israeli juridical interpretation of this issue was also broad: a government official could take a leave of absence to run for an elected post without losing his government position. Should he be elected, he could remain on leave while serving in his new post, as long as he had the permission of his superiors.

Neither of these two interpretations was put to a legal test, since neither was formally challenged. The voter registration committee operated without deviating from the rules laid down by the Jordanian government in the past, 'so that there were very few objections or appeals. The number of local candidates to the municipal council in every city was more than sufficient to hold elections without it being necessary for the local officials of the military government to offer their candidacy.

Preparations for the Elections. It was decided by the military government that the holding of the elections and all preparations for them would be carried out by local officials, who would follow the existing Jordanian municipalities law. The military commanders in the regions were to oversee the work of these officials, listening to the complaints of the public, if any, and explaining to the public the neutrality of the military government in the election process and in the political contests between the various contenders.

Among the most important problems facing the Israeli administration was the need to maintain order while avoiding interference in the elections. For this purpose, an officer in charge of the elections was appointed in each city, representing the supreme administrative function in the electoral process. He had to possess certain essential traits: proper status, a knowledge of the city and its social-familial composition, acceptance by all the local families, and the administrative ability to ensure the proper functioning and control of the electoral process.

In each town, this officer appointed a voter registration committee in accordance with the powers granted to him in his letter of appointment. According to the instructions he received, the *mukhtars* (headmen) of the town were appointed to the committee. Their knowledge of the family interests in the registration of voters, together with the military commander's explanation that this was part of their role as government employees as defined by Jordanian law, led the appointed *mukhtars* to accept their role on the committee and to fulfill it to the general satisfaction of all.

Although the registration of voters was done manually—a method which may perhaps appear outdated and awkward—this method was the best way to ensure the registration of all those who had the right to vote. The limited number of enfranchised voters (resulting from the legal restriction that only those who pay property or business tax may vote or be elected) considerably reduced the awkwardness, and the voter registries were prepared relatively quickly. This was also due to the interest displayed by the committee members and the modus operandi they adopted to avoid futile arguments over the eligibility to vote, together with their desire to prepare a list of voters that would not be contested.

The fact that every *mukhtar*, whether a local leader or the head of a *hamullah* (extended family), was a member of the committee—and thus was acquainted with all *hamullah* affairs and knew the amount of taxes paid by his *hamullah* and by others and, as a result, the number of electoral votes each *hamullah* possessed—allowed each *mukhtar* to protect the rights and interests of his *hamullah* but not to infringe on those of the other families. This modus operandi in fact ensured the preparation of an orderly voter registry that corresponded with existing conditions in each municipality.

The most impressive achievement in the work of the voter registration committees was the negligible number of appeals. On the other hand, equally striking was the very low proportion of eligible voters in relation to the actual population of each city as a result of the taxpaying requirement.

The Elected Offices and the Electoral System. According to the Jordanian municipalities law, which is the law in force in Judea and Samaria at present, the Jordanian minister of the interior was responsible for determining the number of elected positions in each municipal council, though there were quantitative criteria reflecting the size of the population. Nevertheless, he had the authority to use his own discretion in this matter, taking into consideration the number of *hamullot* in each town, their relative strength, and the interests of the central government in Amman.

The electoral system established by law was that of personal, majority, and secret elections. According to this system, each voter could cast several ballots, according to the number of seats up for election. He could select and vote for candidates from several tickets, as long as the number of votes cast did not exceed the total number of seats.

The listing of all the candidates alphabetically on a single sheet greatly facilitated voting as well as tallying the votes. The committee assigned to this task had simply to count the number of names checked off on each sheet, disqualifying those ballots which exceeded the total number of seats.

A committee was appointed for each balloting station, comprising local government officials and nonresident teachers in order to ensure neutrality. Alongside it, a supervisory body was set up made up of the candidates' representatives, who could appeal to the committee or to the officer in charge of the elections in the event of a problem or complaint.

In order to remove all doubts, it was decided that the votes should be tallied at the polling places. Vote-tallying committees were made up of senior officials, some of whom were judges, who were sworn in according to law. Several assistants were also appointed. It was decided that the votes would be counted in public, and in the presence of the candidates or their representatives, and that the results would be announced upon the conclusion of the tally.

The Local Political Atmosphere

Two types of political pressure and coercion were brought to bear on the population of the territories in general and on the heads of the *hamullot* and the local politicians in particular. The Jordanian government, for internal political reasons, did not want the elections to be held. The holding of elections under Israeli military rule appeared to Jordan to constitute a recognition of the existence of that rule and a legitimization of its authority, while emphasizing its liberal-democratic character and its positive relations with the local population. In addition, a shift in the municipal political balance of power would probably bring into power local political figures not necessarily identified with the Jordanian government or supportive of it, thereby decreasing Jordanian influence. All these factors led the government of Jordan to oppose the elections and to advise those who supported or were identified with the Amman government to take no part in them.

The Palestine Liberation Organization. To the leaders of the PLO, holding elections was a clear sign of cooperation between the local population and the Israeli military government, as well as an indication of the positive relations between them and the willingness of the people to recognize the authoritative presence of the military government in the territories. In this view, the holding of elections was the beginning of a political process whereby a local leadership would develop under the military government, either supported or encouraged by it, which would in time undermine the status of the PLO and its leaders, who claim to be the sole representatives of the Palestinian people. Such a process seemed dangerous to the PLO in the long run— that is, should the Israeli military government succeed in interfering in the elections as had been the case under Jordanian rule. Such interference would produce moderate local political forces and even opponents of PLO policy. In time, and with the success of these local leaders elected as the municipal authorities, their status would increase and they would emerge as potential rivals of the PLO—rivals with broad support among the Palestinians living under the military government. They would be likely to recognize the military government's advantages over the former government and be prepared to come to a political agreement with the State of Israel, totally contrary to the basic positions of the PLO and its affiliated organizations.

The local political leadership, including the family heads and local politicians, had other thoughts and interests. Through their day-to-day contacts with the military government, their knowledge of the character of Israeli society, and the high level of political awareness within the local population with regard to the municipal councils, they were led to the unavoidable conclusion that the military government really intended to hold the elections without any interference, in the freest and most democratic manner, provided that they were held according to law. Among the local residents, particularly the young and educated, there was a clear tendency to run for office. The emergence of these new young political forces and their potential assumption of the elected positions would, however, threaten the position of the *hamullah* head and the local politicians. The latter groups would not be able to question the status of the new political forces, thus forfeiting at least one source of their own political power based on the criteria of *hamullah* and class.

Given this internal political situation, the heads of the *hamullot* and the politicians displayed political maturity and an understanding of local politics. Through persuasion and pressure, they convinced the Jordanian establishment that it was in Jordan's interest that they take an active part in the election campaign, thus ensuring their political *hamullah* status. This outcome would be more to the advantage of the Jordanian establishment than the emergence of others on the local political scene who owed nothing to Jordan and were unlikely to recognize it or obey its instructions, if indeed they would even maintain contacts with it. The Jordanian establishment was persuaded but preferred to appear neutral in the election campaign rather than openly support the holding of elections under the aegis of the Israeli military government.

Because of the position of the local population and the dialogue between the local *hamullah* leadership and the Jordanian government, and because of its own internal weaknesses and inferior position in the eyes of the people in comparison with that of the Jordanian government, the PLO was forced to lower its profile and tone down its opposition to the elections (including physical threats directed against the person and property of anyone taking part in the elec-

117

tions). The PLO continued to issue threats and to denounce any-one who participated in the election campaign, but feebly. It directed its threats primarily against those who seemed to be cooperating actively with the military government or who were acting in its name or with its support.

In such a political environment, where local residents enjoyed unprecedented political freedom and where the Israeli military government in physical control of the area confined itself to supervising the election process without otherwise involving itself, the Jordanian government was compelled to avoid trying to exert its influence. The terrorist organizations continued to incite the people, weakly but persistently.

In this environment, the heads of the *hamullot* prepared for a local political struggle on election day. The family leaders and notables headed the election campaign, directing activities, maintaining contacts, and forming internal alliances and agreements in order to ensure their victory. As the deadline for the submission of the names of candidates drew near, it became apparent to all that the elections would be recorded as a highly impressive achievement of the military government, enhancing its image as orderly and progressive.

The results of the elections were very impressive. In a number of cities, the voter turnout was over 80 percent, sometimes over 90 percent. That the heads of the *hamullot* saw to it that members of their families who were away for business, work, or studies should return to their home towns to vote is highly indicative of the attitude toward the elections. The achievement in Samaria was reflected in Judea as well: when elections were held there two months later, the behavior and attitudes of the population were identical.

It is worthwhile noting several phenomena characteristic of political societies in which the extended family stands at the center of society and all political activity takes place around this center and on its periphery.

In the town of Anabta in Samaria, whose municipality has been in existence for about thirty years, each time elections were to be held for the city council, the ruling *hamullah* determined the distribution of seats on the council among the different *hamullot*. This was done by preparing a joint list with the same number of candidates as offices up for election, so that there was no need to hold the actual balloting. This procedure was rooted in the municipalities law, according to which voting is unnecessary where the number of candidates is equal to the number of elected offices. The dominant *hamullah* hoped and expected that it would be able to continue to act in this manner in future elections as well. Its hopes were shattered, however, when, at the last moment before the closing of the list of candidates, it became apparent that the number of registered candidates exceeded the number of offices, and that for the first time in the municipality's history, elections would be held and the voters—and not the head of a *hamullah*—would determine their representatives.

In Nablus, the situation was different. The el-Masry *hamullah*, which was the dominant family in the city, at first preferred for reasons of its own not to present a list of candidates. On the other hand, the Cnaan family, headed by Hamdi Cnaan, the former mayor, did present a list. Other candidates, whose lineage and status had always been considered much lower than those of the el-Masry and Cnaan families, also submitted lists. The el-Masry family, however, sought to undermine the standing of the Cnaan family by supporting its opponents. Among Arabs, the now-almost-certain victory of the rival lists signified the total degradation of the Cnaan family and particularly its leaders.

This maneuver was discovered only after the deadline for the registration of candidates had passed. The Cnaan family, which understood the significance of its humiliation should it suffer an overwhelming defeat by inferior opponents, preferred to withdraw from the elections. The military government came to the assistance of the city by extending the deadline for the submission of lists of candidates, thereby allowing the el-Masry family to present its own candidates. Upon the conclusion of the voting and the counting of the votes, it was revealed that the el-Masry family had won a decisive majority of the offices.

Hebron presented a different situation. There the military government wanted the incumbent mayor, the head of the el-Jabari family, to win the election. Other *hamullot*, however, known to be stronger than the el-Jabaris, would have inflicted a crushing electoral defeat on them. Thanks to various maneuvers and internal persuasion, only one list of candidates was presented, equal to the number of positions open for election and headed by Sheikh-Jabari. This list was "elected" without balloting, in accordance with the municipalities law. (El-Jabari offered his candidacy on the condition that there would be no balloting.)

Appointment of the Mayor. Upon the conclusion of the elections and the publication of the results, the elected council members were summoned before the military commanders. Here it was explained to them that the military government did not intend to force any particular mayor upon them; rather, they were to present a candidate recommended unanimously or by a majority of the council, and this

119

candidate would be appointed mayor of the city by the military governor, as authorized by law. In addition, it was made clear to them that the government did not intend to utilize its legal prerogative of appointing additional members for the city council.

These intentions, and the waiving of the legal prerogatives, surprised most of the local residents and emphasized the extent of the military government's interest in remaining neutral and passive with regard to the internal affairs of the population in Judea and Samaria. Nevertheless, there were those within the military government who called for the immediate cancellation of these prerogatory provisions as a clear and authoritative sign of these intentions.

The 1976 Elections

In the latter half of 1975, as the municipal council members neared the end of their terms, the need for a political decision on the elections again arose. Although opinions were expressed on both sides, it was decided to hold the elections as scheduled.

The Political Atmosphere. The 1976 elections took place in a different political atmosphere from that which had prevailed in 1972. The intervening years had seen the Yom Kippur War and, in its aftermath, the Rabbat summit and its recognition of the PLO as the sole representative of the Palestinian people.

Although the Yom Kippur War, with the separation of forces and interim agreements which followed it, had various effects on the population of the territories, these effects concerned their nationalist aspirations, not the local-municipal political situation. On the other hand, the recognition of the PLO by the Arab states and others on the international scene, including even Jordan (willingly or not), was a determining factor in the local political activity for the upcoming elections. In contrast to 1972, the PLO now approved of holding the elections, encouraged its supporters to run for office, and even backed their candidacy openly. This support had far-reaching significance. It was generally assumed that those who were not known to be supported by the PLO were unacceptable to it, whereas those who did receive its support were its local representatives. PLO activities on the one hand and the passive and hesitant position of the Jordanian government on the other in effect determined the results of the elections in most of the cities of Judea and Samaria.

Family heads who had personal interests in Jordan or close ties with the Hashemite Kingdom preferred to abstain from any public political activity. They wished to avoid expressing political-nationalist positions to which they would later be bound, identified either with or against Jordan, and thus impairing their status or harming their interests vis-à-vis Jordan, Israel, or the PLO. At the same time, they had local interests to protect, which they sought to do by presenting candidates chosen from the second and third rank in the *hamullah* hierarchy, including a proportional number of candidates from the young and intellectual stratum.

Changes in the Municipalities Law. The military government again refrained from making changes in the discriminatory and prerogatory provisions of the Jordanian municipalities law, except for the enfranchisement of women. The result was a relatively significant increase in the number of eligible voters in each city. The change was positively received by the population of the territories, although, since it seemed to run counter to the Muslim-*hamullah* tradition, some feared that it would not be implemented. In fact, however, women were listed in the voter registry, and in most cases exercised their right to vote, although in separate polling booths.

Political Contests and Their Results. Although the major political contests in the 1972 elections centered on local issues and municipal services, the 1976 elections took on a national-nationalistic dimension in addition. Consequently, there soon appeared on the local political platforms previously unknown figures, some of them intellectuals of standing in their communities, and some of them rank-and-file politicians. Most of them were identified with the PLO, some radical in their views and some more moderate.

The events in Hebron are again highly instructive. When it became apparent to the head of the el-Jabari family that he would be opposed by intellectuals from the more powerful *hamullot*, that he would not be able to form a single, joint ticket eliminating the need for an actual election as he had in 1972, and that he actually faced a serious electoral defeat, he decided—at the last moment—to withdraw from all political activity.

Upon the conclusion of the voting and the counting of the ballots, it became apparent that new forces had emerged on the local political map and, thanks to their political identification, had succeeded in being elected to the municipal councils. In this case, too, as formerly, the military government refrained from appointing additional members to the municipal councils, and again appointed mayors according to the recommendation of the elected members of the councils.

Conclusion

It is clear that under the Israeli military government, a fundamental and significant change has taken place in the status of the municipal authorities, particularly of the city councils and mayors. The introduction of a foreign military government undesired by the local population, the severance of local government from the central government in Amman, the policy of the military government in its relations with local governments, the disappearance of certain groups that had previously exerted pressure on the city councils and particularly on the mayors, and the recognition granted to the councils and the mayors by the Israeli military government—all these constituted the basis for a change in the image of the municipal councils in all spheres of activity.

The broadening of the spheres of activity of the city council and the mayor, as a result of the recognition and the status granted to them by the Israeli military government, in turn gave them authoritative status among the population, though not formal status. The urban population came to view the mayor and the councilmen as their representatives, with the power to act in their interests. The political maturity displayed by the mayors, the heads of the *hamullot*, and the politicians in protecting their individual interests enabled them to bring about a change in both the Jordanian government's and the PLO's attitude toward elections under the military government.

For its part, the military government, in adhering to the Jordanian municipalities law and refraining from altering or canceling its discriminatory or prerogatory provisions, while at the same time refraining from applying those provisions or circumventing them through liberal-democratic administrative measures, appears to have abided by the rules of international treaties, law, and custom. Nevertheless, extending the right to vote to women prior to the 1976 elections seems to constitute a fundamental shift from these restrictive norms.

It seems, then, that a fundamental and significant change has occurred in the approach to civil rights and in the procedures for electing representative authorities which will not easily be reversed. On the contrary, it can be expected that the residents of Judea and Samaria will further develop their awareness of their civil rights and will participate in their realization.

5

The Political Economy of the Administered Territories

Shmuel Sandler with Hillel Frisch

Open as it is to widely varying interpretations, economic analysis is often a weapon in the hands of the polemicist. Jamil Hilal, of the Palestine Liberation Organization Research Center in Beirut, describes the Israeli relationship with the territories as a form of economic imperialism.[1] Israel's official economist for the administered territories, Arye Bregman, paints this relationship in much more flattering terms.[2] Political economic analyses differ as widely as do political ideas. Just as each political development necessitates a sui generis assessment, so must every economic indicator be evaluated individually. What is to one observer a positive indicator often points to a negative trend for another.

As a general rule, each critic and adherent of a particular school of thought comes armed with his own set of statistics. In the case of the territories, however, these almost invariably bear the imprimatur of Israel's Central Bureau of Statistics.[3] Israel and its sympathizers are generally considered to be neoclassical, market-oriented, and strongly economic in orientation; its opponents, on the other

The preparation of this chapter was supported by a grant from the Ford Foundation received through the Israel Foundation's Trustees.

[1] Jamil Hilal, *The West Bank: Its Social and Economic Structure, 1948-1973* (Beirut: Palestine Liberation Organization Research Center, 1975).

[2] Arye Bregman, *The Economy of the Administered Territories, 1974 and 1975* (Jerusalem: Bank of Israel Research Department, 1976), pp. 7-9.

[3] The Israel Central Bureau of Statistics is the only institution that systematically collects data regarding population, work-force characteristics, and other economic activities in the territories. Data on GNP, balance of payments, disposable income, etc., represent estimates. Work-force data are derived from periodic surveys and statistical information provided by the various labor exchanges operating in the territories. Both estimates and survey data have been regarded as reliable indicators by all researchers to date.

hand, subscribe to radical economic theories that became popular in the mid-1960s and tend to emphasize the virtues of central planning.[4] While Bregman concentrates on personal affluence, such as GNP growth and the rise in disposable income, and treats the population in a very abstract manner, Hilal focuses on collective structures—the structure of the relationship between Israel and the territories and its historical implications, past and future. Bregman deals with the present, the time dimension logically associated with the status quo. Hilal, whose ultimate objective is an independent Palestinian state, rejects the present while seeking to build the future, drawing conclusions from the past. Each group can claim professional integrity; they are both "committed" to their larger political interests as well as to their respective economic philosophies.

Israel's relationship with the territories is neither the result of a laissez-faire policy nor the product of an imperialist design. Israeli economic policy in the territories has clearly been influenced by both political and economic factors. The background of this policy is best summarized by Larry L. Fabian in his prologue to Brian Van Arkadie's Benefits and Burdens:

> Every Israeli cabinet since 1967, while insisting that there will be no return to the June 1967 borders, has decided not to decide the political future of the West Bank and the Gaza Strip. But government policy, including economic policy, was grounded in three understandings. Israel would not formally annex the territories. Israel would not withdraw from them. And Israel would not allow them to become a net budget burden.[5]

Thus, as Van Arkadie's title suggests, Israel's relationship with the territories has been both positive and negative. How positive and how negative, in any objective sense, depends on with what the existing relationship is compared. Alongside a substantial rise in all major economic welfare indicators, the development of the terrorities' domestic economy was more moderate. While certain sectors were significantly expanded, other sectors did not achieve the same growth rates, resulting in an uneven level of development.[6]

[4] For a representative collection of the radical approach, see Jagdish N. Bhagwati, ed., Economics and World Order (New York: Free Press, 1972). See also Paul A. Baran and Paul M. Sweezy, Monopoly Capital: An Essay on the American Economic and Social Order (New York: Modern Reader, 1966).

[5] Fabian, "Prologue: The Political Setting," in Van Arkadie, Benefits and Burdens: A Report on the West Bank and Gaza Strip Economies since 1967 (Washington, D.C.: Carnegie Endowment for International Peace, 1977), p. 12.

[6] For an analysis of balanced and unbalanced development, see Charles P.

This chapter seeks to examine major economic developments in the territories in two periods—the pre-1967 and post-1967 eras. While concentrating on economic factors, the analysis is not detached from political realities that have a bearing on the subject.

The West Bank until 1967

Few areas in the world have experienced such a rapid rise in the standard of living as has the West Bank. Few areas have received so much external aid per capita—public, private, and to a lesser extent governmental—in the last thirty years. Whether annexed by Jordan or under Israeli control, the West Bank has managed to maintain and even to expand its sources of aid. In so doing, it has been able to live way above its means, consuming much more than it has produced. The extent to which it does so is surprising even more so today when nations around the world face increasing external indebtedness. Yet despite consumer prosperity, a vast improvement in transportation, a concomitant rise in the quality of social and health services, and outstanding gains in education and agriculture, the West Bank remains an underdeveloped region.

Two major interrelated factors have dictated the economic development of the West Bank: politics and geo-economics. Since the 1940s, if not before, the West Bank has been losing economic ground relative to the areas it abuts. Both Jewish settlement (and consequently, Jewish capital) and British investment in infrastructure favored the development of the coastal regions. The British built up the Haifa port and its refineries, and Jews built the petrochemical industrial plants nearby. Both Arabs and Jews played a major role in the development of the coastal areas and were consequently its major beneficiaries.

While events prior to 1948 set off economic processes resulting in a growing economic gap between the West Bank and the coastal areas, they were not sufficient to account for the disparities in the ensuing years. Both the 1948 war and subsequent Jordanian development policies, accompanied by geo-economic realities, were responsible for the underdevelopment of the West Bank.

The 1948 war was followed by the severance of ties between the West Bank and the coastal regions, which then became the State of

Kindleberger, *Economic Development*, 2nd ed. (New York: McGraw-Hill, 1958), p. 57, and A. O. Hirschman, *The Strategy of Economic Development* (New Haven, Conn.: Yale University Press, 1958). A discussion of this subject as it pertains to the territories can be found in Vivian A. Bull, *The West Bank: Is It Viable?* (Lexington, Mass., and Toronto: Lexington Books, 1975), chap. 1.

TABLE 1
POPULATION GROWTH IN JORDAN, 1952–1961

Area	1952	1961	Population Growth 1952–1961 (percent)
Regions			
West Bank	742,000	805,400	8.5
East Bank	495,000	901,000	82.0
Population centers			
East Jerusalem	60,000	60,000	—
Amman	108,000	250,000	230.0

SOURCE: Computed from E. Kanovsky, *The Economy of Jordan* (Tel Aviv: University Publishing Projects, 1976), p. 25; and Yaacov Lifshitz, *Structural Changes and Economic Growth in the Administered Territories, 1922-72* (in Hebrew), Research Report no. 6 (Tel Aviv: David Horowitz Institute for the Research of Developing Countries, 1974), p. 5.

Israel. The economic consequences of this for the West Bank were severe in several respects. First, it lost its major domestic market, which had included both the Arab and the Jewish populations in the coastal and northern regions. Areas in and around Tulkarm and Kalkilya lost their economic functions overnight. Farmers no longer had the advantage of convenient markets located 10 to 20 kilometers from their homes. Artisan industry could no longer supply a relatively affluent Palestinian peasantry, now located in Israel, with their wares. Thousands of workers lost their jobs in cities and industries in what was now the State of Israel. Moreover, the separation of the two regions affected the transportation system of the West Bank, which lost access to the Mediterranean ports of Haifa, Jaffa, and Gaza. Finally, closed borders meant that there would be no spillover effects from economic and industrial development in Israel.[7]

A more decisive factor was the policies of the Jordanian government. When the West Bank was occupied by Transjordan in 1948, it was far more developed than the East Bank. In contrast, when it was reoccupied by Israel in 1967 (and hence separated from the East Bank), it was the lesser developed of the two banks. As table 1

[7] Norman Dlin, "The Geography of the West Bank," in Anne Sinai and Allen Pollack, eds., *The Hashemite Kingdom of Jordan and the West Bank* (New York: Academic Association for Peace in the Middle East, 1977), pp. 193-98; and Van Arkadie, *Benefits and Burdens*, p. 23.

TABLE 2
Gross Domestic Product in the West Bank by Sector, 1965

Sector	GNP (thousands of dinars)	Percent	Percent of West Bank Contribution to Jordan's GNP
Agriculture	12,998	23.9	38
Industry	3,576	6.6	26
Quarrying[a]	646	1.2	26
Construction	3,147	5.8	40
Electricity and water	587	1.1	35
Transportation	3,229	5.9	26
Trade	12,574	23.1	40
Banking and finance	844	1.5	40
Homeownership	4,276	7.8	40
Public services and security	7,492	13.7	35
Other services	5,132	9.4	40
Total	54,501	100.0	36

[a] Stone quarries.
SOURCE: Economic Planning Authority, *Economic Survey of the West Bank* (Jerusalem, 1967), table 1, p. 9.

indicates, while the population of the East Bank grew from 495,000 in 1952 (after the annexation of the West Bank by Jordan and the absorption of all the refugees from the 1948 war) to 901,000 in 1961,[8] the population of the West Bank hardly grew at all. Similarly, while the population of East Jerusalem did not grow at all during this period, Amman grew from 108,000 in 1952 to a quarter of a million people in 1961. Moreover, at the time of the Jordanian occupation, the West Bank had been well cultivated, while East Bank agriculture had been underdeveloped. In the period between 1948 and 1967, although irrigation was developed to overcome periodic droughts, advancement was applied primarily on the East Bank. Consequently, as table 2 indicates, the share of the West Bank's agricultural produce in Jordan's 1965 GNP was only 38 percent. Similarly, although neither area was industrialized in 1948, the rapid industrial expansion since the mid-1950s (an average annual rate of almost 16 percent) took place almost exclusively in the East Bank. In 1965 the share of the West Bank's industrial output in

[8] The period 1952-1961 was chosen because a census was taken in each of those years.

Jordan's GNP was 56 percent, while the total contribution of the West Bank to Jordan's GNP was 36 percent.

To the Hashemites, the West Bank was annexed territory—that is, territory annexed to a kingdom of Jordan whose center was to be Amman. Whether by design or by the imperative of building a government locus in the Amman area, economic development there far outstripped development in the West Bank. Jordan has always been an example of political viability despite economic dependence. In developmental terms, this meant that the government controlled most of the economic activities of the country. As the Amman-Zurqa-Aqaba triangle grew in importance, with Amman-Zurqa as the urban-industrial locus and Aqaba as Jordan's only port, there was a concomitant decline in desire and ability to integrate the West Bank into a meaningful economic relationship with the east. Mazur makes an economic-geographic case for this uneven development which only serves to underscore the interplay between the political-economic and the geographic factors.[9]

The West Bank became, as hinterlands inevitably do, a source of emigration, either to the east or abroad. Within the West Bank itself, some areas suffered more than others. Tulkarm and Jenin lost population to Jerusalem. The "national projects" designed to promote the long-term economic welfare of Jordan, however, were all concentrated on the East Bank, thus attracting the West Bank population to the east. The Ghor canal project and the University of Jordan are two prime examples. As early as the late 1950s, the West Bank had become a labor pool for the Gulf States. University education, financed primarily by Jordan and partially by various organizations ranging from United Nations Relief and Works Agency (UNRWA) to religious denominations, created a relatively highly educated labor pool. This supply of educated workers was able to satisfy the personnel demands of the Jordanian bureaucracy and to fill positions in the field of education and service industries in the Gulf States.

While lack of balanced development between the two banks of the Jordan was the general rule, tourism was a partial exception. Jordanian tourism was a notable success. Amman and Aqaba served as ports of arrival, while the West Bank provided the places of interest. Van Arkadie and others cite substantial growth rates and credit tourism with providing employment for at least 6 percent of

[9] Michael P. Mazur, "Economic Development of Jordan," in Charles A. Cooper and Sidney S. Alexander, eds., *Economic Development and Population Growth* (New York: American Elsevier, 1972), pp. 240-42.

the work force.[10] These figures must be approached with caution, however, as a large percentage of the tourists were undoubtedly expatriate West Bankers. In any event, a thriving tourist trade developed along essentially laissez-faire lines, capitalizing on the existence of high-school-educated and often multilingual youth as a cheap source of labor. Tourism was well suited to traditional investment in real estate, primarily small hotels. Unlike "fun and sun" centers, which require a heavier capital investment, the religious centers of interest already existed. An existing structure that did not have to be "sold" cut down on the need for extensive advertising by the Jordanian Tourist Office. Jordanian encouragement of tourism was nevertheless substantial, making tourism the most capital-intensive sector in the West Bank economy.[11]

Against this background of structural underdevelopment, with the notable exception of tourism, there were nevertheless impressive economic welfare gains. Many of these were the result of exogenous factors. Expatriates, both refugees and Palestinians born on the West Bank, regularly sent money home to their relatives.[12] This money served as a major stimulus to local commercial activity, in part compensating for the absence of any significant state investment. A growing UNRWA presence was also an important factor, both as a source of employment and as a source of disbursements.

Yet welfare gains could not belie the reality of underdevelopment. Emigration remained substantial and unchanged, even during those years of greatest prosperity in the early 1960s. High unemployment levels continued to plague the West Bank. Sector wage differentials reflected a skewed income distribution favoring the few at the top. The West Bank, in short, joined the ranks of many underdeveloped regions: it was a good place to leave.[13]

The Gaza Strip until 1967

Data on the Gaza Strip for the period 1948–1965, however unreliable, suggest an even greater degree of unbalanced development. Egyptian

---

[10] Van Arkadie, *Benefits and Burdens*, p. 26; and Haim Ben Shahar, Eitan Berglas, Yair Mundlak, and Ezra Sadan, *Economic Structure and Development Prospects of the West Bank and the Gaza Strip* (Santa Monica, Calif.: Rand, 1971), R-839-FF, p. 54.

[11] Van Arkadie, *Benefits and Burdens*, p. 29.

[12] "Remittances [in 1965] totaled $6.4 million or 11.8 percent of the West Bank GDP." Van Arkadie, *Benefits and Burdens*, p. 24.

[13] Emigration was equally prevalent among Palestinians born on the West Bank and among the refugees of 1948. See Lifshitz, *Structural Changes and Economic Growth*, p. 9.

TABLE 3
Sources of Income in the Gaza Strip, 1966

Source	Millions of Egyptian pounds	Percent
Gross domestic output by sector		
Agriculture and fishing	5.5	26.2
Industry	0.7	3.3
Trade and personal services[a]	4.3	20.5
Transport	0.5	2.4
Administration and public services[b]	4.0	19.0
Building and public construction	1.0	4.8
Total	16.0	76.2
Transfers from abroad		
UNRWA and other public transfers	4.0	19.0
Remittances from relatives abroad	1.0	4.8
Total	5.0	23.8
Income from all sources	21.0	100.0

[a] Services include banking and insurance; house rents not included.
[b] Including the activities of the Palestinian Liberation Army.
Source: Economic Planning Authority, *The Economy of the Gaza Strip and Sinai* (Jerusalem: Central Bureau of Statistics, 1967), table 6, p. 8.

rule of the Gaza Strip coincided with a period of slow economic growth in Egypt itself.[14] Many of its problems (such as unemployment, acute shortages of capital, soil salinity) similarly beset Egypt as a whole. The state provided neither the means nor the willingness to deal with the Gaza Strip on any kind of preferential basis. National Accounts estimates of 1966 indicate a per capita GNP of 27 dinars, only half that of the West Bank and one of the lowest in the world.[15] Again, as in the case of the West Bank and perhaps even more so, economic welfare gains belied structural underdevelopment. The service sector accounted for over half the GNP. This is in large measure attributable to extensive UNRWA activities, the presence of large army bases, and smuggling. Industry was practically nonexistent (see table 3). Visible

[14] For an analysis of the Egyptian economy, see Bent Hansen, "Economic Development of Egypt," in Cooper and Alexander, eds., *Economic Development and Population Growth in the Middle East*, pp. 22-92.
[15] Ben Shahar et al., *Economic Structure and Development Prospects*, p. 29.

exports were almost exclusively agricultural, with a heavy predominance of citrus.

Against a background of limited unskilled employment opportunities, a high rate of natural increase, and growing unemployment, UNRWA trained what rapidly emerged as one of the most educated young publics in the less-developed countries. In fact, educational attainments were proportionately higher in the Gaza Strip than in the West Bank,[16] and notably higher than in any other country in the Middle East, with the possible exception of Israel. Unable to find work at home, educated youth were natural candidates for emigration.

Israel and the Territories

When Israel took over the West Bank and the Gaza Strip from Jordan and Egypt, the economies of these two territories came into contact with an economic reality that was in many ways revolutionary compared with their previous evolution. The Israeli economy, from which they had been separated for about two decades, had changed drastically since 1948. Moreover, they entered into a relationship that was essentially imposed on them and that did not coincide with their final goal. In general, the economic development in the territories since 1967 has been determined by two major factors: the quantitative and qualitative disparities between their economies and the Israeli economy, and the political uncertainty regarding their future status.

The gap between the economies of Israel and the administered territories was of considerable magnitude. Van Arkadie described the situation as follows:

> Those [the West Bank and the Gaza Strip] are largely agricultural economics made up of small economic units and an unorganized labor force with a low level of technological development, linked to a highly organized economy with a protected industrial sector and a sophisticated level of technology.[17]

This situation can perhaps best be understood by comparing several indicators. The value of Israeli industrial export sales in 1966 alone exceeded the GNP of the two territories combined. Israel's industrial development, like that of the economy as a whole, was rapid in comparison with other countries, including that of developed economies. Industrial output increased by nearly five times between 1950 and

[16] Van Arkadie, *Benefits and Burdens*, p. 57.
[17] Ibid., p. 44.

1966, with an annual growth rate exceeding 9 percent. The number of workers employed in industry in 1966 was 222,000, a figure almost equal to the total employment in the territories combined.[18] While industry in the territories was concentrated mainly in the processing of agricultural produce, the major products in Israel, both for export and local consumption, included machinery, synthetic yarns, rubber and plastic products, chemical and petroleum products, and textiles.[19]

The gap between Israel and the territories was equally evident in agriculture. Israeli farm production increased almost sixfold between 1949 and 1966, as did agricultural exports. A number of factors contributed to this remarkable growth, including the doubling of the number of persons employed in agriculture, a 250 percent increase in cultivated land, a fivefold increase in irrigated land, and a fourfold increase in the use of water. Another important constellation of factors was the rapid increase in capital stock complemented by greater skill, rising efficiency, better organization, and technological innovation, resulting in the tripling of productivity.[20]

In contrast to the rapid development of Israel's agricultural sector relative to other developed economies, agricultural development in the West Bank was in many respects slower, even when compared with other economies at similar GNP per capita levels. A Rand study by four Israeli economists compared the distribution of product by sector in the West Bank with the arithmetic mean of Kuznets's sample. In the hypothetical "average" country in Kuznets's sample of countries with similar levels of income per capita, almost two-thirds of the labor force are employed in agriculture, yet they produce over 40 percent of product, yielding a coefficient of 64.8, significantly higher than West Bank agriculture, with a coefficient of 0.51. The comparison showed that "the share of agriculture was extremely low."[21] While

---

[18] *Israel Economic Development: Past Progress and Plan for the Future* (Jerusalem: State of Israel, Prime Minister's office, Economic Planning Authority, 1968), p. 394. For the data on employment in the territories, see Ben Shahar et al., *Economic Structure and Development Prospects*, p. 21; for GNP data, see pp. 26-27.

[19] *Israel Economic Development*, p. 403.

[20] Ibid., pp. 313-15, 339.

[21] Ben Shahar et al., *Economic Structure and Development Prospects*, p. 33. Kuznets analyzed the distribution of means and shares of product and labor in countries at various levels of per capita income, with the view of assessing the structural features of economies at different levels of development. The sample mentioned comprises countries with an average per capita income of $200. See S. Kuznets, "Quantitative Aspects of the Economic Growth of Nations: II, Industrial Distribution of National Product and Labor Force," *Economic Development and Cultural Change*, vol. 5 (July 1957), Supplement.

almost half the labor force was employed in agriculture, the sector accounted for less than one-quarter of GNP.

The disparity between the two agricultural sectors is best illustrated by the fact that the gross product per person employed in Israeli agriculture was over four times that of the West Bank and six times that of the Gaza Strip.[22] The previously mentioned factors, which played such an important role in Israel's rapid agricultural growth, were almost totally absent in the territories.

Under such conditions, the West Bank and the Gaza Strip could not successfully compete with the Israeli economy. While the territories had little import-substitution industry, Israeli industry was highly developed. Protected by high tariffs, and often competitive without them, the administered territories were an ideal market for Israeli goods, including textiles, detergents, plastics, processed foods, and appliances. Although to the best of our knowledge no study has been made on the direct effects of Israeli business in the territories, there is no doubt that Israeli firms enjoyed the twin advantages of economies of scale and favorable access. Aggregate statistics show that within a period of five years the West Bank had become Israel's second largest export market, second only to the United States. In 1974, 12 percent of Israeli exports went to the territories, a level which has been more or less maintained since that time.[23] As early as 1968, imports from Israel constituted 77 percent of the total imports of the territories, and in 1977 reached 91 percent. Exports to Israel from the territories in 1968 represented 44 percent of the total exports, and in 1977 reached 61 percent (see table 4). Most of the imports have been industrial goods, with agricultural produce constituting approximately 20 percent over the years.

One of the main commodities the territories had to offer in exchange for their trade disadvantage was cheap labor. Although in the first year following the Six Day War Palestinian laborers were not allowed to seek work in Israel, free movement of labor was permitted once the Israeli economy picked up. Laborers entered those sectors with the largest incremental growth and the lowest technological innovation. Construction accounted for the largest share (over 50 percent between 1969 and 1975) of the incoming labor pool, as the building industry experienced its greatest boom since the early 1950s. Others found themselves in the growing service industry as tourism

[22] Ben Shahar et al., *Economic Structure and Development Prospects*, pp. 28-30.
[23] Figures computed from *Statistical Abstract of Israel* (Jerusalem: Central Bureau of Statistics, 1978), table VIII/1, p. 212.

TABLE 4

FOREIGN TRADE OF THE TERRITORIES BY COUNTRY OF ORIGIN AND DESTINATION, 1968–1978

(percent)

Trade Category	1968	1969	1970	1971	1972	1973	1974	1975	1976	1977	1978
Imports from:											
Israel	76.8	80.3	83.7	81.7	84.9	90.1	89.4	91.2	90.3	91.0	89.0
Jordan	7.3	7.8	3.7	3.0	2.8	1.9	1.5	1.2	0.9	1.0	1.0
Overseas	15.9	11.9	12.6	15.3	12.3	8.0	9.1	7.6	8.8	8.0	10.0
Exports to:											
Israel	44.0	36.4	46.2	45.5	48.7	66.3	66.4	64.9	63.3	61.0	60.0
Jordan	43.2	48.3	38.0	32.0	34.5	20.0	24.9	27.2	29.6	34.0	36.0
Overseas	12.8	15.3	15.8	22.5	16.8	13.7	8.7	7.9	7.1	5.0	4.0

SOURCE: Uri Litwin, The Economy of the Administered Territories, 1976-77 (Jerusalem: Bank of Israel Research Department, January 1980; in Hebrew), p. 30; Administered Territories Statistics Quarterly, vol. 9, no. 2 (Jerusalem: Israel Central Bureau of Statistics, November 1979), p. 7.

made significant gains. Their presence in Israeli industry was by and large a later and more selective development.

Exporting labor thus became the territories' main economic activity, and labor by far their major export. In 1974, when earnings from such employment reached their high point relative to total economic activity, they accounted for roughly 27 percent of GNP. Van Arkadie estimates that, given the multiplier effect wrought by the injection of these wages into the West Bank economy, they in effect accounted for nearly half the incremental growth of GNP in the years 1968–1973. These earnings financed Israeli imports to the territories.[24]

Interaction between the two economies subsequently developed along highly specialized lines. Whereas the territories exported mostly labor, Israel's exports consisted primarily of sophisticated and technological goods. This does not, of course, constitute the sum total of the relationship. There are indications that, in recent years, the relationship between the two economies has been becoming more diversified. In this period, labor earnings from Israel accounted for less than 50 percent of total foreign receipts, with the remainder deriving from the sale of agricultural produce and industrial goods. Moreover, in recent years export revenue growth has exceeded growth in labor receipts. The export revenues of the territories grew by 49 percent in real terms over the years 1974–1977, compared with a 25 percent increase in labor earnings from abroad.[25]

Contact between the economies of the territories and the Israeli economy resulted in an accelerated economic growth in the territories. Growth of GNP exceeded an average of 12 percent annually between 1968 and 1978. This figure is even more impressive in view of continued emigration from the territories throughout this period. GNP per capita grew by 11 percent in the West Bank and 9.7 percent in the Gaza Strip (see table 5). This rate of growth surpassed Israel's own remarkable economic growth in the boom years 1955–1964 and 1968–1973 (approximately 10 percent average annual growth), as well as that of other fast-growing economies.[26] The growth in GNP was accompanied by a corresponding expansion of the territories' domestic economy. While notably lower than GNP growth rates, owing to the prominence of labor earnings in Israel, gross domestic product (GDP) grew by an average of 10 percent in the West Bank and 7 percent in the Gaza Strip (see table 5).

[24] Van Arkadie, *Benefits and Burdens*, pp. 163–64.

[25] Figures computed from *Statistical Abstract of Israel*, table XXVII/6, p. 769.

[26] *Israel Economic Development*, p. 10; *Statistical Abstract of Israel*, table VI/3, pp. 164–65.

TABLE 5

ANNUAL GROWTH RATE IN THE WEST BANK, GAZA STRIP, AND ISRAEL,
1968–1978
(percent)

Years	GNP		GNP per Capita		GDP		GNP in Israel
	West Bank	Gaza Strip	West Bank	Gaza Strip	West Bank	Gaza Strip	
1968–78	12.9	12.1	11.0	9.7	10.4	7.3	5.5
1968–73	14.5	19.4	11.8	17.0	9.9	9.9	9.9
1974–78	7.0	6.0	5.2	4.4	5.1	4.5	1.9

SOURCE: Computed from *Administered Territories Statistics Quarterly*, vol. 9, no. 2 (Jerusalem: Israel Central Bureau of Statistics, November 1979); *Statistical Abstract of Israel, 1978*, no. 29 (Jerusalem: Israel Central Bureau of Statistics); *Central Bureau of Statistics Monthly*, no. 1, January 1979, p. 17.

Thus, the impact of the Israeli economy promoted the expansion of the territories' domestic economies in two major spheres. Higher incomes, mainly the result of earnings in Israel, brought in their wake significant increases in levels of consumption, which in turn spurred domestic economic activity. In the area of supply, contact with a vastly superior technological environment resulted in innovations in virtually all sectors of the economy. Productivity gains were especially apparent in agriculture, industry, and construction. The introduction of technological innovations facilitated the expansion of the domestic economy, despite a decline in domestic manpower during the early years following the Six Day War, when an increasing share of the labor force found employment in Israel. The decrease in domestic employment levels was nevertheless slight, owing to the fact that workers employed in Israel came largely from the ranks of the un-employed. Thus, the initial absorption of workers into the Israeli economy reflected little opportunity cost to the economies of the territories.

An additional feature was the expanded opportunities presented by access to the Israeli market once the free flow of goods was allowed. Israel became the dominant importer of goods from the territories; its share of the territories' total exports rose from 44 percent (equal to that of Jordan) in 1968 to 66 percent in 1974 (see table 4). Export growth was registered for industrial as well as agricultural and labor-intensive products, mainly in products in which the territories enjoyed a comparative advantage over Israel. The annual increase in exports for the years 1968–1977 was 8 percent for the West Bank and 20 percent for the Gaza Strip.[27] While prior to 1967 the territories' foreign earnings derived overwhelmingly from tourist services in the West Bank and from services and smuggling in the Gaza Strip, visible exports represented an increasingly larger share of foreign earnings during the post-1967 years despite the tremendous increase in labor earnings during the same period.

The double-digit growth rate that characterized the first six years of economic development has since declined to a more normal but nevertheless substantial rate, hovering around the 6 percent mark. This rate of growth is impressive when compared with Israel's sluggish growth in this period (see table 5). An analysis of the past five years suggests that the 1968–1978 period should be divided into two periods, with 1974 as the dividing point. Several factors can explain the slowdown in growth.

First, after absorbing large numbers of workers from the territories, the Israeli market reached its saturation point, particularly with the Israeli economy itself entering a no-growth period in the wake of the Yom Kippur War. While earnings continued to grow, the number of laborers working in Israel declined (see tables 6 and 7). With Israel's current economic difficulties, the prospects for any significant reversal of this trend in the near future are small. However, the relative inelasticity of Israel's demand for labor in the territories, accompanied by wage rigidity as demonstrated in the last five years, indicates a steady stream of future earnings for the territories.

Second, a steep decline in private consumption in the face of uncertainty has dampened domestic demand. A corresponding decline in public expenditures has also contributed to slower growth.

Third, unusually high savings have not been translated into business investment, although building investment throughout the second period was extremely brisk. A general unwillingness to invest in industry is characteristic of many developing countries where the traditional preference is for real estate.

Fourth, a long-term decline in the comparative labor-wage advantage, accompanied by declining Israeli demand for goods initially subcontracted in the territories, has led to a condition of almost no growth in West Bank industry since 1974. In this respect, the situation in Gaza differed from that in the West Bank. While the Gaza Strip witnessed little emigration, workers from the West Bank sought

[27] Uri Litwin, *The Economy of the Administered Territories, 1976-77* (Jerusalem: Bank of Israel Research Department, 1980; in Hebrew), pp. 8-9.

TABLE 6

Labor Force and Population Characteristics in the West Bank, 1970–1978

Year	Population (thousands)			Labor Force		Labor Force of West Bank Employed in Israel	
	Number	Net outflow	Natural increase	Percent of total population over 14 years	Number employed (thousands)	Percent of total employed	Number (thousands)
1970	603.9	5.0	13.7	36.7	118.4	12.4	14.7
1971	617.3	2.5	15.9	36.3	119.7	21.4	25.6
1972	629.0	5.1	16.8	37.6	126.6	27.6	34.9
1973	646.2	−0.3	16.9	37.4	127.7	30.2	38.6
1974	661.6	2.7	18.1	39.1	139.0	30.5	42.4
1975	665.1	15.1	18.6	36.5	133.9	30.2	40.4
1976	670.9	14.5	20.3	35.4	131.3	28.3	37.1
1977	681.2	10.2	20.5	33.9	128.8	27.6	35.5
1978	690.4	9.4	18.6	34.0	131.5	28.0	36.8

SOURCES: *Administered Territories Statistics Quarterly*, vol. 9, no. 2 (Jerusalem: Israel Central Bureau of Statistics, November 1979); *Statistical Abstract of Israel, 1978*, no. 29 (Jerusalem: Israel Central Bureau of Statistics).

TABLE 7

LABOR FORCE AND POPULATION CHARACTERISTICS IN THE GAZA STRIP, 1970–1978

Year	Population (thousands)			Labor Force		Labor Force of Gaza Strip Employed in Israel	
	Number	Net outflow	Natural increase	Percent of total population over 14 years	Number employed (thousands)	Percent of total employed	Number (thousands)
1970	367.7	3.3	8.8	31.7	62.4	9.5	5.9
1971	375.9	2.4	10.6	30.8	61.8	13.3	8.2
1972	383.5	3.9	11.5	31.5	64.6	27.1	17.5
1973	397.2	−1.6	12.1	32.6	68.1	33.3	22.7
1974	408.5	1.8	13.1	33.6	73.5	35.8	26.3
1975	418.5	3.8	13.8	32.3	72.7	35.6	25.9
1976	429.0	4.3	14.8	33.0	76.3	36.4	27.8
1977	441.3	3.0	15.3	32.3	77.3	35.6	27.5
1978	450.2	5.2	14.1	32.4	80.6	39.1	31.4

SOURCES: *Administered Territories Statistics Quarterly*, vol. 9, no. 2 (Jerusalem: Israel Central Bureau of Statistics, November 1979); *Statistical Abstract of Israel, 1978*, no. 29 (Jerusalem: Israel Central Bureau of Statistics).

employment in Jordan and other Arab countries. Consequently, labor in the West Bank became more scarce and more expensive than in Gaza. In addition, Gaza enjoyed direct investment by Israeli entrepreneurs, while the West Bank did not.[28]

Thus developments in the last five years have led to more conservative prospects for economic growth in the territories. Although a certain leveling off was anticipated after the rapid growth in the first period, the slower pace of development evidenced in the last five years failed to meet expectations. The growth rate projected by Ben Shahar and his associates for the period 1973–1978, for example, varied only slightly from that of the first period.[29] In particular, they seem to have misjudged population growth and labor participation rates. They could not foresee the attractiveness of employment opportunities in Jordan and the Gulf States as a result of the oil boom and other developments more specifically related to Jordan. While Ben Shahar estimated a 3.5 percent annual population growth rate for the whole period, in reality population increased by less than 2 percent per annum.[30] The West Bank has been a major source of emigration especially in the 1975–1978 period. Emigration has traditionally been prevalent among the relatively young and most productive segments of the labor force, and the West Bank has proved no exception. As table 6 indicates, the labor force in the West Bank declined in absolute numbers from 139,000 in 1974 to 131,500 in 1978. Similarly, labor force participation rates as a percentage of the total working-age population declined from 39.1 percent in 1974 to 34.0 percent in 1978. The situation in the Gaza Strip, however, has been more stable (see table 7).

In order to resume accelerated growth, major changes will be needed in areas of economic activity that were only marginally developed in the previous period. These include relatively large-scale investments in infrastructure and developing sources of investment capital and banking institutions to facilitate industrialization in the territories. Efforts will have to be made to reorient the educational structure from a general comprehensive orientation to a more vocational education system. This process has begun under

---

[28] An indication of declining comparative labor-wage advantages can be seen in the fact that earnings of West Bank laborers employed in the West Bank were 60 percent of after-tax earnings of West Bank workers working in Israel in 1968-1969, and 90 percent of such earnings in 1976-1977.

[29] Ben Shahar et al., *Economic Structure and Development Prospects*, table 3, p. 7.

[30] It should be noted that overall growth for the period 1968-1978 exceeded the figure projected by Ben Shahar, who evidently underestimated productivity increases.

Israeli direction, but is still in its infancy.[31] Creating an environment in which such developments can take place is contingent upon altering the political environment. This problem is discussed in the next section. It should be noted, however, that even given an optimal setting, such developments are long-term processes.

Benefits and Limitations of Existing Arrangements

As pointed out in the introduction to this chapter, the economic development of the territories has been determined not merely by economic but also by political factors. In general terms, Israel's policy can be described as being dictated by political uncertainty regarding the ultimate status of the territories. This policy underlies a framework of relationships which did indeed contribute to economic achievements that would be considered positive by any standard of evaluation. At the same time, it has revealed certain limitations that can be resolved only by a more comprehensive political solution.

Israel's policy toward the territories promoted a trilateral economic framework of relationships: (1) economic integration with Israel, (2) autonomy in internal economic activity, and (3) a situation of "open bridges" between the territories and Jordan.[32] This framework produced several advantages. First, economic integration with Israel promoted free trade among the three economies (Gaza, the West Bank, and Israel) and the emergence of what several Israeli economists have called a common market.[33] Under such conditions, unemployment in the territories was reduced to practically nothing, with each economy specializing in those areas in which it enjoyed a relative advantage. Second, while retaining former economic ties, the territories could enjoy the benefits that result from contacts between developed and underdeveloped countries. Thus technology and know-how was transferred to the territories, particularly in agriculture but also in industry. Third, the policy of nonintervention allowed the more traditional commercial network to develop without the threat of competition from the superior economy. Finally, the "open bridges" policy with Jordan assured these economies an additional

---

[31] Bull, *The West Bank*, p. 93.

[32] This relationship is described in Abba Lerner and Haim Ben Shahar, *The Economics of Efficiency and Growth: Lessons from Israel and the West Bank* (Cambridge, Mass.: Ballinger, 1975), pp. 169-74.

[33] Arye Bregman, "The Economic Development of the Administered Areas," in Daniel J. Elazar, ed., *Self-rule/Shared Rule* (Ramat Gan: Turtledove Publishing, 1979), p. 46; and Lerner and Shahar, *The Economics of Efficiency and Growth*, p. 172.

market for their products. Similarly, during periods of economic slack in Israel and economic boom in Jordan or elsewhere in the Arab world, workers could find employment there.

Despite economic gains achieved within this framework, particularly when compared with the record of the pre-1967 period, several negative aspects should be pointed out. Here two pivotal sectors in the territories' economy—industry and tourism—merit special attention.

The record of the last ten years indicates less growth for West Bank industry (5 percent annually). Most of the growth was recorded in the first period; since 1975 virtually no growth has taken place. In contrast, industrial output in the Gaza Strip continued to grow.[34] This growth can in part be attributed to direct investment on the part of Israeli entrepreneurs in an industrial park only a few kilometers from the previous border. The development of this sector has been highly volatile in both regions, since it has been dependent to some degree on Israeli market demand for subcontract material. Moreover, industry was unable to diversify to meet changing consumer demands as disposable income rose. The inevitable result was that more and more incremental income was spent on Israeli products. Nevertheless, both subcontract relationships and higher income levels did have some effect on the changing composition of local industry, as the more technologically based industries, including basic metals and plastics, grew faster than the more traditional artisan industries. In addition, while the industrial labor force increased from 12,000 in 1968 to 14,300 in 1974, only to decline to 13,800 in 1977, total output has increased by 60 percent since 1968. This development suggests that the increase in output was largely the result of technological improvements.[35] Nevertheless, in comparison with the performance of other sectors, industry could have generated a much more rapid growth.

Tourism, which accounted for over 80 percent of the West Bank's foreign earnings in 1966, is a major resource of the region. Its importance is enhanced by the fact that the area is rich in human resources but poor in natural resources. As past experience shows, tourism is labor intensive and highly remunerative. While 70 percent of the tourists visiting Israel include the West Bank on their itinerary,

---

[34] Industrial output in the Gaza Strip grew from 83 million I£ in 1974 to 134 million I£ in 1977 (in 1975 prices). See Litwin, *The Economy of the Administered Territories*, table 6, p. 22.

[35] Figures computed from *Statistical Abstract of Israel*, table XXVII/22, p. 788.

SANDLER AND FRISCH

the overwhelming share of tourist expenditures are made in Jerusalem. Other West Bank tourist centers, such as Ramallah and Jericho, lost their Arab clientele in the aftermath of the war. A notable exception is Bethlehem, whose tourist industry has expanded greatly.[36]

While the requirements for the growth of industry and tourism differ, they share one common need: capital investment. The economy of the territories has consistently been characterized by high levels of savings but low levels of industrial investment. The only area in which substantial investment did take place, notably in the last five years, was in construction.[37] While much of this reluctance to invest stems from a lack of entrepreneurial ability, which is prevalent in many developing countries, the phenomenon must be attributed in part to uncertainty over the political future. To be sure, Israel gave assurances to its commercial banks in order to provide credit to local investors. In addition, it tried to encourage direct Israeli investment by providing political assurances. Both moves were made discreetly, however, as they might have been interpreted as major steps toward annexation.[38] Another potential source of capital was foreign investors, particularly from the Arab oil-producing countries. This potential did not materialize, probably also because of political considerations.

Finally, two other considerations should be pointed out regarding manpower and industrial development. First, as Uri Litwin has suggested, while there was great demand for unskilled labor in Israel in all sectors, there was a demand for skilled manpower in industry on the other side of the Jordan. Consequently, the small technologically skilled labor force that did exist in the territories found employment in other Arab countries. "This situation has contributed to the fact that industry suffered from a relative disadvantage and its development was relatively small."[39] In this respect, the "open bridges" policy has harmed the territories. Second, it should be remembered that industrialization is a long and slow process that requires changes in many areas, such as education, social structure, and institutional organization.[40] A stable political environment is undoubtedly necessary for such a process to take place.

[36] Based on an interview with staff officers in charge of tourism in the military government of Judea and Samaria.

[37] Litwin, *The Economy of the Administered Territories*, p. 26.

[38] This information is based on an interview with Mr. Moshe Sanbar, former governor of the Bank of Israel.

[39] Litwin, *The Economy of the Administered Territories*, p. 14.

[40] Bregman, *The Economy of the Administered Territories*, p. 13.

Conclusions

The economic development of the administered territories since 1967 attests to the benefits derived from contact with Israel. Gains achieved from this interaction should be related both to contact with a more advanced economy and to the framework of relationships instituted by Israel since 1968. An exclusive relationship with either Israel or Jordan would not have served the economic interests of the territories.

The remarkable accomplishments of the territories in the last decade point to the conclusion that the economic relationships which Israel has instituted have proved themselves and should not be drastically transformed under any future political arrangement. The West Bank and the Gaza Strip, regardless of their final status, should for their own economic benefit maintain close economic relations with both Israel and Jordan.

The analysis of economic development since 1967 indicates that while achieving an unusually high economic growth rate accompanied by substantial gains in economic welfare (rise in disposable income), both the West Bank and the Gaza Strip remained underdeveloped regions. This underdevelopment is manifested, inter alia, in their inability to make full use of their human resources and in the low rate of industrialization. For a region that is poor in natural resources and rich in manpower, it is important at this stage to achieve a higher level of industrialization than exists at present. This is all the more important as agriculture becomes more mechanized and therefore less labor intensive.

A major constraint on the development of industry as well as other sectors has been the lack of substantial capital investment. The need for investment has become even more crucial as the territories are slowly losing their comparative labor advantage. Taking into account the limited resources of both Israel and Jordan, it is clear that such needs can be met only by a combined effort of all the parties concerned. In view of the high level of local savings (in 1977 savings in the West Bank alone were four times higher than the value added of its industrial sector) the local inhabitants could play a major role in the industrialization of the territories.[41]

The desire to retain the benefits of the existing framework of interaction, combined with the need for capital investment, requires a multilateral approach. Clearly a prerequisite for such an approach is a political solution for the region.

[41] See Litwin, *The Economy of the Administered Territories*, tables 6, 8, pp. 22, 24.

6

Social Services in the Administered Territories

Avraham Lavine

The social services system that has been developed during the past thirteen years in Judea, Samaria, Gaza, and Sinai was designed partly to respond to new needs arising from social change. Beyond that, however, the system has itself been a major contributor to social change in those areas. Although such change is not per se an expression of improvement in the quality of life nor necessarily the herald of a more desirable social structure, it nevertheless often does have these components. Elements of social change such as dynamism and mobility, innovation and conflict all imprint their image on the changing life of a society and determine the direction it will take in the future. Some features of a process of social change may well clash with long-established behavioral patterns of a strongly traditional society, and the result, while comprising many positive aspects such as modernization, development, and progress, might easily include less positive consequences such as a weakening of family cohesion and a move away from well-respected traditions and values. Each person, depending on his own world view, will welcome or reject particular consequences of social change and the resulting different life-style and social structure.

In Judea and Samaria, Gaza and Sinai, the main components of a continuing process of social change can be identified as: (1) a marked rise in standard of living and a significant decrease in poverty; (2) movement from a predominantly agrarian society to one that is increasingly urbanized and industrialized; (3) an acceleration of a process of westernization and modernization; (4) a change in traditional social and family structures motivated by the three aforementioned factors.

Rapid economic growth, one of the fastest in the world, has characterized the development of the administered areas since 1967.

145

The GNP, which includes the income of administered-area residents working in Israel, has risen by an average of 13 percent for the areas during the period 1968–1978, while gross domestic capital formation has risen by an average of 27 percent for both areas.[1] A good indicator of a substantial rise in the standard of living of the areas is the annual average increase of 9.8 percent in private consumption between 1968 and 1978, as well as an increase in the percentage of households possessing durable goods:

- gas or electric range for cooking: from 7 percent in 1972 to 62 percent in 1978
- electric refrigerator: from 4 percent in 1968 to 38 percent in 1978
- television set: from 2 percent in 1968 to 43 percent in 1978[2]

This rapid development, together with full employment (unemployment dropped from 10.9 percent in Judea and Samaria in 1968 to 0.9 percent at the end of 1979 and from 17.0 percent in 1968 in Gaza and Sinai to 0.2 percent in September 1979),[3] has contributed in a major way, together with the rehabilitation efforts of the social services, to a substantial decrease in poverty and dependence.

Agricultural mechanization and intensified farming methods introduced into the administered areas since 1967 have released labor previously engaged in agricultural production to work in other sectors of the economy. While agricultural output has increased from I£ 135.0 million in Judea and Samaria in 1968 to I£ 3,713.9 million in 1978 and I£ 53.3 million in Gaza and Sinai in 1968 to I£ 1,217.0 million in 1978,[4] there has nevertheless been a significant movement from employment in agriculture, forestry, and fishing to employment mainly in construction, but also in industry (see table 1).[5]

The breakdown in the predominantly agrarian society that existed prior to 1967 has been accelerated by widespread daily contact with a modern, westernized Israeli society. This occurs as workers from the administered areas find employment with Israeli firms, as well as through daily commercial intercourse and free access to Israel by residents of the administered areas. It is living alongside Israeli

[1] *Main Indicators of the Economic Development in Judaea and Samaria, Gaza Strip and North Sinai, 1968-1978* (Jerusalem: Central Bureau of Statistics, August 1979).
[2] Ibid.
[3] *Family Surveys in the Administered Areas* (Jerusalem: Central Bureau of Statistics, 1979).
[4] *Statistical Abstract of Israel, 1979* (Jerusalem: Central Bureau of Statistics, 1979).
[5] *Family Surveys in the Administered Areas.*

TABLE 1
EMPLOYMENT BY SECTOR IN JUDEA AND SAMARIA, GAZA AND SINAI, 1969–1979
(percent)

Sector	Judea and Samaria		Gaza and Sinai		
	1969	1978	1969	1978	Total in 1979
Agriculture, forestry, and fishing	44.8	27.7	33.1	24.0	24.1
Industry (mining and manufacturing)	13.3	16.6	12.5	15.3	18.3
Construction (building and public works)	11.9	21.3	9.6	21.6	22.5

SOURCE: *Family Surveys in the Administered Areas.*

society and having daily contact with it that has posed the greatest challenge to the traditional social structure of the areas. Young people confronted with technological progress and materialism are beginning to lose a long-accepted sense of respect and deference for their elders, who are no longer the inevitable exclusive authority in a generally patriarchal and rural society. The municipal elections held in Judea and Samaria on April 12, 1976, during which 35,000 women were given the vote for the first time, returned younger and more politically oriented officials in contrast to the "elders" who had traditionally led the community. It should be noted, incidentally, that 73 percent of the electorate voted in the 1976 elections—a fairly high percentage of participation in a free and democratic poll.[6]

Although this chapter concentrates on the development of social services in the administered territories as an important element in the process of social change, the global picture of development in these areas must form the backdrop against which social services should be viewed. Moreover, the contrast between the nature of the Arab society today and prior to the Israeli administration that started in

[6] *Judaea and Samaria, Gaza District, Sinai, Golan Heights: A Twelve-Year Survey, 1967-1979* (Jerusalem: Ministry of Defense, October 1979), p. 7.

1967 is of course central to any discussion of conditions resulting from social change in these areas.

In the pre-1967 West Bank, subsistence agriculture and poverty were widespread among the rural and refugee populations, existing alongside urban affluence. The refugee population of the Gaza Strip lived under conditions of deprivation and dependence. The variety of religious beliefs and degrees of practice included a very conservative Islamic traditional way of life, particularly in the Gaza and Hebron districts, and the predominantly Christian character of the Bethlehem region.

While Judea and Samaria prior to 1967 were under Jordanian civil administration and services were delivered by Jordanian civil servants, Gaza came under the aegis of the Egyptian military authorities. Not only did the quantity and quality of social assistance provided in the two areas differ greatly, therefore, but the military administration in Gaza had a different psychological influence on the social motivations of the residents than did the civilian Jordanian government. Generally speaking, social services delivered in all the administered areas prior to 1967 and to all sectors of the population including refugees, constituted the most basic "first aid" relief, ignoring completely any attempt to provide programs designed to change the disadvantaged situation of those in need.

The Jordanian Ministry of Labor and Social Affairs provided social assistance in Judea and Samaria for two categories: border village residents and social cases. Border village residents represented the largest category of people receiving assistance, which was allocated solely on the recommendation of the local *mukhtar* (village representative) to the Jordanian welfare authorities. Living in the vicinity of the border automatically entitled border village residents to be classified as "needy" without having to have a file opened or a social investigation carried out. Social workers normally had little contact with welfare recipients and often knew nothing of their backgrounds or villages of residence. Consequently, the sole form of social assistance offered was in the form of food rations distributed every two to three months, while professional social work help was almost nonexistent.

Social cases represented a minority among those receiving relief. In such cases, in contrast to those involving border village residents, a social worker would indeed inquire into the situation of the needy person, but neither the social worker nor the director of the district office was empowered to decide who would actually receive assistance. In a highly centralized system, all information had to be transferred to Amman, where, under Jordanian law, such decisions were the sole prerogative of the Ministry of Labor and Social Affairs. In addition to a public assistance grant provided by the Jordanian government of an average of five dinars per family per month, or nine kilograms of flour, food rations were also distributed to the needy population by several international organizations.

As already mentioned, conditions prevailing in Gaza prior to 1967 were far less conducive to social development than those in Judea and Samaria. The distribution of food rations was the only type of assistance available there, and all decisions were made by a representative of the Egyptian military administration, to the exclusion of any professional opinion given by a social worker.

It should be remembered that social welfare cases receiving material assistance represented a different population from that residing in the refugee camps, maintained under the auspices of the United Nations Relief and Works Agency (UNRWA). They also provided immediate relief aid and no more.

This is the starting point from which Israeli planners had to determine the direction that social services would take. Progress made in the administered territories, whether in the fields of agriculture, education, health, or social services, owes more to the fact that each of the services offered is the professional responsibility of the appropriate Israeli ministry, than to the undeniable understanding and desire of the military commanders of the various districts to improve conditions of the local population. The staff officers for social affairs in Judea, Samaria, and Gaza are civil servants whose professional activity is directed by the Ministry of Labor and Social Affairs, although they are an integral part of the civil administration of the military government and, in the final analysis, responsible to the military governor in each of the two regions. This professional supervision is a key to the development of social services offered to the population of the areas, since, in this way, social planning and services delivery have a solid foundation in the social work philosophy that is the source of social policy as carried out in Israel.

The social services staff proceeded to construct a social services system that would not simply maintain disadvantaged population groups on the threshold of subsistence but would provide them with the tools to rise above their deprivation to become economically and socially independent. Their underlying philosophy was to motivate and assist individuals, families, and whole communities in caring about their own future and in helping themselves to improve all aspects of their lives. The concept of rehabilitation as pivotal to the solution of social problems was introduced into these areas for the first time.

Three well-defined stages can be discerned in the activity of the social services in the territories which were designed to effect the transfer of emphasis from the provision of relief to the achievement of full rehabilitation for disadvantaged and dependent population groups. Although the three stages undertaken in Gaza were similar to those carried out in Judea and Samaria, the process of development in the former was much more gradual, owing to the differences in social conditions between the two regions.

Within two months of the end of the Six Day War in 1967, all services previously in existence were reactivated, including social welfare bureaus. Social welfare workers were invited to return to work, and all government institutions were reopened. In this initial stage, as well as in the second stage, food rations continued to be distributed at the same levels and according to the same lists of recipients inherited from the previous administrations, even though many of these recipients were not really in need of emergency relief. International voluntary agencies that had been active in providing these food rations were asked to continue carying out their relief activities.[7] At the same time, local charitable societies were also encouraged to resume their social activities.

During the second stage, a comprehensive survey was under-taken of the social requirements of the population of the administered areas, and possible methods of reorganizing services were studied. A prerequisite to the introduction of rehabilitation programs for the residents of the areas was that social investigations be carried out into the individual needs of those who had hitherto been receiving food rations. To this end, explicit guidelines were laid down for the local social welfare workers and in-service training programs were provided to begin raising the level of their social work skills. After the completion of these initial social investigations, the receipt of relief was subsequently based solely upon individual or family hardship, devoid of all political connotations, which had not always been the case under the previous administration. Consequently, the social services provide assistance, for example, even to the needy families of convicted terrorists whose situations are judged purely on the basis of need, regardless of the terrorist activities of a member of their family.

The creation of independent family units that could support themselves on their own earned income, without having to resort to social assistance, became one of the prime goals of the social services. At the end of the second stage it became clearer just which individuals and families would need to continue to receive first-aid relief, and

[7] Food commodities were supplied to Egypt and Jordan under U.S. Public Law 480 before 1967; a modified PL 480 program continues through American voluntary agencies in Judea and Samaria, Gaza and Sinai.

which individuals and families, having a potential for rehabilitation, could be encouraged to embark on programs designed to release them from the social welfare rolls.

In December 1967, six months after the end of the Six Day War, the findings of the social investigations undertaken in the second stage began to be implemented. During the third stage it became vital to strengthen the rehabilitation arm of the social services in the administered areas by augmenting the skills of social workers and of those working with young people, including delinquent youth. Training programs were initiated in cooperation with the Institute for the Training of Social Workers of the Ministry of Labor and Social Affairs for this purpose. Moreover, the Ministry of Labor and Social Affairs began to coordinate the activities of the international voluntary agencies in order to eliminate previous instances of duplication of services and to encourage them to undertake rehabilitation and development activities. These new activities would gradually replace the distribution of food rations as the major activity undertaken by the international voluntary agencies working in the administered areas.

A change in the role and image of the social worker within the social services bureau was essential to the new direction that the social services were taking toward the implementation of rehabilitation activities. Through the decentralization of the various tasks of the social worker, stress was laid on outreach services and the treatment of clients in their own locality and within their own environment. This was done to obviate the need for having the client travel to the district welfare bureau, often over great distances and at considerable inconvenience, which frequently deterred clients from turning to the welfare bureau for help at all. Gradually, the social worker became known within the local community as a professional worker, capable of assisting in the solution of personal and family problems rather than dealing exclusively with the allocation of public assistance. Case work, rehabilitation counseling, and community work were the new tools to be used in solving the problems of individuals, families, and communities. Moreover, decisions on the provision of services to individuals, as well as the choice of treatment methods, were now made by the local and district social services staff rather than by the head of a village or at the ministry level. Using an outreach approach in serving the local population, new social services bureaus were opened in outlying areas that had previously been totally isolated from the mainstream of life in the region, owing to the lack of an adequate road network and proper communications. Six social services bureaus existed in Judea and Samaria in 1967, and six in the whole area of Gaza and Sinai; in 1979, fifteen social services bureaus in Judea and Samaria, including six district offices, and eleven in Gaza and Sinai offered comprehensive personal and community social services.[8]

The three stages described above were an indispensable prelude to the construction of a social services system based on a social work philosophy whose goal is to provide economic and social independence for disadvantaged sectors of the population, as well as to serve special groups in need of assistance, such as the physically handicapped, the blind, the deaf, and the retarded, whose particular needs had received little or no attention prior to 1967.

Through increased employment opportunities in Israel for residents of the administered areas, through individual and family rehabilitation programs carried out by rehabilitation and social workers in local social services bureaus, and through the introduction of standard eligibility criteria for recipients of social assistance, it became possible to reduce drastically the number of food rations that had been distributed up to 1967. By 1973, the 220,000 food rations distributed in Judea and Samaria were reduced to 19,000, and the 92,000 food rations distributed in Gaza and Sinai were reduced to 14,000.[9] Moreover, cash payments were introduced for individuals and families who had no source of income whatsoever and had to rely completely on public assistance. The minimum income level below which a person becomes eligible to receive public assistance is calculated at approximately 40 percent of the average income in the area, including the salaries of workers employed in Israel, for a family of four persons. Further grants are made for each additional dependent according to a fixed scale, and the minimum income level is adjusted periodically to meet the rise in the cost of living. The calculation of the level of public assistance in the administered territories is similar to that used in Israel—that is, about 40 percent of the average income. The reason for this is not only that it is regarded as the minimum level of income necessary to subsist, but also that the provision of public assistance over and above that level might be a disincentive to find suitable employment or to undertake an appropriate rehabilitation program or vocational training. Public-assistance grants are not bound by the constraints of a limited budget, since, should it become necessary, the proposed sum allocated for this purpose in the annual budget for social services may be increased to include all those who

---

[8] *Israel Social Statisticard, 1979* (Jerusalem: Ministry of Labor and Social Affairs, August 1980).

[9] *Society of Change: Judaea and Samaria, Gaza and Sinai, 1967-1973* (Jerusalem: Ministry of Social Welfare, 1974), p. 7.

are in need of this kind of help.[10] Partial public assistance is granted to those who have a small source of income in order to bring them up to the minimum income level, and is usually in the form of supplementary food rations.

In 1967, 198 family units in Judea and Samaria received a total of I£ 1,923 per month in public-assistance grants, and 563 family units in Gaza and Sinai received a total of I£ 5,800 per month. By 1979, 1,089 family units in Judea and Samaria received a total of I£ 2.2 million per month, and in Gaza and Sinai 5,568 family units received public assistance grants totaling I£ 2.6 million per month.[11] The rise in the number of family units receiving cash grants is due mainly to the shifting of emphasis from the distribution of food rations to the provision of monetary grants, to the inclusion of refugees as public-assistance recipients, and also to the necessity of including in an effective incomes maintenance policy all those who might drop below the minimum income level during periods of high inflation. It should be noted that all needy families that receive public assistance have full health insurance paid for by the social services bureaus, in addition to other treatment or rehabilitation services as might be determined by the social worker.

Since 1976, all refugees for whose benefit UNRWA continues to provide services under the Michelmore-Comay agreement signed between the government of Israel and UNRWA on June 14, 1967, may apply to the local social services bureaus nearest to their place of residence and receive all necessary social assistance as provided to all other needy residents in the areas, without prejudicing in any way their status as refugees. Subject to the results of a social inquiry by a social worker of the local social services bureau, a refugee family can receive, for example, the difference between the assistance in the form of food rations received from UNRWA—usually inadequate, especially during the past few years, because of UNRWA's increasing financial difficulties—and the minimum income level. It should be mentioned here that UNRWA has not applied socioeconomic eligibility criteria in the provision of assistance, so that a high proportion of refugees who are not in real need receive an equal share of a continually dwindling cake, thus depriving the needy of sufficient aid. The local social services bureaus received guidelines instructing them to make no distinction between refugees and the rest of the popula-

[10] The annual budget for social services was I£ 2.0 million in Judea and Samaria in 1967 and 60.0 million in 1979. In Gaza and Sinai, it was I£ 3.8 million in 1967 and 76.1 in 1979.
[11] *Israel Social Statisticard, 1979.*

tion but only between people in real need of assistance and those who are able to support themselves independently of the social services.

The delivery of social services in the administered areas is carried out on the district and local levels exclusively by Arab social workers who are residents of Judea, Samaria, and the Gaza district. These include the directors of all district offices as well as other senior staff who hold supervisory positions alongside the small number of Israeli personnel, whose role it is to offer guidance and professional supervision to all those working in the social services network. In 1979, ten Israeli members of the social services staff in Judea and Samaria and 193 local Arab residents were working in the social services, while in Gaza, seven Israelis and 103 local Arab residents were working in the social services.[12] All social workers employed by the social welfare services in Judea and Samaria are graduates in social work, or in a related field such as sociology or psychology, with inservice training experience in social work, while in the Gaza district all are graduates or have taken specially provided courses in social work. Social workers in the administered areas have wide powers in determining the treatment and extent of assistance to be provided to their clients, in accordance with social work practice in Israel and in contrast to the highly centralized Jordanian system of decision making or to that of the Egyptian military administration in Gaza before 1967.

The significance of having social services delivered by local Arab workers is manifold. It is important that the social welfare population be treated by social workers who are thoroughly familiar with the life, outlook, language, mores, and culture of their clients. Furthermore, social workers who possess this familiarity are more easily able to establish the necessary rapprochement and confidence between themselves and their clients that are prerequisites for successful treatment. Moreover, the maximum involvement of qualified local Arab residents in social services delivery is in keeping with the philosophy that the local population should itself be the major source of social development efforts on its own behalf. This is in addition to the policy of the Israeli administration in the administered areas that there be a minimum of Israeli involvement in the everyday life of the population and the greatest possible local participation in the provision of all services.

The declared intention of the government of Israel to achieve equality of services between Israel and the administered areas, represented, in effect, the final thrust in a process that has been striving

[12] Ibid.

to this end since 1967. This is certainly the case in the field of the social services in which the policy of the Ministry of Labor and Social Affairs has been to introduce steadily new, much needed, social services that were lacking under the previous administrations.

Individual and Family Rehabilitation

With the change in emphasis from relief activities to rehabilitation programs, major efforts were invested in persuading welfare recipients and handicapped persons who had a good chance of successful rehabilitation to participate in a program specifically tailored to their needs.

Together with three international voluntary agencies—Cooperative for American Relief Everywhere (CARE), the Swedish Organization for Individual Relief, and the Catholic Relief Services—the Ministry of Labor and Social Affairs established revolving loan funds for the purpose of individual and family rehabilitation. These funds offer loans and grants to those recommended for rehabilitation projects by the local rehabilitation social workers. Each case is discussed separately at a case conference in which participate the local rehabilitation social worker, the director of the district office, the professional supervisor of the social services staff in the area, as well as a representative of the international voluntary agency that contributed to the fund from which the loan is to be made. After a program of rehabilitation has been approved by the case conference, the local rehabilitation social worker follows up the execution of the loan and the progress of the project.

Typical projects include the opening of a small shop or manufacturing enterprise, the purchase of livestock or agricultural equipment, and other suitable activities. Vocational instruction is provided when necessary to prepare the client for his new occupation. Support services are available according to the type of project undertaken. For example, in addition to the purchase of livestock, a loan recipient is eligible for a grant to buy fodder and equipment, as well as for extension services from instructors of the Ministry of Agriculture, including free veterinary service.

To promote the principle of self-help and nondependence, the client is asked to repay the loan he has received on very easy terms over an extended period. In some cases, a small outright grant may be made as an additional incentive. While the project is in its early stages and does not yet provide a sufficient livelihood for the loan recipient, the latter may continue to receive assistance in the form of food rations or a cash payment in order to remove any apprehensions he might entertain about being able to survive the initial period until the project begins to support him and his family without external

155

help. As a result of more than 1,500 rehabilitation programs such as these, former social welfare recipients, who had once stood in line to receive food rations, were shown how they might regain their self-respect and achieve economic independence.[13]

Women are encouraged to help support their families by participating in rehabilitation projects such as the establishment of industrial sewing centers. These centers teach sewing and dressmaking skills and provide employment under sheltered conditions. Supervised by staff employed by the local social services bureau, the centers are profit-making enterprises operating on a subcontracting basis with textile and clothing manufacturers. In this way the centers are able to pay salaries to the women who work in them, with represents an important contribution to the family income, especially in families in which the woman is the main provider.

Two vocational rehabilitation centers for the handicapped are to be opened shortly, one in Gaza and one in Bethlehem. These centers will offer a completely new service to the handicapped and will serve a mixed population of physically disabled, blind, mentally disturbed (not retarded), and other people who can benefit from a process of rehabilitation. This process in the centers in the administered areas will be similar to that in rehabilitation centers in Israel, including intake, assessment, acquisition of work habits, vocational training, placement in the open labor market, and follow-up. For those who are unable to be placed in normal work conditions despite having completed the full rehabilitation process, sheltered workshops separate from the rehabilitation center will enable them to continue to work and earn a living. (A sheltered workshop within the rehabilitation center is undesirable, since it can present too easy an alternative to clients who would otherwise make the extra effort required to succeed in being placed in a normal place of work.)

A positive attitude on the part of disadvantaged population groups toward achieving socioeconomic independence has been continually growing, since a concerted effort on the part of the social services, together with other socially and economically oriented services of the civil administration in the administered areas, has aroused the consciousness of disadvantaged people to realizing their own potential. They have realized that through rehabilitation they might change the social system to which they were bound and which denied them the opportunity to take their rightful place as independent, active members of society.

[13] *Social Welfare Services: Annual Report, 1978-79* (in Hebrew), Judea and Samaria Military H.Q., p. 10; *Twelve Years of Social Services in the Gaza District and Sinai, 1967-1979* (in Hebrew), p. 14.

Youth Vocational Rehabilitation Centers

Patterned on a service that has existed in Israel since 1949, youth vocational rehabilitation centers, called *miftanim*, were established in the administered territories to serve a special population group, namely, twelve- to sixteen-year-olds who are dropouts from the regular school system and who are considered potentially delinquent. For such children, the *miftan* center offers a last chance to become positive and useful citizens, wage earners, and heads of families. The *miftan* program, lasting two to three years, stresses individual attention in classes of no more than twenty trainees. The studies are on a level and at a pace that will alert each trainee to his own capabilities, restore his self-esteem, strengthen his self-confidence, and encourage him to become an active member of society. Although studies are necessarily focused on vocational training because of the low academic capability of the trainees, classes are given in basic studies, including the three R's. Sports, recreation, and social activities also play an important part in the rehabilitation and resocialization program. Vocational subjects taught in the *miftanim*, such as carpentry and metalworking for boys and dressmaking and home economics for girls, enable graduates to find employment that will provide them with a livelihood to support a family, or in the case of girls, prepare them for future life as wives and mothers, working or otherwise.

Some years ago, it would have been unthinkable to establish classes for girls in *miftanim* because of the conservative outlook of this traditional society. Today, in addition to separate *miftanim* for girls, a class for girls exists in the Tulkarm *miftan* alongside two classes for boys. In 1979, fourteen classes in five *miftanim* in Judea and Samaria served 250 trainees, while nine classes in four *miftanim* in the Gaza district served 232 trainees.[14] This does not include two *miftanim* established in El Arish and Firan in Sinai that were handed over to the Egyptian administration, after the return of these areas to Egypt in accordance with the terms of the peace treaty.

Community Rehabilitation

Rehabilitation of the community in the administered areas has taken several forms during the past twelve years. All depend on one of the basic principles of community development—that is, the ability and desire of a group of people who live in proximity to one another to identify common needs and to mobilize their combined efforts in order

14 *Israel Social Statisticard*, 1979.

to satisfy these needs and to advance the community as a whole. The coalition of forces within a communal entity for the mutual benefit of its members was historically a little known phenomenon, particularly among Muslim communities in the territories, which relied almost exclusively on services supplied by central government. Community organization more often found expression among Christian and other non-Muslim minority groups whose need for self-reliance was much greater.

Great emphasis is placed on the activities of local charitable societies as an important element in community development in the administered areas. Ninety local charitable societies existed in Judea and Samaria in 1967, in five main categories: Arab women's societies, Red Crescent societies, societies of religious communities, village associations, and foreign charitable societies. The majority of these societies are organized and operated by women. The social services have encouraged, through professional advice and financial assistance, the establishment of an additional 45 new local charitable societies in Judea and Samaria since 1967, bringing the number to 135.[15] On the principle of self-help within the community, local charitable societies have been motivated to offer new services on the suggestion of the social services. These new services include day centers for retarded children, an institution for the deaf and nonverbal, maternity wings, the expansion of hospitals, rehabilitation facilities, and nutrition centers for instructing mothers in the care and nutrition of their children. All these are in addition to the expansion of existing services such as kindergartens, children's institutions, and centers for the blind.

In Gaza not one such local charitable society existed in 1967. Since then the social services have, working together with the local population, succeeded in bringing about the organization of twelve local charitable societies operating within the community and offering new services that have not existed previously.[16] One such service in Gaza is a residential home for severely retarded children, a population group hitherto sadly neglected both in Gaza and in Judea and Samaria, owing to the social stigma attached by the population of the areas to the presence of retarded children in a family. This attitude created a situation in which no effort whatsoever was made to develop the inherent potential of retarded persons or to attempt to rehabilitate them in any way.

Cases of abuse of retarded children were not unknown. It was

15 Ibid.
16 Ibid.

in this context that the social services sought after 1967 to introduce badly needed professional services for retarded children. In addition to day-care centers for the retarded opened by local charitable societies and international voluntary agencies at the encouragement of the Ministry of Social Welfare, the ministry opened the first diagnostic center for the retarded in the administered areas, in 1978, in El-Bire, near Ramallah, where a multidisciplinary team assesses the treatment requirements of retarded children. The center is open two days a week offering diagnostic, counseling, and psychological guidance services. A residential home for severely retarded children has already passed through the planning stage and will be opened in the Ramallah district. This is a major step forward in services for the retarded in Judea and Samaria, where community care of the retarded, developed during the past thirteen years, has not until now provided an answer to the needs of those retarded children requiring institutional care.

Increased activity in the field of rural and agricultural development, especially in the villages of Judea and Samaria, has provided an excellent vehicle for community organization. Village residents who had never considered the possible benefits of combining forces in order to develop the infrastructure of the village and to advance its services have been aroused to the advantages of cooperation among separate social units within the community. The community worker, working closely with the various elements in the village, brings them to the realization that much progress can be made in enhancing the standard of living of the whole community, whether it be the construction of an access road to the main road network, the installation of an adequate water pipe system or sewage system, the building of a community center, school, or clinic, or other projects that bring many hitherto isolated and backward rural areas into the era of mechanization. Subsequently, the community worker persuades the various separate units in the community, often using a specific project as a catalyst, that by working together much is to be gained. Thereafter, the representatives of the village are encouraged to identify their own needs and determine their own priorities, as well as to approach, on their own initiative, governmental or international voluntary agencies that are prospective partners in village development projects.

The emphasis is on self-help and maximum participation by the villages in both the funding and execution of projects. Eventually, the combined effort of all members of the community toward a common goal engenders a spirit of solidarity, communal pride, and independence. Moreover, increased contacts with officials of the various civil services provide local leaders with experience in representing community interests in their dealings with different branches of the bureaucracy that might be involved in future development of the village. Although in the early stages the initiative for rural development projects came mainly from the suggestions of the community workers, after the projects gained momentum and as community service efforts began to bear fruit, the village residents themselves began to take the initiative in promoting the development of their local communities.

Community work in the Gaza Strip has, during the past eight years, focused on communities in new neighborhoods for families relocated from refugee camps. The Israeli administration, in reaction to the subhuman conditions under which the refugee population of the Gaza Strip had been living for almost twenty years in refugee camps maintained by the UNRWA, undertook a program of relocation of refugee families to newly constructed housing projects in nearby areas in the Gaza Strip. For the first time, people who had learned to become totally dependent on food rations and the basic services provided by the UNRWA were offered the opportunity to regain their self-esteem and attain social and economic independence. New housing purchased on easy terms is the basis for the change, replacing perpetual squalor and total reliance on relief. To accommodate political realities, families thus relocated are not required to relinquish their status as refugees. By 1980, 5,850 families had been relocated in new housing.[17]

It is considered essential to the normal functioning of the newly established communities to arouse in the residents a sense of communal pride and responsibility and of the desirability to organize themselves to help themselves. The community workers work together with the residents, identify the natural leaders among them, and encourage the formation of neighborhood committees that can take their affairs into their own hands and can define the needs of the community which they will then proceed to try to supply. This necessitates establishing and developing contacts with a wide variety of government and social service agencies; gradually, communities composed of former residents of refugee camps who had no previous experience of communal affairs are organizing themselves, though not always without internal difficulties and arguments, into representative and active neighborhood committees. By negotiating with

[17] The total refugee population of the administered areas is 310,000, or 27.6 percent of the total population. That number includes 205,000 persons in Gaza and northern Sinai, representing 46 percent of the population, and 105,000 persons in Judea and Samaria, comprising 15.4 percent of the population.

municipal and government agencies, these committees have succeeded in improving services to the neighborhoods and in constructing, on their own initiative, communal facilities such as places of worship and community centers that offer a wide range of services for preschool children, youth, and adults. The initial totally negative attitude of the majority of the residents of the new neighborhoods, created by years of living in a refugee camp, has been modified only through the patience and tenacity of the local community workers, whose task it is to motivate the residents to work toward assuring their own progress and prosperity.[18]

Educational Summer Camps

In 1969 educational summer camps were introduced for disadvantaged children from Judea and Samaria, Gaza, and Sinai. The camps enable children to spend a vacation by the seaside supervised by local Arab teachers and instructors. A program of educational and recreational activities has been prepared which includes tours to different parts of the country. Since 1975, summer camps have taken place at the permanently established site in the National Park in Ashkelon on the Mediterranean coast. Every year 1,200 youngsters from Gaza and northern Sinai and 600 from Judea and Samaria attend ten summer camps lasting eight days each.[19] Two of the six summer camps for children of the Gaza area are for girls. This represents a radical change in social attitudes of a highly conservative and traditional Gazan community, particularly since the request that girls be allowed to attend their own summer camp came from the community itself.

International Voluntary Agencies

Since the situation in Judea, Samaria, and Gaza cannot by any stretch of the imagination be compared to the dire conditions of people in overpopulated, underdeveloped, undernourished, and often catastrophe-beset countries to whose plight is drawn the attention of international philanthropic, voluntary, and relief agencies, it is understandable that international voluntary agencies do not grant highest priority to the implementation of programs in the administered territories. This is all the more true since rapid economic growth

---

[18] *Community Work in the Gaza Strip* (Jerusalem: Ministry of Labor and Social Affairs, June 1980).
[19] *Israel Social Statisticard, 1979.*

TABLE 2
INTERNATIONAL VOLUNTARY AGENCIES ACTIVE
IN THE ADMINISTERED AREAS

American Near East Refugee Aid (ANERA)
American Save the Children Federation/Community Development
  Foundation
Amideast
CARE
Catholic Relief Services
Christoffel Blinden Mission
International Red Cross Committee
Lutheran World Federation
Mennonite Central Committee
Near East Council of Churches
Nordic Children's Fund
Norwegian Refugee Council
Quakers (American Friends Service Committee)
Svenska Jornalen
Swedish Free Church Aid
Swedish International Relief Association
Swedish Save the Children Federation (Radda Barnen)
Swedish Organization for Individual Relief (IM)
Terre des Hommes
United Nations Development Programme (UNDP)
United Nations International Children's Emergency Fund (UNICEF)
UNRWA

and social development, together with full employment, have removed completely the urgency for relief programs that existed prior to 1967. Nevertheless, twenty-two international voluntary agencies (see table 2) do in fact cooperate with the Ministry of Labor and Social Affairs in carrying out programs for social and economic development in the administered areas in accordance with the general social policy for the areas described in this chapter. The main fields of activity of the international voluntary agencies are the distribution of food rations, rural, agricultural, and economic development, day care for the retarded, primary health care, nurses training, nutrition, education and child care guidance, and the care and the rehabilitation of epileptic children and other special population groups.

In 1967, four international voluntary agencies which had been carrying out programs under contract to the government of the Hashemite Kingdom of Jordan were requested by the new Israeli administration to continue working in the territories but in a manner in keeping with its new social policy.[20] The four agencies agreed to do so, and in September 1967 the government of Israel endorsed their contracts with the Jordanian government. To this day, these contracts are honored by the government of Israel, including provisions allowing the agencies to enjoy exemptions from taxes, customs duties, and all other levies that would otherwise apply to them. Since 1967, nine additional international voluntary agencies (including UNRWA) have been granted the same customs and tax exemptions on materials and equipment used in activities carried out in the administered areas, while some also have program and administrative expenses shared by the government.[21] In this way, as well as by direct funding of joint projects, the government of Israel contributes financially to the activities of the international voluntary agencies.

Jordanian law, still the prevailing legal system in Judea and Samaria, demands that the Ministry of Labor and Social Affairs assume responsibility for supervising the activity of all local and foreign voluntary agencies and charitable societies.[22] This professional supervision makes it possible to avoid duplication of services, maintain required standards, and channel the combined energies of the organizations on the basis of mutual agreement and cooperation, to activities that have high priority. Where an international voluntary agency is interested in carrying out projects which come within the field of responsibility of other ministries such as Agriculture, Health and Education, the Ministry of Labor and Social Affairs acts as a liaison between the agency and the ministry concerned.

Four American voluntary agencies are currently carrying out programs in the administered areas in various fields, including rural, agricultural, economic, social and community development, using Economic Support Funds allocated by the United States Congress.[23] The regulations for use of these funds, averaging $3 million annually, require that projects be carried out through private voluntary organizations rather than government agencies. The legal status of the

[20] Catholic Relief Services, Lutheran World Federation, Mennonite Central Committee, and Near East Council of Churches.

[21] American Save the Children Federation, CARE, International Red Cross Committee, Norwegian Refugee Council, Svenska Jornalen, Swedish Free Church Aid, Swedish Organization for Individual Relief, Swedish Save the Children Federation, and UNRWA.

[22] Charitable Associations and Social Institutions Law (no. 33), 1966.

[23] "Economic Support Fund Programs in the Middle East," Report to the Committee on Foreign Affairs, U.S. House of Representatives, April 1979. The agencies are Amideast, ANERA, Catholic Relief Services, and the Community Development Foundation.

Ministry of Labor and Social Affairs and the social policy requirements of the ministry necessitated that an acceptable modus vivendi be found by the voluntary agencies concerned that satisfies these requirements and yet makes it possible for the agencies to operate within the framework laid down by the U.S. Congress. At this writing, the agencies using Economic Support Funds are carrying out projects in cooperation with the Ministry of Labor and Social Affairs.

It should be noted that international voluntary agencies are often less eager to carry out projects in the Gaza district because of the greater difficulties they face in obtaining the local communities' cooperation as active partners in development efforts. An additional factor in the concentration of international voluntary agencies (which are often religious organizations) in Judea and Samaria is the attraction of Bethlehem and Jerusalem as holy places.

Of all the international voluntary agencies working in the administered areas, the activities of the Quaker-sponsored American Friends Service Committee seem to be the most politically oriented— a factor which influences the nature of its activities as well as its attitude toward the Israeli government agencies. Other foreign voluntary agencies do not for the most part let political views interfere with humanitarian programs whose goal, as is that of the Ministry of Labor and Social Affairs, is to work toward the social and economic advancement of the population.

In a discussion of social developments in the administered areas, some words should be devoted to the social advancement of women and to their changing status in a traditional society. Although, according to Muslim Sharia law, a woman may be divorced against her will, during the past few years, social workers have made efforts to intervene by treating family problems in order to prevent deterioration of relationships that might lead to divorce. In the event of unavoidable divorce, a number of alternative rehabilitation programs are proposed to the divorced woman so that she will be able to support herself in her new situation.

Family-planning centers now exist in all the main cities in Judea and Samaria as well as in many of the larger villages, despite the highly sensitive nature of this subject in traditional Arab society. Sixty-two well-baby clinics serve all the main cities and 140 villages in Judea and Samaria, compared with 23 in existence in 1968.[24] Within the framework of the well-baby clinics, the opportunity is taken to offer classes to women in home economics, reading, and child development and nutrition.

[24] *The Development of the Administered Territories, 1967-1979*, Report of the Military Government Judea and Samaria, November 1979, p. 16.

AVRAHAM LAVINE

The changing role of women in society in Judea and Samaria is indicated by an increase in the number of women who go out to work,[25] as well as an increase in the participation of women in communal life. The majority of members of local charitable societies are women, numbering more than 4,000, who are carrying out social programs that include, among many other services, day-care centers for children, which enable mothers to go out to work. In the 1976 municipal elections in Judea and Samaria, women were enabled to vote for the first time,[26] a great step forward in the enhancement of their status as active members of society.

The rapid social and economic development of the administered areas and their confrontation with westernized Israeli society has brought about two less positive phenomena. The first is a rise in the need for services for the aged, who have until now always been regarded as an integral part of the Arab extended family. The change to a more modern life-style has had a negative influence on the attitude of a society that traditionally cares for its aging members within the family circle. Although the requests for placements of the aged in residential care are increasing, this phenomenon has by no means as yet assumed epidemic proportions. In Judea and Samaria, nine homes for the aged are in existence, serving about 250 residents, in all.[27] The social services are endeavoring to expand and improve community care of the aged in order to prevent and reduce the need for residential care.

Another less desirable consequence of accelerated development and contact with the modern westernized society is an increase in the rates of juvenile delinquency. Notwithstanding the efforts invested by the social services in the prevention of delinquency through community and rehabilitation programs for young people, the number of crimes committed by juveniles has been on the rise. In 1974, 1,697 crimes were committed by juveniles in Judea and Samaria while in 1978–1979, 1,873 crimes were committed by juveniles.[28] In the Gaza district 180 crimes were committed by juveniles in 1971, rising to 544 in 1978.[29] On the other hand, the number of young offenders sentenced to spend some time in homes for juvenile delinquents is small. The social services in Judea and Samaria maintain a home for juvenile

[25] According to Family Surveys in the Administered Areas, 29,400 women residents of the administered areas were employed in September 1979.
[26] Judaea and Samaria, Gaza District, Sinai, Golan Heights, p. 7.
[27] Social Welfare Services: Annual Report, 1978-79, p. 23.
[28] Ibid., p. 35.
[29] Twelve Years of Social Service in the Gaza District and Sinai, 1967-1979, p. 20.

delinquents that has a capacity of fifty residents, but in 1978 only sixteen offenders were maintained there.[30] The goals of this home are to offer socioeducational and rehabilitation services to the young residents, to help them start life anew on leaving the home after completing their sentences. An observation and diagnostic center for juvenile delinquents in Ramallah treats about 300 young people annually who are referred there by the court prior to its making a decision.[31] As a result of the professional opinion offered by the center to the court, a small number of young offenders are sentenced to residential care while others are referred to alternative services such as probation or youth vocational rehabilitation centers.

In Gaza a residential home which offers observation and diagnostic services as well as the social and vocational rehabilitation of offenders had 169 people referred there for observation prior to the court's decision between April 1978 and March 1979. Another 89 youngsters received sentences during this period to remain in the home for a fixed period.[32]

The development of social services in the administered areas has served as a major catalyst in the evolution of new attitudes that have stimulated a desire in the population for modernization and progress, thus creating a different approach to their traditional society. Full employment, an increase of wealth among all sectors of the population, and comprehensive social and rehabilitation services have gone a long way toward eliminating poverty in the administered areas, and at the same time have opened up a wide range of possibilities to a large sector of the population that had previously lived on a level of mere subsistence. The considerable rise in standard of living and development of the infrastructure and economy of the territories have generated new aspirations among those who have recently been exposed to new sources of wealth; these represent a direct challenge to the traditional social structure.

Close contact with a modern, westernized Israeli society has had a radical influence on previously accepted norms within a traditional way of life. For example, the formerly unchallenged acceptance of patriarchal authority no longer stands firm in the face of the widened horizons, augmented ambitions, and growing economic independence of the younger generation. The challenge for a society that undergoes development and radical change in its socioeconomic structure is to

---

[30] *Social Welfare Services: Annual Report, 1978-79*, p. 25.
[31] Ibid.
[32] *Twelve Years of Social Services in the Gaza District and Sinai, 1967-1979*, p. 24.

preserve the worthwhile features of the traditional value system while taking advantage of those positive elements offered by the new structure. The challenge facing the populations of Judea and Samaria, Gaza and Sinai, demands that great wisdom and skill be exercised by the residents of these areas and their leaders in order to achieve the desired equilibrium in the situation of great potential that has been created during the last thirteen years.

Given a rising standard of living and economic prosperity, together with increasing social mobility and freedom of expression, it was not unnatural for the members of a largely underprivileged, highly traditional, and fairly closed society to build up gradually their self-confidence and assert themselves through public organization and political expression. Had the policy of the Israeli administration in the late 1960s and early 1970s been to sow and nurture the seeds of political organization in the administered areas as carefully as it did in the economic and social fields, would it now be left to hostile elements outside these areas to reap the harvest?

PART THREE

Planning for the Future

7

The Administered Territories and the Internal Security of Israel

Rephael Vardi

The question of internal security in the administered territories relates to the means of suppressing and undermining hostile organizations and subversive action, of preventing disruptions to civilian life, and of preventing the achievement of the broader aim of the dissolution of Israel as an independent political entity through internal and external armed terror and violence of various kinds. The first section of this chapter examines Israel's past experience with internal security problems. The second analyzes the lessons of this experience and its implications for the future, particularly in light of the possibility that full autonomy will be granted to the inhabitants of Judea and Samaria and the Gaza Strip in accordance with the Camp David agreements.

For the present purpose, I will make the following distinction between external (or comprehensive) and internal security. External security refers to the protection of Israel's borders and the maintenance of its territorial integrity and the security of its population from attack by any regular foreign army controlled by one of the states at war with Israel, whether bordering on it (such as Jordan and Syria) or not (such as Saudi Arabia and Iraq), from the territory of one or more of these states. Internal security, on the other hand, relates to any military or paramilitary action by armed organizations (including regular armies) along or within the borders of the state or any subversive or hostile action, whether systematic or sporadic, whose military objective is injury to the person and property of civilian and military targets. The intent may be to disrupt orderly life in the country; to incite a segment of the population against law and order on an ethnic, religious, or national basis; to cause chaos in civilian life, taking lives and inflicting injuries as an aim in itself; to create nests of violent resistance and civil disobedience in the administered territories and within Israel; or to incite the government and the security forces to reprisals against individuals and groups as a means of deepening hostility and reducing the chances for peaceful coexistence between the majority and the minority in the state—all this in order to achieve the national-strategic aim of the terrorist organizations to bring about the dissolution of Israel as an independent political entity and establish a Palestinian Arab state in its place.

Since its establishment, Israel has faced acts of armed sabotage, usually directed against civilian targets—public transportation, rural settlements, workers, and unsuspecting vacationers. These actions severely disrupted the lives of the people, as well as civilian activities and development projects. At various times, such actions were taken by the regular armies of the neighboring countries—Egypt, Jordan, Syria, and to a lesser degree, Lebanon—and by irregular armed groups inspired and directed by the regular armies of these states. It is instructive to review several of the characteristics of these actions during the years 1950–1979.

Threats to Internal Security during 1950–1979

During the period 1950–1956, the regular Egyptian forces and the Palestine Liberation Army (PLA) under Egyptian control fired intermittently, day and night, on the Israeli border settlements from their positions along the border between Israel and the Gaza Strip, using small arms, mortars, and artillery.[1] Irregular forces infiltrated from the Gaza Strip into Israeli territory, especially at night, to mine roads, sabotage buildings and water installations, ambush vehicles, and attack workers in the fields. In the latter part of this period, 1955–1956, these actions by the fedayeen grew in number, striking at public transportation on the Tel Aviv–Jerusalem highway and the surrounding settlements, causing casualties also among schoolchildren and women.[2]

[1] The units of the PLA were set up by the Palestine Liberation Organization (PLO) in the early 1950s and attached to the armies of Egypt, Syria, Jordan, and Lebanon as regular units. After September 1970, the battalions of the PLA in Jordan were incorporated into the Jordanian army. After the outbreak of the civil war in Lebanon, the Palestinian battalions were transferred from Egypt to Lebanon, so today there are battalions of the PLA only in Syria and Lebanon.

[2] Fedayeen in Arabic means suicidal fighters. This was the name given to the armed band that operated out of the Gaza Strip under the direction of Egyptian intelligence.

During the same years 1950–1956, the Jordanian army fired at will from its positions on the walls of the Old City of Jerusalem, dominating a considerable portion of western Jerusalem, into the heart of the city, causing loss of life and damage to property. Traffic on the western approaches of the Tel Aviv–Jerusalem highway was at the mercy of this army, which fired periodically on moving vehicles. At night, armed bands would infiltrate into settlements in the mountains and the coastal plain, reaching as far as the outskirts of Tel Aviv, where they carried out acts of murder and sabotage. Road mines and ambushes were frequent, and large areas along Israel's borders, particularly in the Hebron mountain area, were unsafe for both daytime and nighttime travel. Consequently, these areas were largely deserted except for army patrols, which invariably met with fire from the Jordanian army and from the Arab villages on the other side of the cease-fire line. The exercise of Israeli sovereignty and control over these areas was thus made very difficult.

The Syrian army shelled the settlements of Upper Galilee from its positions and fortifications on the Golan Heights, causing casualties and heavy property damage and interfering with agricultural work in the fields, regular traffic on the roads, and such vital development projects as the conveyance of water from the Jordan to southern Israel. Approaching the settlements in the area involved great personal risk. Commando units of the Syrian army laid ambushes and periodically attacked settlements to commit acts of murder or sabotage. These actions continued and even increased in intensity in the years prior to the Six Day War, particularly during the laying of the national water carrier from the north to the south of the country. The entire region east of Zemach to Al-Hamma along the Yarmuk River within Israel's international border and the armistice line was in fact under Syrian control from 1951 to 1967.

Following the Sinai Campaign of 1956, Egypt altered its policy of guerrilla and border warfare against Israel. The activities of both the regular army and the irregular armed groups were discontinued. Jordan also altered its policy, although its army remained in its former positions in Jerusalem and along Israel's borders. The army ceased its direct involvement in border incidents, and the Jordanian government, moreover, made marked efforts to curb attacks by irregular forces from its territory into Israel. Despite these efforts, however, armed bands continued from time to time to infiltrate from Jordanian territory into Israel, causing injury to citizens and damage to property. In 1965, the Al-Fatah organization was established, and its military arm, El Asifah, began systematic acts of murder and sabotage inside

Israel. The major base for the organization's activities was Judea and Samaria, then under Jordanian rule.

The Six Day War and the occupation of the Golan Heights, Judea and Samaria, Sinai, and the Gaza Strip by the Israel Defense Forces (IDF) afforded greater strategic depth for Israel's defense and removed the settlements within Israel's pre-1967 borders from vulnerability to attack by the armed forces of these states.

As a result, the 1967–1970 war of attrition between Egypt's regular army and the IDF along the Suez Canal was conducted far from any Israeli civilian settlements. During these years, the Jordanian army engaged the Israeli forces in the Jordan Valley, primarily with artillery fire, directed as well against the new settlements established there. The Syrian army fired periodically on the new settlements on the Golan Heights, and Syrian commando units attacked the settlements there, resulting in serious interchanges of fire and military confrontations. At times, though infrequently, the Syrians allowed terrorist actions from territory under their control or allowed the passage of armed units affiliated with the PLO on their way to targets in Israel.

The post–Six Day War period was characterized by the growth and consolidation of armed PLO-related groups and an increase in acts of subversion and sabotage in the administered territories and in Israel. Later, these groups extended their activities to include Israeli and other targets outside Israel and throughout the world—primarily in Asia and Europe but also in the United States and Latin America.

Until 1970, Jordan served as the major base for organizing, equipping, and dispatching terrorist units to Judea, Samaria, and Israel. Since the September 1970 civil war in Jordan, during which the PLO's armed organizations were suppressed by the Jordanian army, Jordan has ceased to serve as a permanent base for these activities. Indeed, the Jordanian army has in the meantime consistently taken firm action against attempts at terrorist organization and activity from Jordanian territory into Israel, Judea, and Samaria. Despite these efforts, which were generally sincere, the army has not succeeded in preventing the use of Jordanian territory as an arsenal for munitions and explosives smuggled from Syria to Jordan and across the Jordan River to terrorist units in Judea and Samaria. Despite intensive intelligence and preventive activities, moreover, it has not succeeded in preventing the occasional infiltration of armed units into Jordanian territory, where these units have organized themselves for acts of murder and sabotage in the administered territories and in Israel.

During this period, Syria adopted a different policy. Except for isolated cases, it has not permitted activities by PLO groups from its territory into Israel. Even in these isolated cases, the action was carried out with the authorization and under the supervision of the Syrian army. On the other hand, it allowed the organization and placement of forces of the PLA in its territory, under the supervision of the Syrian army, and permitted the PLO-affiliated organizations, particularly the one which arose under its aegis, El Saiyka, to set up training and supply bases within Syria, and even aided in the supplying and training of these forces.

Syria also encouraged the PLO's armed units to establish bases in Lebanon, transforming that country into the primary base for all armed attacks by the PLO against Israel. These actions threatened the very sovereignty and integrity of Lebanon, resulting in a bloody civil war and the effective takeover by the Syrian army of most of the country (except for a narrow strip in southern Lebanon bordering on Israel). Since the civil war, and particularly since the Syrian takeover of Lebanon, the terrorist organizations have achieved a recognized status in the country and have completely taken over large areas, where they set up their bases and enjoy unlimited freedom of action against Israel. Today, the terrorist organizations in Lebanon are equipped with the best Soviet infantry weapons, including anti-tank and antiaircraft missiles, mortars, artillery, armored cars, and tanks.

A further characteristic of the post–Six Day War period has been the attempt to establish clandestine armed terrorist groups within the administered territories themselves, in order to establish bases of armed resistance and to inspire violent resistance and civil disobedience among the local residents. The role of these groups has been to engage the IDF forces in the administered territories, to intimidate and impose their authority on the population, to prevent cooperation with the military government, and to set out from the territories to perform acts of murder and sabotage within Israel itself. At the same time, attempts were made to organize terrorist units from among the Arab residents of Israel. In the years 1967–1969, repeated attempts were made to establish permanent bases in the mountain areas, in caves and mountain settlements in the districts of Jenin, Tulkarm, Hebron, and the areas east of Nablus and Ramallah. Through great effort and considerable losses, the IDF succeeded in wiping out these bases.

Throughout this period, the infiltration of armed units via the Jordan River into the Jordan Valley and the mountain settlements continued until the closing of the river crossings by the IDF on the one hand and the liquidation of the terrorist bases in Jordan by the

Jordanian army on the other. From then on, terrorist activity has been based in small clandestine cells in the cities and villages, the primary task being to set off bombs and booby-trap devices, either according to instructions received from the terrorist organization centers in Lebanon or on the terrorists' own initiative. At first, terrorist units operated primarily in the territories themselves and in Jerusalem, causing casualties among the IDF forces and among the Jewish and Arab citizens in the territories. In recent years, these organizations have altered their tactics. Because of the numerous victims within the Arab population itself, terrorist activities in the territories were substantially reduced while those within Israel proper were expanded. The open borders between Israel and the administered territories, the free and uncontrolled movement of tens of thousands of workers, tradesmen, and visitors from the territories and Arab countries in Israel, the temporary dwelling of thousands of Arabs from the territories in Israel, their familiarity with the objectives and targets, and their knowledge of Hebrew—all these greatly facilitate "hit and run" attacks and the placing of explosive charges in buses, markets, population centers, streets, and stores. Such actions have increased in recent years, causing many casualties.

The Gaza Strip became a center for terrorist activity during the 1969–1972 period. Terrorist units established themselves in the refugee camps, in the villages, and especially in the orange groves of the region. From here they set out to attack IDF forces in the Gaza Strip itself and civilian settlements nearby and in Israel. Only through concentrated and continued action did the IDF succeed in routing terrorists from the Gaza Strip in 1972, achieving relative calm since then. Here, too, as in Judea and Samaria, the terrorists operated out of small clandestine cells and redirected their activities to Israeli territory. The terrorist activities in the cities and settlements south of Tel Aviv and within Tel Aviv itself orignated in units based in Gaza, which, like their counterparts in Judea and Samaria, are free to act largely because of the ease with which they can travel and mingle with the population after the completion of an attack.

Despite the substantial successes of the Israeli security forces in their diversified war against the terrorist groups, Israel could not put a complete stop to their activities. This failure can be attributed to the terrorists' methods of organization, secrecy, and communication, the concealment of explosives, the variety of attack methods used, and especially to their ability to find shelter and to mingle with the population in the administered territories where they are like "fish in water." The integration of the terrorists within the population in which they live, their ordinary and innocent occupations (workers, students, farmers), the sympathetic conspiracy of silence in their environment or the fear of reprisals should they be handed over to the IDF, the ease with which they mingle with the local population in the territories, and the difficulty in distinguishing between them and the Israeli population—all these greatly facilitate their activities. Moreover, setting out from one's home to commit an act of sabotage and returning home after its completion are to all appearances innocent activities, especially in the case of delayed charges hidden in containers which appear equally innocent. Neither is the concealment of the weapons and explosives difficult. Since the quantities are small, they can be hidden in stone fences, caves, holes dug in the ground, and even in the houses themselves in the labyrinth of the casbahs of Nablus, Hebron, and other towns, not to speak of the villages. Moreover, deadly explosives can be improvised at home from easily obtainable materials which serve normal civilian purposes, and the charges can be prepared close to the time of the action and all signs of them concealed afterward.

Implications for Future Security

Israel has learned some lessons and drawn a number of conclusions from its bitter experience with constant terror during these years. The basic lesson is that it is impossible to maintain orderly life, industrial and agricultural development, and large-scale immigrant absorption in Israel without ensuring internal security.

In order to ensure internal security, it is not sufficient to fight terror within Israel and along its borders. Rather, it is neccessary to extend the war to the territory of the states that grant support and protection to terrorists, aiding them with training, equipment, and weapons, and serving as staging areas for acts against Israel. The war against terror must therefore adopt an offensive rather than merely a defensive strategy. It must be well-planned, aggressive, and continuous wherever terrorists are to be found, using all means available and engaging the terrorist forces in their own self-protection. The concern for the safety and defense of their bases will limit the terrorists' freedom of movement and action and interfere with their actions against targets in Israel.

A third lesson is that the burden of responsibility for terror originating in the neighboring states must be placed on the states themselves, and they must suffer the consequences through reprisals, based on the principle of self-defense, against military objectives within their territory. Israel cannot rely on the readiness of other states (such as Jordan) to take action of their own free will against terrorists;

it must maintain a constant deterrent threat against these states in case their own actions should flag or be ineffective.

It is necessary also to establish effective early warning and control mechanisms along the borders and an internal security network in the cities and settlements and to provide for the permanent protection of the beaches, public institutions and facilities, schools, and centers of population throughout the year. Israel must provide for the early detection of terrorists and explosive charges and deal immediately with all incidents. Also, there must be continuing education of the public to be on the alert for terrorist actions and particularly to aid in the detection of explosive charges. At the same time, the public must learn to maintain self-restraint following the perpetration of such atrocities, to avoid taking the law into their own hands and retaliating against those who may be innocent.

Another important implication is the need for a network of relations and a system of "checks and balances" with regard to the population of the administered territories aimed at creating a buffer between them and the terrorists and thus preventing active cooperation. Although the local residents may not hand over the terrorists to the security forces, they may well refrain from sheltering them, thus forcing them to protect themselves by transferring their operations to other areas. (Implementing this policy has noticeably reduced acts of terror within the territories themselves.) Economic and social freedom and a higher standard of living, freedom of expression and movement, and the fear of losing these benefits were placed on one side of the scale, with prompt and severe punishment for offenders and those who aid them on the other. Although there have been ups and downs in the active cooperation of the local residents with the terrorists (as there have been in the policy of the IDF toward the local population), on the whole, most of the population has refrained from actively aiding the terrorists or from being recruited in large numbers to their ranks.

With regard to exposure to acts of terror, it is immaterial whether a settlement is located near or far from the border. With the perfection of the means of penetrating Israel's borders from the sea, and at times even from the air, and particularly given the terrorists' considerable freedom of movement in Israel, at least for those living in the administered territories, every settlement is in danger of attack. On the other hand, the strengthening and extension of security settlements limit the terrorists' living space, freedom of movement, and ability to hide.

At the same time, it should be recalled that the maintenance of internal security constitutes an appreciable economic, military, and psychological burden on the Israeli population. A fixed number of the defense forces, including army, police, and security services, devote their time to protecting the public and fighting terror. A special voluntary organization—the Civil Guard—was established, encompassing tens of thousands of members whose role is to maintain day-to-day security in the settlements. In addition, thousands of reserve soldiers are engaged in the protection of the beaches, cities, and settlements. It is doubtful whether there is another country in the world where proportionately so many citizens are engaged daily in maintaining internal security.

Still, Israel must be prepared for an extended war against terrorism. The massive financial and moral support provided by all the Arab states (here no distinction should be made between the Rejection Front—the radical wing of the PLO—and other Arab states), the high degree of security which the terrorists and their organizations enjoy in these countries, where they can set up military bases undisturbed, the political and material support of the Soviet Union and the countries of the Eastern bloc, the readiness of the Western international community to recognize the PLO as an equal member in the community of nations, and the minimal sanctions applied to acts of terrorism and their perpetrators in these countries—all these help ensure that terror will continue for many years. To this list should be added the reserves of manpower available to the PLO for the recruitment of terrorists.

Finally, even if autonomy should be established and accepted by some of the Palestinians (at least those living in the administered territories), there is no doubt that terrorism on the part of those groups which do not accept this solution will continue and perhaps even intensify. Even if the PLO as an organization were prepared to accept such a solution for a period of time, the rejectionist organizations within it would continue perpetrating acts of terror and sabotage against Israel and against Arab collaborators within the autonomous area. This will be all the more true should only a small segment of the Arab population in the territories take part in the autonomy administration. This segment would be subject to pressures, threats, and acts of terror by the opponents of autonomy to no lesser extent than Israel itself.

Remaining Problems of Internal Security

Several major problems of internal security remain in the present and for the future, particularly in light of the possibility that full autonomy will be granted to the population of the administered territories in accordance with the Camp David agreements and the peace treaty with Egypt.

The First Problem: Intelligence. Success in fighting terror requires a highly developed, reliable, continuous, up-to-date, and prompt intelligence network which operates in real time and which is controlled by the party interested in putting an end to the phenomenon of terror. This requires early-warning intelligence, preventive intelligence, and operational intelligence capable of dealing with terror in all its stages: pre-action organization, the detection and apprehension of arms, and the foiling of terrorist activities before they are carried out; the immediate detection of the perpetrators, abettors, dispatchers, and munitions after the terrorist action is carried out in order to prevent both its successful exploitation and the increased activity which follow such successes; prompt and efficient investigation of suspects in order to uncover their associates, abettors, weapons, and caches of explosives. Such an intelligence network requires organization, efficient management, determination, initiative, and imagination in its methods of action, and especially complete and centralized day-to-day control and uncompromising devotion to the task.

As the primary factor in the fight against clandestine subversive forces, the intelligence network cannot be controlled from afar or by proxy. The party in charge of intelligence may have the best intentions, but if it does not have a vital interest in the outcome of the intelligence actions—if it does not view it as a life-and-death issue—it will not succeed. Even when the intelligence is completely controlled by an interested sovereign government, it encounters serious difficulties in detecting underground and terrorist cells. (It will suffice to note the example of the relatively limited success of the Italian security authorities in taking effective action against the Red Brigades and other terrorist groups of both the left and the right.) On the other hand, when there is a slackening in the control over intelligence in a sovereign state interested in wiping out terror, acts of subversion and latent and overt terror increase to the point where the state loses complete control of the situation. It can be assumed that the growth in acts of internal terror and sabotage in Syria today are partly the result of the weakening of President Assad's and his government's control over intelligence. This is all the more true where the intelligence service is in the hands of a party whose interest in wiping out terror is at best questionable and which at worst actively cooperates with the terrorist organizations. The inference is quite clear: the intelligence service and its sources must be controlled by the party most interested in fighting terror (in our case, Israel), when possible, with the material and sincere cooperation of local intelligence service and agents.

The Second Problem: Freedom of Action of the Antiterrorist Forces.
Although intelligence is basic and central to the fight against terror,
it will not succeed if the interested party cannot act quickly on
intelligence information to subvert terrorist actions before they are
carried out, apprehending those responsible together with their
arms, or, alternatively, to seek out and arrest the perpetrators after
the completion of such actions. This requires reliable army and/or
police forces and special units trained in antiterrorist action.

Even if another party—such as the self-governing authority,
which is not the party directly interested in fighting terror—should
possess such forces, properly trained and of sufficient numbers,[3] and
even if this party should possess the political desire to undertake
antiterrorist action, there is no certainty that these forces, drawn from
the same people from whom the terrorists themselves arose, will
act with absolute devotion to subvert terrorist actions. The terrorists
they are bound to fire on or arrest belong to their own people, perhaps
even their own families. Moreover, not a few of those designated for
antiterrorist action may well identify with the aims of the terrorists.
It will be easy for the terrorists to recruit informers from within
these forces who will warn them of every movement and action
planned by the local police, thus enabling the terrorists to escape, to
change their places of hiding and weapons caches, and to shift their
area of operations or target of activity. Members of these forces can
also be expected to aid terrorists by providing shelter and escape
routes even after their apprehension. Experience has shown that
reliability, loyalty, unlimited devotion to the cause, and the un-
equivocal national and personal interest of the antiterrorist forces are
vital to the success of military and police actions, especially when they
involve personal risk of life. (The local policeman or soldier may well
ask himself on each such occasion why he should risk his life to
prevent actions by his brothers against Israelis.)

Thus, we cannot escape the conclusion that an effective war
against terror requires that the interested party—Israel—bear most of
this burden. It must enjoy freedom of action within the autonomous
area—when possible, through maximum cooperation with the local
police force. Within the framework of this responsibility, the Israeli
security forces will patrol the borders, especially along the Jordan
River, in order to prevent the infiltration of terrorists and the
smuggling of arms and explosives.

[3] It is reasonable to assume that this was the intention of the formulators of
section A, paragraph 2, of the Camp David agreements in saying that the self-
governing authority would have a "strong local police force."

The Third Problem: Authority to React against Terrorists. No less important than the foregoing is the question of the authority over the investigation of suspects, the place of and responsibility for their detention, the guarding of the detained terrorists during the investigation, and their imprisonment after trial.

The power of investigation. The investigation of detainees is vital in obtaining information for the exposure of collaborators, abettors, places of hiding, and arms caches. It is especially important to ensure immediate action on information obtained through investigation, before members or collaborators can be warned and thus have time to hide, to change their place of hiding, or even to leave the region or the country. Similarly, it is important to take prompt action to uncover arms, explosives, and documents. In whose hands should these powers be placed? In the hands of local investigators who are of the same people as those they are investigating? Will such investigators make the necessary effort to report to the interested party all the information thus obtained? Will they not alter or obscure it in such a way that information obtained through investigation will be useless in follow-up action against the terrorists? Even if we optimistically assume that the local authorities responsible for the investigation will be sincere in their desire to take proper action, can we rely on the investigators themselves, or will their sympathies lie with those they are investigating?

These difficult problems can be solved by: (1) placing the investigation wholly in the hands of the Israeli security forces; (2) leaving the entire investigation in the hands of the local authorities; (3) entrusting the Israeli authorities with parts of the investigation (for example, the operational investigation immediately after the incident); or (4) having the representatives of the Israeli security forces participate in all stages of the investigation along with the local authorities. The implementation of the last two solutions will be possible only with the establishment of sincere and continuing cooperation and mutual feedback between the local authorities and the interested party, not only at the highest level but at all levels.

Placing the investigation wholly in the hands of the Israeli security forces in all matters related to acts of terror and sabotage would be effective in the investigation itself and in the immediate application of its results. Its shortcoming lies in its repudiation of the interchange of information and cooperation between the local police and investigators and the Israeli authorities, possibly resulting in the concealment, obstruction, or loss of important information conveyed to local investigators. Yet in leaving the entire investigation in the

182

hands of the local authorities, Israel would run the risk of serious disruptions to antiterrorist activities, obstructions or delays in the transmission of information, and, no less serious, the intentional transmission of misleading information.

From the point of view of Israel's security, the first solution is preferable. Alternatives (3) and (4) are also possible, whereas the second is liable to become a serious obstacle to security, nullifying all the efforts of the war against terror.

Authority over arrest and detention. It would be natural for the power of arrest to be placed in the hands of the local authorities empowered to do so by law. The same is true of detention, determining the place of detention, and guarding the security detainees and prisoners. Even if we assume that the local authorities will maintain a policy of cooperation, serious questions arise. Will the local police force exert its authority on all occasions, and in time, to arrest suspects in terrorist actions? Will it arrest the true suspects? Will it detain them long enough to complete the investigation? Will it guard them properly before their trial, and afterward should they be sentenced to imprisonment? Will it detain and imprison them in secure places, preventing their escape or release through external action?

Here, too, the preferred solution is collaboration between the Israeli forces and the local authorities. There are two alternatives available: (1) leaving the responsibility and authority for these matters completely in the hands of the local authorities; and (2) granting independent powers of arrest to representatives of the Israeli forces, along with the authority to set up and maintain detention installations for security detainees and prisoners within the administered territories or in Israel and to determine the procedures for guarding them and regulations for their treatment. From the point of view of Israeli security, the latter alternative is preferable, although this solution, like that described above, has certain essential limitations which are not necessarily in the sphere of security and will be dealt with below.

Law and justice. Above and beyond the issues discussed previously, the question arises, What laws should be applied in the autonomous territories in the case of security offenders and in the war against terror? Who shall have the authority to enact security legislation and to amend it periodically in accordance with changing circumstances and needs? What penalties will be set by law for different security offenses? Who will have the authority to establish courts to try security offenders, and what will their powers of jurisdiction be? What procedures will be adopted by the court, and who will be its judges?

On the surface, the natural, convenient, and simple solution to these questions is to retain the existing local system of laws—Jordanian in Judea and Samaria, Egyptian in Gaza—and the local civilian court system which functions according to these laws. In reality, however, the existing legislation and local court systems as they existed prior to the Six Day War in the administered territories were not adequate for the purpose of maintaining internal security and combating terror. It is for this reason that authority is today wholly in the hands of the IDF. The most salient proof of this is that the military government has been obliged to rely on special security legislation and on a system of military courts established by that legislation in order to deal with security offenses and offenders.

The question of what laws should be applied can be solved in the following ways: (1) retaining the existing security legislation, in whole or in essence, and empowering the local courts and judges to abide by it; (2) abolishing the existing security legislation and enacting new legislation directed toward an effective war on terrorism by the self-governing authority (if it is granted legislative powers)[4] or any other body[5] authorized to do so by the agreement establishing autonomy or as an integral part of the agreement itself; (3) continuing the existing legal situation without change, that is, retaining the existing security legislation and leaving jurisdiction in the hands of the existing military court system, made up of Israeli army officers; (4) retaining the security legislation, or amending it, and establishing special courts composed of local and Israeli judges; or (5) applying Israeli law and using Israeli courts for the trial, judgment, and imprisonment of those suspected of acts of terror against Israel.

From the point of view of Israel's national security, the primary implication of alternative (2) is the removal of the existing legal and judicial basis which has proved vital to effective action against terrorists and acts of terror. If authority in this matter is transferred entirely to the self-governing authorities, it is doubtful that any legislation will be enacted directly serving the war against terror. Even if the local authorities should independently enact such

---

[4] It is not the purpose of this paper to express an opinion on the granting of primary legislative powers to the autonomy authorities, but only to examine its effect on security.

[5] Such a body might be a joint committee of the signatory parties to the agreement established specifically to deal with this matter.

legislation, it is unlikely that it would be as effective as that which presently exists. In this case, it is of course preferable that security legislation should be enacted by a different body or as an integral part of the agreement, on the condition that it meet the needs of the war against terror and that it be respected and maintained by the self-governing authority.

On the other hand, retaining the existing security legislation and its adoption by the local authorities (even if pre-agreed changes should be incorporated in it) will both demonstrate their sincere intention to take effective action against terror and place a legal-judicial tool in their hands for its execution. Such a solution would raise the question of who has the authority to make changes in the security legislation. Should this authority remain exclusively in the hands of the local authorities, they might, in the course of time and for a variety of reasons, make changes that would render action against terrorism (whether by local or Israeli forces) very difficult, limit the courts' authority to inflict punishment, and might ultimately completely abolish the security legislation without enacting other legislation in its place. This solution would, of course, necessitate the placing of total or partial restrictions on the legislative powers of the local authorities (should they be granted certain legislative powers).

From the point of view of internal security, and as long as terrorist actions continue, the preferred alternatives are those that retain the existing security legislation, with the provision that it cannot be changed by the local authorities without the consent of the interested party. Thus, legislative power in matters of security would in fact remain wholly in the hands of the Israeli military authorities—even if certain legislative power should be granted to the local authorities, which is still very doubtful.

The question of the powers of the courts is no less problematic. Should the local courts be empowered to adjudicate on the basis of the existing security legislation, the administration of justice may be severely impaired. The court system, and the judges themselves, may be exposed to threats, pressures, or temptations that would impair their ability to judge, even if they in fact desired to fulfill their role properly. Such a situation would seriously damage the effectiveness of antiterrorist activities.

It would therefore be preferable for the trial of security offenses to remain in the hands of the existing Israeli military judicial system. Alternatively, this problem might be addressed by the establishment of mixed courts, representing both the Israeli and the local parties. This would guarantee two objectives: a fair trial for the offender and effective justice in the war against terror.

Then there is the question of who should conduct the prosecution. Local prosecutors, like their colleagues in the judiciary, would be open to pressures and threats: those who so desire can easily avoid presenting the evidence accurately and in full, thus endangering the conviction of serious security offenders who would at best receive light sentences. Here, too, a possible solution would be the collaboration of local and Israeli prosecutors, unless the prosecution is left wholly in the hands of the Israeli authorities.

In all the alternatives mentioned above, there remains the question of the authority to pardon or to lighten the sentence of security offenders sentenced to terms of imprisonment. Placing this authority in the hands of the local authorities, even if they should be sincere in their desire to cooperate in the war against terror, would expose them to pressures and threats (similar to those exerted on the local judges and prosecutors), and the result may be that the offender who enters prison through the "front door" after conviction will be set free through the "back door" by means of a pardon or a mitigation of the sentence. It seems that here, too, the desirable solution would be to grant the local authorities limited authority to pardon or to lighten sentences, or to establish joint Israeli and local authority, unless authority is left in the hands of the Israeli authority responsible for the war against terror.

It is also possible that following the arrest of suspects in the administered territories, they will be held in existing or special detention centers in Israel under the auspices of the Israeli prison service. The suspects would be brought before Israeli courts, whether military or civilian, in accordance with Israeli law, and if convicted would serve their sentences in Israeli prisons, as is the case today for some of the prisoners residing in the territories. This is of course a remote possibility, from the point of view of both international law and the desired relationship between the self-governing authority and the State of Israel. It is very doubtful whether such an arrangement can be agreed upon in the autonomy talks. It should be recalled that, to date, Israel has refrained from transferring to Israel the trial of offenses committed in the territories, at a time when government in the territories is wholly in Israeli hands (except in cases where residents of the territories or foreigners perpetrated actions within Israeli territory or against an Israeli target abroad and were brought to trial in Israel). Although such a solution could provide simple answers to the questions of law, jurisdiction, and imprisonment (subject to appropriate legislation by the Knesset),[6] solving most of

[6] Residents of the territories suspected of perpetrating attacks in Israel are

the problems raised above as well as being expedient for the self-governing authority, which would be exempt from dealing with such delicate issues, it is doubtful that such an agreement can be reached in the autonomy talks.

Thus, it seems that the solution must be found within the framework of the laws and powers of legislation, jurisdiction, and imprisonment now existing in the territories, while limiting the powers of the self-government authority to amend the security legislation and protecting the powers of the IDF in matters of internal security. Mixed Israeli and local courts can provide a possible solution to the question of jurisdiction, including pardons and the mitigation of sentences. Cooperation between the Israeli security forces and the local forces is also most desirable in the areas of arrest, investigation, prosecution, and imprisonment, on the clear condition that in disputed cases, the decision will remain in the hands of the Israeli security forces.

Conclusion

The question where to place responsibility for the components of the war against terror in the administered territories after autonomy is achieved entails not only the practical, operative, and technical issues discussed above, but also a fundamental ethical question: Is it right to place in the hands of the local authorities responsibility in a sphere which means constant war between brothers, where a substantial portion of the local public in the territories is likely to identify with the terrorists and their aims? This public will view the war against terror as one that is not their own, recoiling from it and from the need to act as policemen in order to ensure the safety and protection of a neighbor for whom they feel no sympathy. Even if they are willing to take this upon themselves, will they be able to carry out this task over an extended period of time? In view of this, it seems inevitable that internal security should remain wholly in the hands of the Israeli security forces. At the very least, responsibility and authority should be shared by both parties in such a way that each side will be able to fulfill its part without daily imposing on the local bodies difficult and even impossible decisions.

---

brought to trial in Israeli courts in accordance with the regulations enacted in 1967: Extension of Emergency Regulations (Judea and Samaria, the Gaza Strip, the Sinai Region, and the Golan Heights)—Jurisdiction and Legal Aid—1974. These regulations have been extended by the Knesset every two years. In cases of offenses committed outside Israel's jurisdictional borders against an Israeli target, the offender can be brought to trial in Israel, in accordance with section 5 of the Penal Code 1977.

On the other hand, what meaning will the autonomy arrangements for self-government have if an external force has the right, whenever it deems fit and at its own discretion, to enter the domain of the individual to conduct searches and arrests, to bring citizens to trial, and to imprison them for security offenses? Will not the entire idea of autonomy thus be meaningless? This would undoubtedly constitute a significant restriction of individual and civil freedom (though this would also be true were the war against terror to be properly conducted by the local authorities), causing daily interference in civilian life and infringing on the local population's ability to conduct a fully autonomous life. Is there not a danges that the Israeli forces, on the pretext of maintaining internal security, will interfere also in the conduct of other internal affairs in the absence of a clear line distinguishing between what contributes to security and what does not? It may be possible to define what is to be permitted and forbidden in these areas in the autonomy agreements and security legislation. However, it is doubtful whether such distinctions can be maintained in practice, in the heat of pursuit.

Not imposing any restrictions might well subject both the individual and the public at large to the arbitrary decisions of the security forces, whether warranted or not. On the other hand, subjecting every action by Israeli forces to the agreement or approval of the local authorities is likely to impede effective antiterrorist action.

In opposition to this cardinal question, there stands another question raised at the beginning of the discussion. Can Israel, which has had to endure countless acts of terror which have constituted a constant threat to its internal security, to the lives and property of its residents,[7] and to orderly life in the state, be able to entrust its internal security to an external force which may not be at all interested in effectively fighting terror and, even if it were, whose hands would be tied—if not politically, then at least from the point of view of ideological and emotional identification?

We have now seen how difficult it is for a sovereign state such as Jordan to supervise and control terrorist organization, infiltration, and action from its territory into Israel. This is the case even though Jordan has a strong interest in not allowing its territory to be used as a base for terrorist actions against Israel and has a loyal army that

[7] According to the data of the IDF history department, from April 1967 through February 1980 there were 3,174 terrorist attacks in the territories and 1,306 in Israel. The casualties in these attacks were 230 Israeli citizens killed and 3,303 injured. In 1973-1979, 31 local Arab residents were killed and 1,961 injured in terrorist actions in the territories. All this is in addition to enormous damage to property both in Israel and the territories.

has made and continues to make sincere efforts to prevent terrorist action. We have also seen how difficult it is for such sovereign states as Italy and Spain (in the Basque region), which are determined to eradicate terror in their countries.

Whatever autonomy arrangements are agreed upon, there is no doubt that the danger to Israel's internal security will be greater after the establishment of autonomy than it is today, especially if the two-way freedom of movement of people, workers, goods, and vehicles between Israel and the territories continues. Judea, Samaria, and the Gaza Strip can easily become strongholds, bases, and hide-outs for terrorist groups opposed to Israel, enabling them to act with relative security within Israeli territory, which they cannot do today. Internal security is thus no less crucial to the maintenance of orderly life in Israel than is external security. It is hard to imagine how internal security can be effectively maintained within the 1967 boundaries alone. This proved ineffective in the past when Israel found it necessary to initiate punitive and reprisal actions in the territory of the neighboring countries in order to curb terrorist actions and to force the sovereign Arab states to take action against the perpetrators of these acts.

The proposal to restrict the Israeli security forces' freedom of action to the area within the 1967 boundaries is tantamount to closing Israel's borders, barring any movement from the territories into Israel or placing severe restrictions on entry into Israel, with all that this implies for the maintenance of the economic link between the territories and Israel and the gradual development of normal and peaceful relations between the people of Israel and the residents of the territories. Such a solution could only increase the mutual alienation, hatred, and hostility, and as a result further incite terrorist actions from the territories against Israel.

The question, then, is, What is preferable? The preferable solution seems to be autonomy with limited security responsibility. This places internal security, with a certain amount of local cooperation, in the hands of the Israeli authorities. With all the disadvantages this entails, there remains the hope that, with the consolidation and strengthening of the autonomous entity on the one hand and the success of the war against terror on the other, there will be less need for direct action by the Israeli defense forces within the autonomous area. Under such circumstances, interference in the orderly lives of the local residents and the management of internal affairs would be minimal. This solution seems preferable to the military and political chaos that might result from the inability of the "strong" local police forces to deal effectively with terror, forcing Israel to dispatch army units to regain control over terrorist bases and centers of violence in order to fulfill its vital interest in maintaining internal security and protecting the lives of its citizens. Such a development would essentially nullify the whole idea of autonomy. It is reasonable to assume that Israel's ability to ensure internal security and tranquillity within its borders and the autonomous area in the short run will be of primary importance to the normalization of life in Israel and the administered or autonomous territories and, in the long run, to the peaceful coexistence between them.

8

The Palestinian Features of Jordan

Mordechai Nisan

The Hashemite Kingdom of Jordan has been intimately involved in matters relating to Palestinian Arabs, the areas of Judea and Samaria, and a workable relationship between Jews and Arabs in the land of Israel (or Palestine) for well over thirty years. That time has seen an ongoing attempt to define clearly the character of "Palestinians," their peoplehood, and their possible statehood. There has been correspondingly little effort in defining "Jordanians" and their political identity. Consideration of the latter question provides an important and perhaps new slant in dealing with the corresponding issues regarding Palestinian Arabs.

The history of modern Jordan is rooted in two factors which have played a dominant role in that country's life until today: foreign intervention and military force. Both the strengths and the weaknesses of the kingdom are derived from these factors, and they have proved vital to the very survival of the regime of King Hussein, who took power in 1953.

On May 26, 1921, Winston Churchill, as British colonial secretary, authorized the creation of the Emirate of Transjordan on the eastern side of historical Palestine. By imperial fiat the British Mandatory regime entered into what was then defined as a "temporary arrangement" for a period of six months. Abdullah, the son of Sharif Hussein of Mecca, became the ruler of approximately three-quarters of historical Palestine (the area from the sea to the desert on both sides of the Jordan River)—the territory set aside for the realization of a Jewish national home as promised by the Balfour Declaration. It was not only Abdullah's religious sensitivity but also his political sense that brought him to declare, "He [God] granted me success in creating the Government of Transjordan by having it

NOTE: The research for this paper was made possible through the support of the Leonard Davis Institute of International Relations at the Hebrew University of Jerusalem.

separated from the Balfour Declaration."[1] For the moment, the new Arab entity had a purpose, albeit a negative one, but it was not clear it had a positive identity in national and political terms.

Prior to the Churchill-Abdullah meeting in Jerusalem, where Transjordan was officially recognized, Abdullah had ridden north from the Hejaz through Maan and into Amman with a few thousand warriors. His Bedouin tribesmen constituted a military force in a land that had been without law and order since the collapse of the Turkish Empire in the First World War. Nomadic incursions and tribal warfare had for many years denied orderly rule even when the Ottoman regime still existed. In an area of about two hundred thousand people, with no special national identity, with no government institutions, Abdullah's forces became the organizational backbone of the future Transjordanian state. Transjordan was an army before it was a state, and Jordan, its successor in 1950, would be a state before becoming a nation.

The links between Transjordan and the western portion of Palestine were diversified and intense in the period prior to 1948. Abdullah carried his family's dream of a Greater Syria, including Syria, Lebanon, Transjordan, and Palestine, which would be the center of a united Arab kingdom throughout the Middle East. His particular interest in western Palestine and its Arab population was first expressed no later than 1934, when he suggested annexing the territory to save it from the Zionist movement. In 1937 the British Peel Commission raised the idea of Abdullah's taking over the Arab parts of Palestine, apparently because there seemed not to be any other Arab figure west of the river with sufficient authority, strength, and stability to do the job.

At the same time Palestinian Arabs west of the Jordan continued a tradition going back to Turkish times of serving in the East Bank's administration. Families from Nablus (Shechem), such as the Tuqans and al-Hadis, occupied key positions in the Transjordanian government erected after 1921 under Abdullah. This elite movement eastward was accompanied by larger population movements in the same direction resulting from fear of the Turkish military draft in World War I, Zionist competition in land acquisition, and the poor Palestinian economy in the 1920s. In this way, Transjordan played an important role as a protector of Palestinian Arab interests and as a focus for their collective needs.

[1] Howard M. Sacher, *The Emergence of the Middle East: 1914-1924* (New York: Alfred A. Knopf, 1969), p. 404.

A number of historical works on the period point to a specific British intention regarding the ultimate purpose of Transjordan. Palestine west of the river became the sole field for Jewish national aspirations following the 1922 decision to "postpone or withhold" the application of the Mandate in the eastern part of Palestine. Transjordan was consequently identified as the home of Arab national aspirations in Palestine. Sir Alec Kirkbride, who served as the British minister to Jordan after 1948 but whose career began in Transjordan in the 1930s, has written that the east side of the river was considered for the "resettlement of Arabs once the National Home for the Jews in Palestine . . . became an accomplished fact." [2] Christopher Sykes also has suggested that a plan existed to transfer Arabs from the west to the east bank of the Jordan.[3] In all this it appears that the imperial creation of Transjordan was seen by the British as a future political framework for Palestinian Arab aspirations. A state that has often been defined as "artificial" would thereby acquire national content and political purpose.[4]

Events during 1947–1948 led to a situation whereby Jordan became the Arab successor state in Palestine. The Arabs rejected the United Nations Partition Resolution, a Jewish state arose, and the remainder of Palestine was conquered and annexed by Transjordan. The area taken was called the West Bank. Adding 2,165 square miles to the 35,550 square miles on the East Bank, the West Bank constituted just 6 percent of all Jordanian territory. The approximately 300,000 population of the East Bank rose to about 400,000 following the influx of 90,000 refugees who fled western Palestine and crossed the river during the 1948 war. In addition, approximately 200,000 or 250,000 Arabs leaving the territory of Israel had entered the West Bank, augmenting its population to about 700,000 people. Jordan— so called since the change of name from Transjordan in April 1949— was geographically centered on the East Bank (94 percent of its territory) and demographically centered on the West Bank (64 percent of its population). The political significance of these developments was not long in dawning: they served to alter the face of Abdullah's sleepy desert emirate established in the courts of princes and in the tents of warriors.

[2] Sir Alec Kirkbride, *A Crackle of Thorns* (London: John Murray, 1956), p. 19.
[3] Christopher Skyes, *Cross Roads to Israel* (London: Collins, 1965), p. 61.
[4] See Naseer M. Aruri, *Jordan: A Study in Political Development, 1921-1965* (The Hague: Martinus Nijhoff, 1972), pp. 5-6; Morroe Berger, *The Arab World Today* (Garden City, N.Y.: Doubleday, 1964), p. 192.

Palestinian Features

An analysis of Palestinian aspects in Jordanian society and statehood touches on the gap between the country's official identity and its unofficial reality. Jordan is a Hashemite kingdom whose regime is rooted in a hereditary dynasty headed by a king who rules for life. According to this political foundation, which resembles a medieval European belief in the divine right of monarchy,[5] political transformations should not affect the structure of government or the direction of policy in Jordan.

The formal definition of the regime does not always reflect the underlying social realities, and the discrepancy between the two spheres is an index of the regime's representative function and political stability. While the annexation of the West Bank in 1950 aggrandized the Hashemite rule in Transjordan, adding territory, population, and prestige, it also introduced potentially unstable elements into the rather sturdy political structure on the east bank of the river. Ever since, Jordanians have continued to evaluate the relative costs and benefits deriving from their involvement with the Palestinian Arab question.

Demography. Although the figures vary according to different sources, the predominant impression is that Palestinians constitute over 50 percent of the Jordanian population. Aruri, Schmelz, Sinai, and others estimate the Palestinian component to be from 50 to 65 percent of approximately 1.8 million people on the East Bank.[6] The Palestine Liberation Organization (PLO) in 1971 referred to 960,000 Palestinians in Jordan; in 1974 they referred to 1 million Palestinians; and in 1975 Arafat claimed that in Jordan there are "more than a million Palestinians."[7] The massive movement of Palestinians eastward since 1948 has left the more indigenous Transjordanian stock a minority. This migration reversed the trend of a century or more of

---

[5] The Hashemite family claims direct descent from the house of Hashim, the tribal clan of the prophet Mohammed. His service as the messenger of Allah accords the Hashemites with a divine right to special political status.

[6] See Anne Sinai and Allen Pollack, eds., *The Hashemite Kingdom of Jordan and the West Bank* (New York: American Professors for Peace in the Middle East [APPME], 1977), p. 36; A. Shmelz, "Demographic Development of Arab States in our Region" (Hebrew), *The New East*, vol. 1 (1973), pp. 29-45; and Uriel Dann, "Regime and Opposition in Jordan Since 1949," in Menachem Milson, ed., *Society and Political Structure in the Arab World* (New York: Humanities Press, 1973), pp. 145-81.

[7] *International Documents on Palestine, 1975*, reported in *Al Thawra*, Beirut, January 1, 1978.

migration from the East to the West Bank. In essence, the same population stock reversed course.

While Jordan ruled the area from 1949 to 1967, about 400,000 Arabs moved from the West Bank to the eastern side of the river. This massive population movement was not forced by the regime, nor was it a product of political tension. Two basic reasons explain it: the economic strength of the East Bank as an investment center and job market, and its political centrality as the kingdom's capital and focus of governmental activity. Large numbers of Palestinian Arabs moved, seeking better jobs and greater personal opportunities. The linguistic-religious-ethnic-social affinity between the two banks made this process quite tolerable. The short distances involved—from Nablus to Amman is only 45 miles—also made the move relatively unproblematic. The move resembled a change of address from one part of a familiar landscape to another, rather than an uprooting experience as refugees have known.

The East Bank population rose as that of the West Bank fell. In 1952 the East Bank contained 587,000 people, compared with 742,000 on the West Bank. By 1961, the East Bank had grown to 879,000 and had surpassed the West Bank figure of 801,000.[8] The demographic advantage enjoyed by the West Bank following the annexation had disappeared and seemed unlikely to return. By 1967, before the Six Day War, the East Bank population reached slightly over 1 million, while that of the West Bank was static at approximately 800,000. To sum up: the percentage of Jordan's population residing on the East Bank rose from 36 in 1949, to 45 in 1952, to 52 in 1961, and to 58 in 1967. The geographic predominance of the East Bank was now complemented by its demographic predominance.

The impact of the 1967 war generated a continuation of the historical process of a population exodus to the East Bank. During and immediately after the military hostilities, 200,000 Arabs left the West Bank—about one in every five inhabitants of the territory sought security and prosperity on the East Bank.[9] This rapid increase of the Palestinian population in the East Bank was not an isolated development, dramatic as it was. From 1968 to 1978, West Bank migrants to the East Bank numbered about 100,000; during the years 1974–1977 the annual exit from the West Bank reached 15,000 peo-

---

[8] Moshe Efrat, *Palestinian Refugees: Social and Economic Research, 1949-1974* (Tel Aviv: Tel Aviv University, 1976; in Hebrew), pp. 21-30.

[9] Peter Dodd and Halim Barakat, *River without Bridges: A Study of the Exodus of the 1967 Palestinian Arab Refugees* (Beirut: Institute for Palestine Studies, 1969), p. 1.

ple.[10] Not all the migrants remained in Jordan, for the economic opportunities of Kuwait, Saudi Arabia, and other lands with large job markets beckoned Palestinians to their shores. But Jordan, on the East Bank, has always been the major destination for Palestinian migrants.

By the end of the 1970s the population of Jordan on the East Bank was nearing the 2 million mark, while the West Bank population was close to what it had been thirty years earlier (700,000). The population of the East Bank had become more and more Palestinian, housing almost three times more Palestinian Arabs than the West Bank. Jordan was the demographic center of the Palestinian population.

Politics. In order for Jordan to demonstrate its claim to be the Arab successor to Palestine, the Hashemite regime opened its political system to Palestinian elements. This development was not a necessary democratic response in the light of demographic developments just discussed, but rather a political response to legitimize Jordan's territorial annexation of the West Bank and its desire to speak for the Palestinian Arabs after 1948.

Immediately following the takeover in 1949, three Palestinians from the West Bank were brought into the Jordanian cabinet, and a year later five of the eleven ministers were Palestinians. Loyal elements were co-opted into senior government positions, though the powerful and sensitive Ministry of Interior was withheld, by and large, from Palestinians. Of a total of eighteen prime ministers appointed by the king, six were Palestinians: Tawfiq al-Huda from Acre, Samir al-Rifa'i from Zefat, Ibrahim Hashim from Nablus, Husayn Fakri al-Khalidi from Jerusalem, Ahmad Tuqan from Nablus, and General Muhammad Da'ud, also from Jerusalem. Palestinians were welcomed into Jordanian cabinets to the extent that they served the regime's purposes.[11]

It is noteworthy that two attempted coups were organized by Transjordanian figures: Tal in 1949 and Nabulsi in 1957. The Palestinians Da'ud and Tuqan were appointed to be prime ministers in 1970 when the regime faced a dire threat from PLO factions seeking to undermine Hashemite rule. This turn of events points to the firm cohesion that developed in Jordanian ruling circles between traditional East Bank forces and Palestinian elements.

However, if the regime is thwarted in its attempt to represent the Palestinian Arabs—as after Rabbat in 1974 when the PLO was

[10] *Ha'aretz*, February 12, 1977; and *Rus Al-Yusuf*, June 6, 1978.
[11] Clinton Bailey, "Cabinet Formation in Jordan," in Sinai and Pollack, *Jordan and the West Bank*, pp. 102-13.

recognized as the "sole legitimate spokesman for the Palestinian people"—then Jordanization rather than Palestinization defines the political system. Palestinian cabinet membership dropped to four of twenty after 1974. It may be recalled that Jordan had included seven Palestinians in its eleven-man delegation to the Geneva Conference a year earlier in December 1973.

After the annexation of the West Bank, the Jordanian House of Representatives was composed of twenty members from each bank, increasing to thirty from each in 1962. The Senate totaled twenty, then thirty, members, and West Bank representation was usually half that number. After Rabbat, Hussein dissolved the Jordanian Parliament as if to signify his acceptance of the PLO's sole role in speaking for the Palestinians. Yet that is accurate primarily with regard to the West Bank, but not the East Bank. The Senate continued to exist with seven members of Palestinian origin, *all* from the East Bank. In 1978 a National Consultative Council was established in place of the House of Representatives: of sixty members, thirteen were Palestinians—but they, too, were all from the East Bank. In Jordan proper, Palestinians still have a major political role to fill; they are an integral and legitimate element in the regime.

In 1954 all Arabs in Jordan who were former residents of Palestine were accorded citizenship. Since 1960 all Palestinians, wherever their place of residence, can receive Jordanian citizenship. This is a concrete and clear expression of Jordan's self-perception as the Arab successor state in Palestine.

King Hussein's quest to legitimize his regime in Palestinian eyes, and in the eyes of the Arab world generally, finds expression in an old dynastic practice of linking marriage and politics. His third wife, Alia, who died in a plane crash in 1977, was the daughter of the Tuqan family from the West Bank. The Crown Prince Hassan, the king's brother, also married a woman from the West Bank, from the town of Jenin. While personal and not only political motives may have been operative, the king is no doubt sensitive to the need to symbolize publicly in his own life the link between the two banks, and particularly the role of Palestinians on the East Bank.

In this discussion it should not be forgotten that it was a Palestinian who killed King Abdullah, Hussein's grandfather, in 1951; the Palestinians led popular and party opposition to the regime in the 1950s and 1960s; and PLO factions created a kind of fedayeen "state within a state" in the late 1960s and then confronted Hussein with an open threat to his very life and rule in September 1970.

Palestinians have been co-opted into the top echelons of power in Jordan. Even former opponents associated with Hashemite enemies, like Anwar Nusseibh of Jerusalem, were brought in to serve in senior government and diplomatic posts. Yet this process has its limits—as in 1970 when 4,000 Palestinians in the ranks of the PLO were killed by a king hungry for life and fighting to rule. There is only one realistic standard for the political role of Palestinians in East Bank life: so long as they help to legitimize and strengthen the Hashemite regime, they shall be raised to power; but if they threaten the regime and endanger its very survival, they shall be dismissed and, if necessary, eliminated.

The introduction of so large a number of Palestinians into the Jordanian system on the East Bank has a definite self-destructive quality to it. It may not be an automatic suicidal device, yet the attempt to legitimize the regime seems almost the same as destroying it.

Society and Economics. The influx of large numbers of Palestinians into Jordan introduced a more advanced and educated socioeconomic element into East Bank life. The basis for Palestinian social and economic dominance is rooted in the superiority of their way of life over that of the weaker, more backward traditional elements in Transjordan. Some statistics clarify this point: in the 1930s Palestinian schools enrolled 52 percent of school-age children, compared with 28 percent on the East Bank. Between 1932 and 1944, the number of schools in western Palestine rose from 299 to 406, while the number on the East Bank remained static (157 to 155). In 1943, 34 percent of Palestinians lived in cities, while only 22 percent of Transjordanians did.[12] It was from among such Palestinian elements that large numbers crossed the river into the East Bank after 1948.

During all the years of Jordanian rule in the West Bank, economic development was overwhelmingly directed toward the East Bank. In the 1950s, two-thirds of the import licenses issued went to the East Bank and just one-third to the West Bank.[13] In June 1967 about 90 percent of the country's industrial establishments were on the East Bank.[14] In the active environment of prosperity on the East Bank, the Palestinians became the pillar of Jordan's economy, forming the banking, industrial, and commercial elite. Refugees (or migrants) from 1967 who arrived in the East Bank brought with them

[12] Aruri, *Jordan: Political Development*, pp. 33-36.
[13] Shaul Mishal, *West Bank/East Bank: The Palestinians in Jordan, 1949-1967* (New Haven and London: Yale University Press, 1978), p. 21.
[14] "Is Jordan's Economy Dependent on the West Bank?" *The Israel Economist*, vol. 23, no. 10-11 (October-November 1967), p. 225; Elias Tuma and Haim Darin-Drabkin, *The Economic Case for Palestine* (London: Croom Helm, 1978), chap. 8.

"great assets of manpower and skills,"[15] In addition, the Hashemite regime spent $160 million on rehabilitation programs to ensure that they would become fully productive elements in East Bank life.

It is an instructive human lesson that such people, notwithstanding their "newcomer status," could become the dominant elite through their experience, education, and initiative. In the socioeconomic sphere, as in others, the West Bank's loss became the East Bank's gain. The two banks are engaging in a constant competitive struggle, a kind of zero-sum game to determine the ultimate locus of Palestinian power. The victory may go to the East Bank, but it will be due not to its older Transjordanian and Bedouin elements, but to the newer, more recent Palestinian forces.

For the last few years Jordan has had hardly any unemployment to speak of (2 percent at most).[16] Foreign workers, such as Pakistanis, have been brought in to fill jobs. The economy has been strong generally throughout the 1970s. The annual growth rate in the industrial sector is 23 percent. Tourist strength on the East Bank has grown far beyond the country's capacity even when the West Bank was part of Jordan: compared with the 617,000 visitors in 1966 (which includes visitors to the West Bank), over a million visitors arrived in the East Bank alone in 1976.[17] Many of these were Lebanese sojourners fleeing from the violence of the civil war. Jordan now symbolized prosperity and stability, two key characteristics that made the East Bank a viable option for many Palestinians.

The Army. The army has been the backbone of the Hashemite regime, a servant of the state, an instrument for quelling political opposition, and a force for stability amid far-ranging social and political changes. Because of its functions and sensitive political identification with the regime, the army's most strategic posts have been reserved for trustworthy loyalist elements. Loyalist elements are not usually Palestinian; however, Majali, the chief of staff, is one.

Before 1970 about half the army was composed of Palestinian personnel, yet they were for the most part assigned to administrative and logistical units. Key army commands—artillery, operational ground forces, infantry—have usually been in Transjordan Bedouin hands. Since 1970, following the civil war, Palestinian numbers in the Jordanian army dropped and traditional elements tightened their control even further.

[15] Penelope Turing, "Jordan: A Sense of Purpose," *Middle East International*, vol. 86 (August 1978), pp. 25-26.

[16] *Al-Dustur*, Jordan, June 25, 1979, and July 7, 1979.

[17] Turing, *A Sense of Purpose*.

King Hussein has been successful in making safe major decisions touching on military matters involving Palestinians. Two are note-worthy: first, he refused to allow Ahmad Shukeiry, the first head of the PLO, to draft Palestinians into the Palestine Liberation Army in 1965 for fear that this new force could turn against his regime in Jordan itself. Second, he dismissed two close associates who held high army ranks, Sharif Nasser and Zeid Ben Shaker, prior to September 1970 because they were noted for their tough anti-Palestinian stand. At that point Hussein was trying to neutralize the Palestinian threat by searching for an accommodation with PLO forces. Hussein decided well in both cases. In the first, he refused to compromise and came off with his feet on the ground; in the second, he compromised momentarily but then proved he could act with both authority and vengeance. In both cases, a united, loyal army stood behind him.

The Palestinians have a place in the Jordanian army so long as their commitment to the regime remains firm. Let us recall that many Palestinians were involved in the Jordan effort which resulted in the massacre of 4,000 PLO terrorists in 1970.

Amman. The city of Amman has grown from a small town of 35,000 people in 1948 to a city of respectable size during the last thirty years. It reached a population of 108,000 in 1952 and jumped to 250,000 by 1961; before the 1967 war the city contained about 340,000 inhabitants; the population grew to a half-million by 1970 and approximately 670,000 in 1976. This rapid growth is due to the overwhelming influx of Palestinians over the years. Today two-thirds of Amman's residents are of Palestinian origin.

Two brief remarks capture the change that has taken place in the capital of Amman. In the 1950s, Peter Young, a senior British officer who served in the Arab Legion (as the Jordanian army was then called), remarked that the "traditional costumes of Palestine are common in the streets of Amman." [18] This rather quaint impression refers to the arrival of refugees after 1948. The second remark is from a report in the *New York Times*, August 3, 1975, calling Amman "the largest Palestinian city in the world." This definitive statement is a factual recognition of the primacy of the Palestinian element in the city as in no other Arab city in the Middle East. This is no longer the folklore of the 1950s but the vibrancy of the 1970s.

Amman is the political and economic center of Jordan. The status of Jerusalem was intentionally restricted during the 1949–1967 period by a regime that did not want to tolerate any competition with

[18] Peter Young, *Bedouin Command* (London: Kimber, 1956), p. 148.

Amman's singular political role in the kingdom. Government offices were transferred out of Jerusalem (the West Bank) and brought to Amman (the East Bank).[19] It was in Jerusalem, we remember, that Abdullah was assassinated.

Amman quickly became the economic hub of Jordan. In the first half of 1965, for example, no new industrial enterprises were established outside of Amman, and all major commercial and banking outfits are located there.[20] Indeed, the demographic growth of the city is testimony to this development. This is the city, one may say, that the Palestinians built.

Palestinian Identity

Our first examination of Palestinian features in Jordan has focused on the objective changes brought about during the last thirty years. The second examination of Palestinian identity as a predominant national definition of Jordan draws on the subjective attitudes expressed by Jordanian and PLO spokesmen. There is a rather close correspondence in Jordanian and Palestinian circles in absorbing and articulating the fact of the Palestinization of Jordanian life. Both sides, however, point to very different practical political conclusions; their shared perceptions do not produce shared visions.

Jordanian View. On March 1, 1950, King Abdullah issued a royal decree to forbid use of the word "Palestine" in official documents.[21] Prior to that, he had apparently suggested that his country be called the Kingdom of Palestine, but the British persuaded him to drop the idea. During the years of Hashemite rule over the West Bank, the regime consistently opposed the slogan of a "Palestine entity" and even tried to force the founding congress of the PLO to meet not in Jerusalem, as it eventually did, but in Amman. Jordan sought to eliminate any emerging Palestinian identity that could dangerously undermine the regime's legitimacy and hold on power.

Nevertheless, Jordan has been caught in a strange paradox: it rejects any separatist Palestinian trends within its territory, denies the Palestinian quality to Jordan in an official sense—yet recognizes as an unofficial reality a profound linkage between Palestinians and Jordanians and sees in that linkage the very essence of what the

---

[19] Eliezer Be'eri, *The Palestinians under Jordanian Rule* (Jerusalem: Hebrew University, 1978; in Hebrew), chap. 3.

[20] Aruri, *Jordan: Political Development*, p. 67.

[21] Mishal, *West Bank/East Bank*, pp. 1-2.

kingdom is about. Power must remain, however, in traditional Hashemite hands—those of King Hussein, whose family origins are rooted in the soil of the Hejaz in the Arabian Peninsula.

In 1962 the government of Amman published a white paper, *Jordan: The Palestine Problem and Inter-Arab Relations,* in which it recognized that the problem of Palestine "is the problem of the Jordanian homeland and the Jordanian family and the Jordanian citizen." More than any other Arab state, Jordan is integrally connected with the Palestinian issue: it is "the heir of Palestinian sorrow and hopes," and its future is linked indissolubly with that of Palestinian Arabs.

It has long been held that Palestinians and Jordanians are really "one people" (as Abdullah remarked in annexing the West Bank in 1950) because of their ethnic identity. In his plan of March 1972 for a federal pact between the banks, Hussein defined Jordan in the following manner: "This Arab country belongs to all, Jordanians and Palestinians alike. When we say Palestinians we mean every Palestinian throughout the world, provided he is Palestinian by loyalty and affinity." [22] The geographical division of Jordan into "banks" from 1949 to 1967 did not hinder an ethnic intermingling that succeeded in blurring the distinction between Palestinians and Jordanians. In this same spirit, Prime Minister Rifa'i referred in 1975 to the close union between the two banks—"a union that is now difficult to distinguish between what is Palestinian and what is Jordanian." [23] The only distinction that remains significant lies in the Hashemite hold on power, which explains why Hussein conditioned his willingness to accept all Palestinians with the proviso that they be "loyal" to the regime.

The Palestinian Jordanian citizen on the East Bank has become an integral and legitimate participant in political life there. The conviction of a Palestinian role in Jordan converges at times with a belief not only in the oneness of the two peoples but also in their shared destiny and struggle against Israel. Hussein articulated this in a dramatic manner after the battle at Karameh in March 1968 when, at that East Bank town, PLO and Hashemite units together fought off an Israeli raid. The king said, "We are likely to reach a situation in which we will all be fedayeen." Not only are Jordanians and Palestinians one people; they have one policy against a common

[22] Sinai and Pollack, *Jordan and the West Bank,* p. 134
[23] *International Documents on Palestine, 1975* (Beirut: Institute for Palestine Studies, 1977), p. 385.

enemy. The regime can hardly disassociate itself from the anti-Israel effort when it is led by Palestinian forces who, after all, are a majority in the East Bank and a legitimate factor in Jordanian life.

After a long period of open hostility and lack of contact—due to the 1970 war in Jordan and the 1974 Rabbat decision—Hussein met Yasir Arafat in 1978 for the first time in over seven years. The readiness of the regime to identify itself with Palestinian efforts against Israel is useful to avoid domestic unrest within the country. As Hussein admitted in 1967, had he not gone to war, Nasser would have overthrown his regime. An external war can be expedient, or even necessary, to avoid an internal war.

Jordan's "moderate" image in the context of the Arab-Israeli conflict is certainly questionable in a substantive sense. Following the Six Day War, Hussein, in an address at Georgetown University, raised the hope that "developments in the Arab world would one day lead to the de-Zionization of Israel." He thought peace would come when "Arabs and Jews can live together, as they have in the past, in peace, friendship and religious liberty." [24] This formula for co-existence hearkens back to the era when there was no Jewish state and Jews endured a minority status under Arab-Muslim rule, and it looks forward to the PLO version of a "secular democratic state in Palestine" in place of Israel.

Yet beyond the issue of Jordan's moderateness or absence of it lies the dilemma of Jordan's national, ethnic, and political character: its self-defined Palestinian quality makes it almost impossible for Jordan to make a settlement with Israel at the expense of the Palestinians. Even if Jordan's orientation toward Israel was authentically moderate, it must be very careful not to threaten its own political survival by taking steps for peace with the enemy of the Palestinians. A Palestinized Jordan, unable to make concessions to Israel in an effort to further peace, is a major block on the road to a settlement in the region. Alternatively, a Palestinized Jordan provides a solution for "the stateless Palestinian people" and takes the sting out of their frustrations and demands. This would make a peace settlement more feasible.

Jordan has absorbed the changes brought about by the influx of Palestinians into the East Bank into a new national definition. The regime is ready to see the country as a home for the Palestinians, while it is careful at the same time to keep them an arm's length away from a hold on true power.

[24] *New York Times*, November 7, 1967.

The PLO's View. One of the major questions about the PLO is whether their aims include taking over, not only Israel, but the kingdom of Jordan as well. The insignia-map of the PLO limits Palestine to the western portion alone; the East Bank does not appear as a national Palestinian goal. The National Covenant refers to Palestine, in article 2, "with the boundaries it had during the British Mandate" as an indivisible territorial unit. This is ambiguous because the Mandate formally included the eastern side of the river, though Transjordan was recognized as a separate unit from 1922 on. No doubt the PLO does not mind clouding the issue in order to avoid certain problems and gain advantages, possibly of time and aid.

The overall thrust of subsequent and substantive PLO attitudes, however, does identify the East Bank as a Palestinian entity and part of the homeland to be ruled, eventually, by true Palestinian elements. This approach is grounded in three sets of reasons.

Ethnic oneness. Jordanians and Palestinians are considered by the PLO as "one people," declared Farouk Kaddumi, the head of the movement's Political Department in March 1977.[25] This has been a recurring theme in PLO circles for many years. For the purposes of the struggle, the Fedayeen Consensus Agreement in May 1970 recognized "that the people in the Palestinian-Jordanian theater are one people." The same point was made even more radically by Zuhair Mohsin, the *Saika* (a military organization within the PLO under Syrian sponsorship and leadership) leader who was assassinated in the summer of 1979:

> There are no differences between Jordanians, Palestinians, Syrians and Lebanese. . . . We are one people. . . . The Palestinian state would have the right to act for all Palestinians in the Arab world and elsewhere. Once we have acquired all our rights and the whole of Palestine, we may not put off, for a moment, the re-unification of Jordan and Palestine.[26]

There is no reason for the very same people to live under different regimes in what are different parts of the very same country. There are no ethnic boundaries, and there would be, therefore, no political or territorial ones.

Even today, there is a strong sense that Palestinians who do not reside in the East Bank still accept it as home. One of the most revealing statements to indicate this came from Leila Khaled, "the lady terrorist" of the Popular Front for the Liberation of Palestine

---

[25] *Newsweek*, March 14, 1977.
[26] *Trouw* (Holland), March 31, 1977.

(PFLP) faction, who lived for many years in Lebanon and later trained in Kuwait. Upon arriving in Amman once, she declared in a personal, emotional way, "It felt good to be a Palestinian in one's homeland." [27] And this came from a woman born in Haifa! The East Bank, and Amman, the capital, were instinctively conceived to be *Palestinian* in the widest and most encompassing sense, even though the leadership at the top is non-Palestinian. Indeed, this is in accord with the demographic, political, and social reality of centuries.

National rights. At the eleventh meeting of the Palestinian National Council in 1973, a political program was drawn up that recognized that the Palestinian majority in Jordan possesses national rights. This justified the free development of the Palestinian movement in the East Bank, not as foreign intervention but as domestic mobilization. At the twelfth meeting in 1974 the call went forth for the establishment of "a democratic national authority" in Jordan that would bring to fruition complete cooperation among all elements for the Palestinian revolution. The implicit message was that Hussein, with his concern for power, blocked the road to use of all forces for the purpose of the PLO-Palestinian struggle.

Before the 1970 civil war and particularly after its dismal termination from the Palestinian point of view, PLO figures called openly for the overthrow of the "lackey Hashemite regime." Amman's historical relationships with Britain and America, and its not infrequent encounters with Palestinian opposition, led the PLO to the view that Jordan's current regime was almost as foreign and illegitimate in the region as was Israel's. In the 1960s the PLO slogan was: "We must liberate Amman before we liberate Tel Aviv," or, "The road to Palestine passes through Jordan." This claim to the East Bank reflected a Palestinian interest in ultimately eliminating, as *Fatah* (the mainstream and dominant military body in the PLO) member Abu Ayad said in December 1973, "the Israeli occupation and the Hashemite oppression." [28] Only then would the entire Palestinian homeland be ruled by its legitimate owners.

Military tactics. Blocked from using the West Bank as a staging area to launch assaults against Israel, the fedayeen see in Jordan a natural and expedient territory from which to generate a military campaign against the enemy. The vital consideration in this approach is not the regime's political illegitimacy but the country's

[27] Leila Khaled, *My People Shall Live* (London: Hodder and Stoughton, 1973), p. 118.
[28] Abu Ayad reversed the order of events: eliminating "the Hashemite oppression" is supposed to be the condition for ending "the Israeli occupation."

geographic location. Abu Mazer, head of the Department of National Affairs in the PLO, referred to the special concern of the movement for Jordan—"based on the large numbers of Palestinians there, its physical location, and the national ties with it." [29] Jordan is the venue for the attack against Israel, as when an attack was attempted from the Jordan Valley on the East Bank during 1968–1970.

In 1979 renewed contacts between Hussein and the PLO once again touched on the fedayeen demand to operate militarily from Jordanian territory. The request was not granted. The PLO's military presence in Jordan produced political complications for the regime in the late 1960s. Hussein will undoubtedly be careful to prevent a repetition of that situation. Still, from the PLO's viewpoint, the role of Jordan in the Palestinian campaign looms large in importance.

In summary, the PLO contends that from an ethnic, national, and military perspective, Jordan is a necessary and legitimate field for Palestinian activity. The narrow map used by the PLO, limited to western Palestine, does not reflect the true territorial ambitions of the movement. In 1966 Shafiq al-Hut, PLO representative in Lebanon, declared, "Jordan is an integral part of Palestine, exactly like Israel." And in 1974 Yasir Arafat, in a letter to the Jordanian Student Congress, wrote, "Jordan is ours, Palestine is ours and we shall build our national entity on the whole of this land after having freed it of both the Zionist presence and the reactionary-traitor [Hussein] presence." [30] It seems that Jordanians will be Palestinians, if they are not already, whether they like it or not.

Both Jordanian and PLO spokesmen perceive in Jordan a Palestinian entity, a homeland for the realization of the national aspirations of the Arabs who, west of the river, have not succeeded in establishing practical rule. The objective developments during the last thirty years have not outdistanced a subjective appreciation of their significance. There is no lag in Jordan's and the PLO's political understanding of Palestinian features in, and penetration of, the East Bank.

There are places, however, where an intellectual lag is found, with the expected political consequences. During discussions in March 1979 concerning an Israeli-Egyptian peace settlement, Ariel Sharon, Israel's minister responsible for Jewish settlement in the territories, confronted President Carter with the following information:

[29] *Al-Siyasa*, Kuwait, July 28, 1979.
[30] *Washington Post*, November 12, 1979.

"There *is* now a Palestinian state," Sharon said. "It is called Jordan. It consists of three-fourths of the land mass of Palestine as determined by the League of Nations. Palestine was partitioned by a British trick in 1922, in violation of the mandate turned over to England by the League of Nations. Of the 2 million people living in Jordan, nearly all are Palestinians. If you count the Bedouins as Palestinians—and why not, they were born there—then everyone in Jordan is a Palestinian, except maybe the Hashemite King Hussein, because his dynasty was imported by the British from Arabia. So a Palestinian state on the West Bank would be a *second* Palestinian state."

Carter turned to his national security adviser, Zbigniew Brzezinski, "Is what he says correct?"

Brzezinski agreed that the area now known as Jordan had originally been part of the Palestinian mandate.[31]

It was Sharon who waited for a Palestinian takeover of Jordan during the 1970 civil war and ever since. Beyond any other reactions, the logic of that position would not have been lost on King Hussein and Yasir Arafat.

Conclusions and Implications

The raison d'être of Jordan has been clarified as the creation of a Palestinian order on the East Bank. Initially an artificial country, established by British imperial decree, with unclear boundaries and no national identity, Jordan has taken major strides in trying to build a new collectivity that might be termed "Jordanian-Palestinian." It is a state in search of a nation to fill it with content and purpose; nation building is proving, however, to be a more arduous and problematic task than erecting a state apparatus.

The traditional Transjordanian elements climbed the political ladder by force of ascription, while newer Palestinian elements have garnered influence in economic, social, administrative, and educational fields by virtue of achievement. The ongoing discontinuity in Palestinian experience—political power at the highest level is unattainable—leaves the Jordanian system burdened with stresses. It is not clear that the regime can keep the lid on Palestinian political frustrations indefinitely. Aruri referred to the Palestinians in Jordan as "subject to the state but not psychologically members of the nation."[32] If such a situation persists, it could erupt like hot political lava.

[31] *New York Times Magazine*, April 8, 1979.
[32] Aruri, *Jordan: Political Development*, p. 7.

It is worth stressing that, in spite of the prominent Palestinian features and identity in Jordan, King Hussein has not refrained from lashing out at Palestinian opponents when necessary. It is not unlikely that he would do more of the same in the future.

The unstable elements in the system may be growing, however, and while this may necessitate drastic steps, it could also limit Hussein's maneuverability. The Iranian revolution has introduced a religious element that could be used to undermine further the ideological basis of the regime's legitimacy. The "Muslim Brothers" appear to be the only active party in Jordan, and this with Hussein's consent and assistance. In June 1979 Dr. Said Al-Tal, minister of communications, declared that political reforms would soon be introduced based on a number of categorical principles, the first being, "Islam is the foundation of political life in Jordan." [33] In addition, there have been reports on the distribution of leaflets in a few refugee camps calling for a coup against the regime.

There have been voices in Jordan advocating abandonment of the Palestinian issue and giving up the idea of recovering the West Bank. Crown Prince Hassan fears increasing Jordanian involvement with the Palestinians any more than already exists, and he may favor a settlement with Israel based on this kind of thinking. There is no way to determine if this is the hidden line of the regime.

There is little doubt that the center of Palestinian political gravity is today on the East Bank. This entity has a strong, united political leadership, a disciplined army, a solid economy, and a growing population that provide it with the major ingredients of national viability. The West Bank will continue to orbit around the Jordanian sun across the river.

The Hashemites serve as the West Bank's "big brother"—transferring money and salaries westward, welcoming visiting West Bank political figures and mayors, articulating West Bank aspirations, and maintaining the impression that they will struggle for the Palestinian victory against Israel. A minister for the occupied territories continues to function in Amman.

The West Bank, compared with the East Bank, has not created a strong national leadership with regional authority, nor has it advanced in economic and demographic terms compared with its eastern neighbor. The West Bank is an appendage of the East Bank; it is geographically contiguous yet is the weaker partner in Arab endeavors on both sides of the river. It is not a political center, a focus of power; rather, it is stuck between two solid, well-organized states,

[33] *Magazine*, Lebanon, June 30, 1979.

Israel and Jordan, each seeking influence over it. The future of the West Bank—even in PLO thinking—is that of a marginal area linked to a more powerful core centered either in Israel's Jerusalem or in Jordan's Amman. The PLO's vision, which is first and foremost a call for the refugees' return to the coastal region of Israel, also leaves the West Bank in a secondary status.

The links between the two banks are likely to continue. Factors rooted in history, geography, economics, politics, and family considerations ensure that East Bank–West Bank connections will not cease. Today, nearly half of West Bank exports go to Jordan, in spite of the open market and strong economic links that characterize Israel–West Bank relations.[34]

The Palestinian entity of Jordan has not eliminated traditional PLO ambitions to contest Hashemite control over the East Bank. In essence, the real PLO-Jordanian contest is over the East Bank and not the West Bank. The eastern portion of Palestine, for formidable objective reasons, is the big prize. It is interesting to recall Hussein's vain attempt to convince Sadat in the summer of 1974 not to recognize the PLO as the representative of *all* Palestinians, and certainly not those on the East Bank. In the same year Hussein asked Kissinger whether the United States would recognize a PLO government-in-exile. Kissinger assured the king that America would not.[35]

A search for a stable and realistic solution to the Palestinian issue and the West Bank would be an isolated and partial endeavor if the Palestinian entity on the East Bank is ignored. The West Bank is part of a larger and stronger Palestinian Arab world across the river. Jordan is in Palestine and is Palestinian. The Palestinians are in Jordan and define its character.

The mayor of Nablus, Basam Shaka, has used a simpler formula to capture the essence of Hashemite-Palestinian relations: "They are Arabs and we are Arabs." In cryptic ambiguity the point is finally clarified.

---

[34] Israel, Central Bureau of Statistics, *Administered Territories Statistical Quarterly*, vol. 9, no. 1 (1979), Jerusalem, p. 6.

[35] William B. Quandt, *Decade of Decisions: American Policy toward the Arab-Israeli Conflict, 1967-1976* (Berkeley and London: University of California Press, 1977), p. 234.

9

Shared Rule:
A Prerequisite for Peace

Daniel J. Elazar

Permanent and Transient Elements in the Search for Peace in the Middle East

The problem of the Palestinians and the territories of Judea, Samaria, and Gaza, which has surfaced as the major stumbling block in the negotiations between Israel and Egypt, should indicate to all involved that new ideas are needed that break through the barriers of conventional thinking regarding the principal points at issue in the Israeli-Arab conflict. Yet such new thinking must recognize certain constants in the Middle East situation that seem to have been ignored by most if not all of the parties involved, not least the United States. Four such points stand out.

    1. The most enduring elements in the Middle East are not its territorial states as they presently exist but its peoples, those ethno-religious communities which, in their most comprehensive form, share a kinship manifested through a common creed. In the long history of this, the most ancient historical region in the world, empires, states, provinces, even cities have come and gone, but the peoples have persisted. Not only do the Jews have a recorded continuous presence in the region for nearly four thousand years, but other peoples—the Armenians, the Copts, the Arabs, the Kurds, the Maronites, to mention only a few—have histories stretching back two thousand years or more. Even such relative latecomers as the Turks have been in the region for no less than a millennium. These peoples have made their adjustments to different political structures, sometimes being their creators, sometimes their subjects, but as peoples they have persisted while states have come and gone. In fact, the Middle East is a mosaic of long-lived peoples who have used various political

devices over time to achieve as much political self-determination as possible.

Precisely because of the ancient character of the peoples of the Middle East, "instant peoplehood" as has been claimed for the Palestinian Arabs is suspect. The Palestinian Arabs have indeed come to constitute a "public" within the Arab nation, an extended group sharing a common interest and affected by a common set of externalities. They may even become a separate people in due course. Yet peoples in the Middle East take form over centuries, not in a decade or two, and the truly legitimate structures, whether states or churches, are those created by these ancient peoples.

All the evidence indicates that modernization has not eliminated the primacy of ethno-religious identity, but rather has sharpened certain of its aspects. Those who thought that the imposition of new categories of statehood would undermine the old order have discovered, often through bloody civil war or massacre, how mistaken they were. Thus, any settlement must recognize the permanence of ancient peoples and the precedence of their rights while remaining dubious about those who claim statehood on the basis of fifteen or thirty or even fifty years of national self-identification.

2. Even more than states, boundaries in the Middle East have been highly impermanent, rarely lasting more than a generation or two under the best conditions. The Middle East consists essentially of oasis areas surrounded by deserts, with the struggle between the desert and the sown areas as one of its few constants. The carving up of those oasis heartlands that are of such continuous geographic identity as exists in the region and the division of the territories in between has been a regularly recurring effort.

Not a single boundary in the Middle East today is as much as a hundred years old. To take the Israeli case, the oldest boundary is that between Israel and Sinai, which was drawn in 1906. Israel's northern boundaries were established only in the early 1920s, while its eastern boundaries have never been formally established except on an interim basis. The same is true for the boundaries between Syria and its neighbors, Egypt and its neighbors, not to speak of Jordan, which does not even have a historical heartland known by that name.

This has been a recurring pattern; it is not simply a phenomenon of modern nation building in the region. Even during the days of imperial rule, boundaries changed regularly as a result of external and internal wars, and the imperial powers were constantly redividing the territories within their domain. The Ottoman Turks redrew the provincial boundaries in what was known as Syria and Palestine on the average of twice every century. The whole purpose of boundaries in the Middle East has not been to encompass geographically fixed nations but to provide security for the peoples of the various heartlands or for the powers able to make their needs felt at any given time. To repeat, in this region peoples are constant, not boundaries.

3. Not only are peoples more persistent than political structures and boundaries in the region, but the peoples are so situated that homogeneous states have rarely if ever been attainable. Excluding Egypt (where the Coptic minority tends to be concentrated in the largest cities), one can at best identify homogeneous areas the size of relatively small provinces or medium-sized American counties. In urban areas, peoples have usually been substantially intermixed, separated at most into neighborhood groupings. In rural areas, the division has often been on a village-by-village basis, which leads to great complications when trying to draw boundaries on a more than local level. History has demonstrated that every successful political arrangement in the region must involve the satisfaction of some majority people along with the maintenance of the communal rights of the minority peoples within the same jurisdiction. Thus every polity in the region is, in some respects at least, a compound one, with no possibility of becoming an ethnically unitary nation-state as called for in European theories of nationalism, without resorting to expulsion or genocide.

4. As a consequence of the foregoing, peace has existed in the Middle East only under conditions when now-conventional notions of sovereignty have been drastically limited and principles of shared power have operated in their place. The various empires that have succeeded in bringing peace to the region, particularly the ancient Persian Empire and the more recent Ottoman Empire, were built on principles of local autonomy. The autonomy was at times ethnic, at times a combination of ethnic and territorial factors, but under this principle, each of the peoples within the imperial system was granted or guaranteed some significant measure of cultural, religious, and even political self-determination or home rule within the imperial framework. The rulers of these empires recognized the aforementioned "constants" or "facts of life" in the Middle East for what they were. Unfortunately, the historical record shows that only where there have been dominant empires have these peaceful relations obtained, albeit at some cost to all but the imperial rulers. In those periods—which have come at repeated intervals—when the region has been broken up into separate states or small imperial domains, consistent interstate warfare has been the general rule, with all that such warfare has

213

meant for the stability of populations and, most particularly, of boundaries.

Today, we are once again in a period in which the region is divided among many states. The result is once again what it was earlier, and not only with regard to the conflict between Israel and its Arab neighbors. In the post–World War II generation—the first generation of independent statehood for most of the states in the region— there were civil wars in Cyprus, Ethiopia, Iraq, Iran, Lebanon, Sudan, and Yemen; revolutions based on ethno-religious differences in Lebanon and Syria; interstate conflicts or border clashes between Egypt and Libya, Iraq and Iran, Ethiopia and Somalia (not to mention Eritrea), Syria and Turkey, Syria and Jordan; and such foreign interventions as the Egyptian War in Yemen of the mid-1960s, which added a new twist to the general pattern of regional conflict through the use of poison gas.

None of the peoples in the region would wish for a return to imperialism, even in the name of peace. Nor would any of the states in the area wish to sacrifice its independence for that reason. The record has once again demonstrated, however, that the system of fully sovereign states as developed in modern Europe is not appropriate for the Middle East. Thus new inventions are necessary to achieve peace within the framework of modern nationalism and, one hopes, democracy. Such inventions must derive from the spirit of the region, not be foreign transplants likely to be rejected by the region's bodies politic. In the development of these new inventions, it is also possible to learn from old imperial solutions, even if these cannot be applied as they were in imperial times.

Two particular arrangements stand out as having had recurring success in imperial peace systems of the past. One is the principle of ethnic autonomy or home rule—what in the Ottoman period was known as the millet system—and the other is the principle of extraterritorial arrangements whereby particular groups can be protected by external powers with which they have an affinity—what were known in Ottoman times as capitulations.

While both the millet and capitulation systems have been roundly rejected by newly sovereign states jealous of their prerogatives, significant remnants of the millet system in fact persist in every one of these states, and the outside intervention of brethren or great powers has been tacitly reaffirmed. Even the most extreme among them have discovered that unless they are willing to exterminate minority populations or drive them out—the pattern followed by the first new states in the region early in the twentieth century—it is necessary to come to some accommodation with them. All but the most extreme rulers have found that it costs less to do so by giving them formal or informal cultural and religious autonomy in some spheres and even legal powers in matters of personal status (marriage, divorce, and inheritance are the most common of these) rather than to try to force them to give up ways of life that stretch back in continuous form to antiquity.

With a few exceptions, these accommodations have not been constitutionalized in writing because of the reluctance of the new states to limit their sovereignty formally, but, for all intents and purposes, they cannot be changed without civil war or great upheaval. To the extent that they become constitutionalized over time, it will mean that while not every group that has an identity of its own can have a state in the complex pattern of the Middle East, each can have the wherewithal to preserve its own integrity.

Extraterritorial arrangements are in greater disfavor in the newly established states of the Middle East, principally because they smack of colonialism. Indeed, were they to involve overt intervention from outside the region, they would be just that. Extraterritorial arrangements among neighbors are another matter, however. Even now, a number of such arrangements prevail on the Egyptian-Sudanese border, where they have been formally incorporated into the settlement between the two states.

Viewed in this light, the Israeli request for extraterritorial arrangements in eastern and southern Sinai after the return of the peninsula to Egyptian sovereignty was not a radical new departure within the Middle East. It was, rather, an inventive approach for dealing with the disputed borderland region that has separated the Judean and Egyptian oases without the need for clear-cut boundaries since time immemorial, an approach that could foreshadow a new era of a peaceful interstate system in the region. The request was a step toward rationality in a situation where simple-minded exercise of sovereignty can only lead to repeated wars; it deserved a better hearing from the United States and Egypt than the out-of-hand rejection it received.

The Israeli government's concessions on the sovereignty issue reflect a perception, perhaps only intuitive, perhaps more, of the limitations of the sovereignty concept in the Middle East. While no state in the area wishes to give up the essence of its sovereignty, it is quite proper to think of Israel's recommendation as a first step toward creating shared arrangements on the peripheries of sovereignty that can foster peace, in part because they overcome the jurisdictional problems that have always arisen on the peripheries of the many oases that compose the region and in part because the problems can be solved by so intertwining the various parties that war becomes difficult and unprofitable for all.

A Workable Solution for Israel, Jordan, and the Territories

Similar inventiveness is possible with regard to Judea, Samaria, and the Gaza district, only there it must take yet another form. Nearly a decade ago, Moshe Dayan stated a simple truth long recognized by the Israelis at least: "We must recognize the fact that we have two peoples living in the same land, each desirous of preserving its own national and cultural integrity." However Eretz Israel/Palestine is defined, few thoughtful people disagree with such a statement. In essence, this is the problem whose solution is the key to peace in the area. How can both peoples who are fated to live in physical proximity create a life together that will enable them to preserve their respective national and cultural integrities?

Israel's security needs rule out simply returning the territories to Jordanian (or Egyptian) rule. The existence of a substantial Arab population with nationalistic aspirations rules out any unilateral Israeli action to incorporate the territories into the Jewish state without providing a satisfactory means of self-determination for their Arab inhabitants. A Palestinian state west of the Jordan River is also not a reasonable option. For one thing, the creation of a second Arab state within the historical Land of Israel/Palestine ignores the Palestinian character of Jordan, where today at least half the Palestinians live. Such a plan would actually permanently divide rather than unite them. Even disregarding Israel's own need for secure borders, such a state would be too small and poor relative to its neighbors to be viable. Hence it would be extremely vulnerable to extremist control. Under the best of circumstances, it could not help but be a nest for continued terrorist activity. One need only consider the situation in Ireland to understand why. The Irish Republic has no interest in encouraging trouble in Northern Ireland. Quite the contrary, the Irish government would like to avoid trouble. Even so, with all the good will in the world, it cannot prevent the Irish Republican Army (IRA) from using the republic's territory as a staging ground for terrorist activities in Ulster and as a haven afterward, except perhaps through draconian measures that would be intolerable to its own citizens. Even if it were responsibly led, a small, poor Palestinian state could not be expected to have nearly the same desire for peace as Eire and would be even less able to control its "crazies."

216

The conventional response to the problem has been a repartition of the land west of the Jordan River, whether through a complete Israeli withdrawal to the pre-1967 lines (the Arab position), a withdrawal with "minor territorial adjustments" (the American position), or a major redrawing of the boundaries along the lines of the Allon Plan (the position of the Israeli Labor party). It is this response which has proved to be inadequate—a "nonstarter" in one way or another—and which Camp David has effectively jettisoned.

From Partition to Sharing. The framework of peace signed by Carter, Begin, and Sadat in the final dramatic moment of the Camp David summit marks a turning point in the direction of Israeli-Arab accommodation in more ways than one. Not only does it put both parties on the road to a peace settlement, but it also changes the basis for making peace within Eretz Israel/Palestine that has prevailed for the past two generations by necessitating some combination of self-rule and shared rule for Jews and Arabs (or Israel, the Palestinian Arabs, and Jordan) within the land.

Since the Churchill White Paper of 1922, which detached Transjordan from the "Jewish national home in Palestine" provided for by the League of Nations Mandate, the whole thrust of efforts to achieve accommodation between Jews and Arabs has been based upon partition of the land between them. The Peel Commission report of 1937 carried the partition idea a step further with a plan to divide Cis-Jordan (western Eretz Israel/Palestine) as well. While it was never implemented, the idea was revived in the 1947 United Nations partition plan, which was adopted as the basis for establishing Jewish and Arab states in the Cis-Jordan area. In fact, the Israel War of Liberation restored the connection between Arab-occupied Cis-Jordan and Transjordan, and the armistice agreements signed between Israel and the Hashemite Kingdom of Jordan in 1949 ratified a partition status quo between the two, encompassing all but a fraction of the historical land of Israel, which held until 1967.

The Six Day War destroyed that status quo by placing Israel along the Jordan and removing Jordanian rule west of the river (and, for that matter, Egyptian rule in the Gaza Strip). It did not solve the problems of peace in the land, however, because the Arabs who had settled in the territories formerly occupied by Egypt and Jordan were not prepared to be annexed by Israel. Rather, the war stimulated a sense of Palestinian identity which had hitherto been relatively dormant. Had the Palestinian Arabs been willing to acquiesce to citizenship in an enlarged Israel, then the partition solution of 1922 would have been restored. This, indeed, became the goal of certain substantial elements on the Israeli political scene, including Menachem Begin's Likud, which was to gain power in the May 1977 elections.

On the other hand, the then-ruling Labor party, while unable to fully crystallize its position, leaned toward a repartition of the territory west of the Jordan on terms more advantageous to Israel from a security point of view. This position was embodied in the Allon Plan, which was based on the premise that the heavily populated hill country in the heart of Judea and Samaria, with its large concentration of Arabs, would be returned to Jordan in some way while Israel would annex a wider band of territory along the western foothills plus the Jordan Valley. In fact, the proponents of this plan had no more success in persuading the Arabs or, for that matter, Israel's own friends, of the acceptability of this more modest repartition than those who espoused the Likud position had with regard to their plan. The Arabs insisted on a return to the pre–Six Day War borders, and even the Americans supported that demand for all intents and purposes. Stalemate ensued.

The Israel-Egypt peace treaty broke that stalemate, substantially with regard to relations between Israel and Egypt and now at least potentially with regard to relations between Jews and Arabs within the Land of Israel/Palestine. A major element in breaking that stalemate is a shift away from partition as the basis for a settlement and a search for other alternatives. Simply put, partition has reached a dead end. None of the three partition schemes on the table is acceptable to more than one of the parties involved. In current diplomatic slang, they have become "nonstarters."

The first formal break in partitionist thinking came with Begin's announcement of his autonomy plan in December 1977. That plan, although purposely limited, for the first time formally suggested that the solution to the problem did not lie in partition but in some combination of self-rule and shared rule. Rejected at first by the Arabs, it was accepted by the Americans as a possible basis for an interim arrangement and, with some significant modifications, became the basis for the interim arrangement agreed upon for a five-year period at Camp David. Each of the two parties to the conflict accepted this new framework for its own reasons, reasons which are still to a great extent contradictory in their expectations.

It is precisely because of these contradictory expectations and the impossibility of satisfying them through partition that a shift of direction toward federative solutions has begun. It remains to be seen whether this initial shift can be utilized to achieve a peace that sufficiently reconciles the contradictory expectations to bring peace. But the framework does provide a basis for moving toward achievement of the classic goal of federative arrangements, namely, to enable the several parties to the arrangement to have enough of their cake and to eat enough of it as well.

The Revival of the Federative Option. The shift from the pursuit of partition to the pursuit of federative arrangements raises to new importance a theme that has been played in a minor key throughout the history of the Israeli-Arab conflict. Since 1917, at least sixty different proposals for federative solutions have been advanced, including such well-known ones as that of the Brit Shalom group led by Martin Buber and Judah Magnes in the early 1940s and the minority report of the UN Special Commission on Palestine in 1947. None of these got far because they were all based upon expectations of Jewish-Arab cooperation which were unrealistic at the time. Between 1948 and 1967 voices for federative solutions were muted, although they did not entirely disappear. A few remained to build their paper castles in the sky.

After the Six Day War, the search for federative solutions received new impetus. The idealists reemerged with beautiful plans that continued to ignore stubborn realities, but even more cautious realists began to suggest that the federative option was the only one that offered any promise of movement at all. Shimon Peres endorsed the pursuit of federative options in a vague way within two years after the war, later elaborating a plan for a redivision of the entire Cis-Jordanian area into multiple Jewish and Arab cantons. Moshe Dayan suggested a functional solution for the administered territories that would involve shared rule by Israel and Jordan. Even Yigal Allon at one point suggested that the West Bank areas to be returned to Jordan be linked with that state in a federation, with the whole confederated with Israel.

Unfortunately, none of these plans nor those put forward by others outside of political life such as this writer, produced any echoes in the Arab camp. As has been said, Israel found no partners. Now for the first time, there is a slim but real possibility that partners will appear on the scene.

A detailed look at the text of the framework for peace in the Middle East, with all its ambiguities and opportunities for interpretation in one direction or another, indicates how this is so. On the one hand, the framework provides for "a self-governing authority . . . freely elected by the inhabitants" of the West Bank and Gaza on a transitional basis under the supervision of Israel, Jordan, and Egypt. What is suggested here and for the future final settlement is a Palestinian entity that will not be a sovereign state, and hence will have to be linked with some state—which state is not specified. The provision for Jordan's entry into joint arrangements with Israel leaves the possibility open for a link to Jordan, Israel, or both.

Knowing Israel's position about full evacuation of the territories and the Arabs' position about full relinquishment of any part of them, only one option remains, namely, some kind of shared arrangement. This is further enhanced by the specific involvement of Jordan, Egypt, and Israel in any decision involving the Palestinians' future along with the representatives of the Palestinian inhabitants of the territories. The provision for joint committees and security forces is a first step in the direction of some kind of shared-rule arrangement, even though they are to be established on a five-year interim basis only at this point.

All told, the Camp David agreement is a major step toward some combination of self-rule and shared rule, which is characteristic of all federal arrangements and which could lead to the solution of the major governance problem of the Israeli-Arab conflict, provided that the parties to the agreement recognize the possibilities inherent in such arrangements and the severe limitations, if not impossibility, of any other approach.

A solution suggested in some quarters is the creation of a "Palestine" entity in the West Bank and the Gaza Strip which would then be linked with Jordan in a federal relationship of some kind. This would do little to solve the fundamental problems of Israel's security, just as full Jordanian control could not (or did not) restrain terrorism between 1949 and 1967.

On the other hand, an Israel-Palestine federation, which is sometimes proposed by well-meaning people, is practically unworkable at the present time. The history of federalism shows that it takes two to federate. That is to say, both parties must be willing to accept the bargain creating the ties between them in the proper federal spirit and have a strong desire to live up to its provisions if the federation is to have any chance of success. This does not seem to be a realistic possibility under present conditions. Moreover, inequality in such arrangements can be tolerated when the inequalities are more or less balanced or dispersed among a number of units (as is the case in the United States or Canada), but a confederation of one strong and one weak unit can only lead to frustration and repression or rebellion and war, particularly when such sharp ethnic and ideological differences are involved.

Framing a Federal Arrangement. The actual development of a self-rule/shared-rule arrangement will require the utmost sensitivity to the needs of the various parties involved. It will have to deal with four principal factors: peoples (or nations), publics, territory, and states. Each of these four represents a separate element in the overall equation.

The two peoples involved, Jewish and Arab, must maintain the maximum amount of independence, on a separate basis, since there is little at this point that would encourage them to opt for any degree of sharing if that were not guaranteed. The Jewish majority in Israel wishes to preserve the Jewish character of that state and their own Jewish identity, while the Arabs wish to exercise self-determination to the fullest possible extent.

Within the Arab nation, the Palestinians have come to constitute a separate public, perhaps only in opposition to Israel or in response to their own peculiar needs of the past generation or two, perhaps on a long-term basis in the manner of the Syrians, Iraqis, or Egyptians. As a public they must be given maximum feasible self-rule within a larger context of sharing. Whatever the fate of the administered territories, the Palestinians, as a public rather than a people, cannot hope to attain more than that. The great and persistent reluctance of the Arab states to do more than give lip service to the idea of a separate Palestinian state—which there is every reason to believe that they basically oppose—is indicative that even if Israel were to agree to a full withdrawal, the Palestinians are to be tied to some larger Arab entity even more than other publics within the Arab nation. Thus the fact that their self-rule must come within a shared Jewish-Arab context should not be considered as unsettling in the long run as it appears to the Palestinian Arabs at this point. The spread of the Palestinian Arabs on both banks of the Jordan River augurs well for the transformation of the Palestinian public into the dominant force in the Arab state sooner or later, and the limited yet very real linkage with Israel on the West Bank could serve to protect them from the designs of other Arab states or leaders. Geographically and demographically, Jordan is part of Palestine (or Eretz Israel); politically it will become a Palestinian state sooner or later.

The territory now shared by both peoples, on the other hand, should be subject to the maximum feasible amount of shared rule, since the several claimants all have legitimate claims with regard to it. Israel has a historical right, which has a certain status in international law, while the Palestinians have a right of occupancy strongly supported in international politics. The only way to satisfy these conflicting claims is through sharing the territory in some way. Since peoples in the Middle East have never depended upon territory to legitimize or even maintain their existence, but only use it as a form of accommodation, the provision of self-rule for them as peoples does not preclude shared rule by two or more peoples over the same territories which they may occupy or in which they have rights vested simultaneously.

Finally, the two states involved, Israel and Jordan, will wish to maintain their own independence and status as politically sovereign entities. At the same time, they should be linked through limited shared functional arrangements as necessary to provide the structural and institutional cement for the entire arrangement. Thus, their separate existence would also be guaranteed along with the Palestinian entity but in a situation in which those functions which should be handled in common, whether control of water resources, tourism, a customs union, or whatever, would be handled by limited-purpose joint authorities.

Right now that portion of the land that is the focus of the dispute is already in joint tenancy. The two states are already "in place" to provide a framework for a federative arrangement. In fact, over the course of the last decade, the basis for an arrangement has been established de facto and is working, at least on a technical level, despite public political posturing to the contrary. The Palestinian Arabs in the territories may have to make do with an "entity" that is less glamorous symbolically than a "state," but they will have taken a giant step forward into self-rule in such a way that if the federative elements are strengthened, so, too, will their chances for full equality in a partnership of one kind or another grow.

If a viable solution is to be achieved out of the momentum generated at Camp David, the various sides must be prepared to explore options along these lines, moving forward into initial forms that may be less than any of the parties would wish but which will open the doors to a developmental process that could transform the entire land with its states and peoples.

A NOTE ON THE BOOK

The typeface used for the text of this book is
Palatino, designed by Hermann Zapf.
The type was set by
Hendricks-Miller Typographic Company, of Washington, D.C.
Thomson-Shore, Inc., of Dexter, Michigan, printed
and bound the book, using Warren's Olde Style paper.
The cover and format were designed by Pat Taylor,
and the figures were drawn by Hördur Karlsson.
The manuscript was edited by Janet Marantz, and
by Claire Theune of the AEI Publications staff.

Selected AEI Publications

AEI Foreign Policy and Defense Review, (six issues $12; single copy, $2.50)

A Conversation with the Exiled West Bank Mayors: A Palestinian Point of View (15 pp., $2.25)

United States Relations with Mexico: Context and Content, Richard D. Erb and Stanley R. Ross, eds. (291 pp. $7.25)

A Conversation with Ambassador Tahseen Basheer: Reflections on the Middle East Process (24 pp., $2.25)

A Conversation with Ambassador Hermann F. Eilts: The Dilemma in the Persian Gulf (19 pp., $2.25)

A Palestinian Agenda for the West Bank and Gaza, Emile A. Nakhleh, ed. (127 pp., $5.25)

What Should Be the Role of Ethnic Groups in U.S. Foreign Policy? John Charles Daly, mod. (28 pp., $3.75)

U.S. Policies toward Mexico: Perceptions and Perspectives, Richard D. Erb and Stanley R. Ross, eds. (56 pp., $4.25)

Modern Diplomacy: The Art and the Artisan, Elmer Plischke (456 pp., $9.25)

Prices subject to change without notice.

AEI Associates Program

The American Enterprise Institute invites your participation in the competition of ideas through its AEI Associates Program. This program has two objectives:

The first is to broaden the distribution of AEI studies, conferences, forums, and reviews, and thereby to extend public familiarity with the issues. AEI Associates receive regular information on AEI research and programs, and they can order publications and cassettes at a savings.

The second objective is to increase the research activity of the American Enterprise Institute and the dissemination of its published materials to policy makers, the academic community, journalists, and others who help shape public attitudes. Your contribution, which in most cases is partly tax deductible, will help ensure that decision makers have the benefit of scholarly research on the practical options to be considered before programs are formulated. The issues studied by AEI include:

- Defense Policy
- Economic Policy
- Energy Policy
- Foreign Policy
- Government Regulation

- Health Policy
- Legal Policy
- Political and Social Processes
- Social Security and Retirement Policy
- Tax Policy

For more information, write to:

AMERICAN ENTERPRISE INSTITUTE
1150 Seventeenth Street, N.W.
Washington, D.C. 20036